THE AVIATOR'S BATHROOM READER
TWO HOLER

The following quotes [included in the Aviator's BathroomReader #1] were so good it was decided to include them in this, the Aviator's Bathroom Reader #2. Most of those quoted have since 'Gone West' and are no longer available to review the second volume.

Dieses Buch ist wunderbar. Wen ich zurückkehrte von schiessen einige tapfer und mutige englische Piloten runter und auch ein paar französchische feiglinge. Nach dem Abendessen nehme ich mir die Zeit und geniesse einige Kapitel von den Buch. Lachen hilft mir, mich zu entspannen und lerne dabei auch ein paar Sachen. Ich empfehle das für jeden Piloten, nur natürlich nicht für die französchisen Flieger.

[This book is wonderful! After returning from shooting down some brave British pilots - and a few cowardly French ones - I sit down after dinner and enjoy a few sections. Laughing helps me relax...and I learn things, too! I recommend this for every aviator...except, of course, the French ones.]

Pour le Merite "Blue Max" Prussia 1712 –1918

- Manfred Freiheer von Richthofen [The "Red Baron" -highest scoring ace in WWI with 80]

I wish I had this book along on my Atlantic flight. There were a lot of long, boring hours where some entertainment would have been welcome!
- Charles A. Lindbergh [First to fly solo across the Atlantic Ocean]

If my brother and I had this book back then, we would most likely have made our first powered flight in 1902 instead of 1903.
- Orville Wright [Pilot of the first powered takeoff of an airplane]

This is the best ****ing book about flying I've ever read! It's got ****hot pilots, stupid ****ing pilots, and a lot of ****ing good lessons we can all learn from. If you don't come away with some ****ing good smarts after reading this, then you're just an *******.
- Florence "Pancho" Barnes [Movie pilot, adventurer, owner/operator of the "Happy Bottom Riding Club" near Muroc Lake, CA. – now Edwards AFB]

I really don't care for all the parts about flying airways, the rules and regulations and stuff. I mean, isn't the sky open and free? That's the way it should always be. The funny parts were okay though, I guess.
- "The Great" Waldo Pepper ['Barnstormer' pilot]

We need more material like this so when I send my boys over Hitler's Reich they have the knowledge and skill to make it back safe and alive. Send me more assets like this!
- Frank "12 O'clock High" Savage, BGen [918th Bomb Group, 8th AF]

You can't get to fly the big ones until you can fly the little ones. This book will help you do that.
- William Boeing [Airplane designer and builder]

This book is the best way I've seen to make the mundane knowledge found in the FARs and AIM come to life so it can be recalled by pilots when they need to have it at their fingertips. It will assist in making todays' fliers safer and more capable. And by the way, that story of me saying "Good luck" to Mr. Grindowski when I was standing on the moon is a fabrication: A funny one, yes, but a fabrication.
- Neil Armstrong [First human to set foot on the moon and a true hero]

I offered Drew one million dollars for the rights to his book. I was going to turn it into a blockbuster picture starring my newest bombshell actress. He wouldn't sell. It seems some people just can't be bought: Too bad for him.
- Howard Hughes [mega-billionaire, movie producer and pilot]

I make the best airplanes of the war and the Allies call them a bad name. Well, in the next one all those "Fokkers" – as you call them – will be flying Messerschmidts. And I'll be sitting at home enjoying books like this one.
- Anthony Fokker (German WWI aeroplane designer/builder]

Reading; it gives the mind a chance to pause and, with the mind's eye, extend one's awareness far ahead where mere sight cannot take you. I continue on into the black of night; blacker even than over the Sahara on a moonless night; guided only by that small glimmer of light far ahead, which is the dawn. The dawn of my awareness, the dawn in recognizing inspiring passages of knowledge, the dawn of a new day high in the calm before the coming storm that is my life on the ground.
- Antoine de Saint-Exupéry [Author of Conquest of the Air, Night Flight, The Little Prince]

You know, I played a number of characters in the movies, all of whom were pilots. And then as a pilot myself I got to fly some of the most up-to-date planes the US Army Air Corps – later the US Air Force – had at the time. Reading this book won't get you a part in the movies, but it may keep you from being mentioned negatively in the newsreels.
- Jimmy Stewart, BGEN, USAF (ret.) [Actor and pilot]

I wish I had read this book before coming down out of the mountains.
- John Denver [Songwriter and performer, pilot]

This book has its ups and downs, like my work.
- Igor Sikorsky [Inventor of the first practical helicopter]

Okay, you SOB's – read this here book from cover to cover – yeah, the footnotes too – and maybe, just maybe, you'll make it off this stinkin' island and back home to yer loved ones in one piece!
- Gregory "Pappy" Boyington [VMF-214, WWII Pacific theater ace]

Chaps, the information you will find herein is bloody good! Remembering what the author presents (although he does get a wee bit 'skanky' at times) may well keep you from becoming 'Fokker Fodder'.
So chin up, Lads, and God Bless the King!
- Major Billy Bishop, VC, Royal Flying Corps/Royal Air Force
[Major Bishop, RAF, was the highest scoring Allied ace of WWI with 72 victories. His son, who flew in WWII, liked to say that between his father and him, they shot down 74 German planes. – Ed.]

Learn from the mistakes of others because you'll never live long enough to make them all yourself.
- James H. "Jimmy" Doolittle, Lieutenant General, USAF (ret.)
[Famed pilot, record breaker, leader of the 'Doolittle Raid' on Tokyo in 1942 and another true hero]

As Army Aviator #2 since 1913, I've seen 'em come and I've seen 'em go. The ones who stayed put their all into it; living, breathing, eating and sleeping aviation. This book will help in that endeavor, enrichening the lives of all who dream of a life in the sky.
- Henry H. "Hap" Arnold, General of the Air Force (5 stars)

US Signal Corps 1913 Military Aviator (Awarded to the first 14 military aviators, of which Lt. Henry Arnold was #2, from his estate.)

Real Quotes From Real Readers

The 'Aviator's Bathroom Reader' is now getting attention from Europe!

Thanks for sending a copy of your book! I am looking forward to making her wonder what I'm chuckling at while in the bathroom. Flying remains a dream and passion of mine and I hope to get my PPL [Private Pilot License] someday. I'll write you when I pass my checkride! Tally Ho!
- Joel Rosen, Hendon, London, United Kingdom

When once you have tasted flight, you will forever walk the earth with your eyes turned skyward, for there you have been, and there you will always long to return.
- Leonardo da Vinci

Aviators Love the Bathroom Reader!

THE AVIATOR'S BATHROOM READER
TWO HOLER

Drew Chitiea
Master Flight Instructor - Emeritus

Colorado Skymaster, LLC
Centennial, Colorado

Photographs of the wings and badges pictured herein by Peggy Long.

The wings & badges pictured herein reside in the author's collection.

The Aviator's Bathroom Reader Two Holer
First Edition
Copyright @ 2022, Colorado Skymaster, LLC
All rights reserved. No part of this publication may be reproduced, photocopied, stored in an unauthorized retrieval system, or transmitted in any form or by any means – including but not limited to: electronic, photocopy, audio/video recording without the prior written permission of the copyright holder. This novel is a work of fact and fiction. While most of the book is factual, some of the names, characters, quotes may be the product of the imagination or may have been used fictitiously.

ISBN: 978-0-578-29605-0

This book is dedicated to my "brother of a different mother" – Robert Brownson 'Brown' Cabell, CW5, US Army (ret.), 1950 – 2018, and to all the other aging warriors seeing their mortality 'in the wire' [closer than it has ever been since 'those days'], and to those who have 'gone west' already on their last mission. In the movie "The Bridges of Toko-Ri" [Korean War aviation epic], the skipper of the aircraft carrier from which the pilots flew on their last mission remarks "Where do we find such men?"
Where, indeed?
May God welcome with open arms those men and women who stepped forward, left their friends and families behind, and dedicated their lives, their fortunes, and their sacred honor to this country. May God bless them, and may God bless America!

"Bit by bit it comes over us that we shall never again hear the laughter of our friend, that this one garden is forever locked against us.
And, at that moment, begins the true mourning which, though it may not be rending, is yet a little bitter.
For nothing, in truth, can replace that companion. Old friends cannot be created out of hand.
Nothing can match the treasure of common memories, of trials endured together, of quarrels and reconciliations and generous emotions.
It is an idle thought, having planted an acorn in the morning, to expect to sit that afternoon in the shade of an oak.
So, life goes on.
For years ago we planted the seed, we feel ourselves rich; and then come other years when time does its work, and our plantation is made sparse and thin.
One by one, our comrades slip away
Depriving us of their shade."

- Antoine de Saint-Exupery
Wind, Sand & Stars, 1939

TO MY READERS

For Those of You with A.I.S. (Acronym Impairment Syndrome)

Throughout this book you will come across many acronyms pertaining to various aviation matters (V.A.M.'s). "B.F.D." you might think, I know 'em all and perhaps even invented a few when I was at (Fill in the blank) back in (Fill in another blank). That might be well and good (W.a.G.) for you old greybeards, but think of the young ones coming along, those foolish new guys (F.N.G.'s) whose heads are yet empty of the wisdom represented by trusty old acronyms (T.O.A.'s).

So when you, my faithful reader (M.F.R.) come across one of those T.O.A.'s, please refer to the Acronyms List (A.L.) of the Appendix Section (A.S.) of this book just to make sure that the meaning you understand of the acronym in question (A.i.Q.) is indeed the actual meaning of the acronym in question (A.M.o.t.A.i.Q.).

This will further your enjoyment of this book (E.o.t.B.) and perhaps even clear up misconceptions of misunderstood acronyms (M.o.M.A.) which have persisted since the days of your being the F.N.G.

Oh, there is a dictionary in the appendix section as well, for those words unique to aviation, presented for the same reason.

ACKNOWLEDGEMENTS

I wish to commend to you, the reader, the following persons who have contributed to this volume 2 of the *Aviator's Bathroom Reader*.

Captain Dave English, for his two fine books containing a myriad number of quotes concerning flying and aviation. Many of the quotes contained on the pages herein were discovered - and lifted - from his books. These quotes are illustrative and should be thought-provoking to the thinking pilot - in one quote the commenter mentions flying with one's head, not just muscles. One can find these, and many other quotes about aviation, in the following books:

Slipping the Surly Bonds, McGraw-Hill publishers, © 1998 by Dave English
The Air Up There, McGraw-Hill publishers, © 2003 by Dave English

"Captainette" Christine Wolff, Starduster biplane [named 'Bright Spirit'] pilot and aviatrix extraordinaire who coined the phrase - and epitomizes same - "The mind can do strange things when you're not paying attention to it." When she's not paying attention to her mind, she comes up with the most amazing ~~shit,~~ thoughts and ideas which keep all around enthralled and asking of her, "Where did THAT come from?" She contributed two of the stories herein, swearing they both are true. Y'all can take them with as big a shaker of salt as required.

'Captains' Spencer Mamber, David Senn, Dennis Koontz, Paul Sciera, Tom Burlace, Gerry Baker, 'Craigie' Johnston, JJ Grindrod, Bill Porter, Richard Smith ["Catkiller 22"] and others of their ilk who have passed on stories of daring-do [or is it daring doo-doo?]. The stories all began, surprisingly, with "I knew this guy once who ..." and went on to tell the story - as if it wasn't anything they personally had done, experienced first-hand, or been a party to; always a vague 'someone else's' actions and mumbling something about the 'statute of limitations' or some such BS.

The Denver Hangar of *The Ancient and Secret Order of Quiet Birdmen.* An ancient and secret order no-one has ever heard of; why? Because we're so quiet. But a more accomplished group of military, airline, and civil aviators you'll never find. Many listed items in these pages come from the individual and collective memories of these great pilots; some retired, some still treading the hallowed halls of the heavens. Usually these memories come to the fore of mind after liberal application(s) of a 90-proof 'Safety Award'. If you ever are privileged to sit in one of these sessions, grab your ass ... ahhh ... hat and marvel at what these intrepid aviators have experienced - and lived to tell the tale.

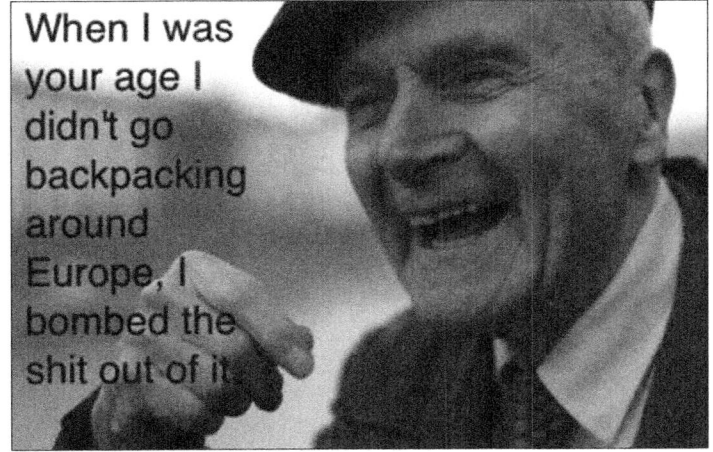

UNDERSTANDING & FORGIVENESS

Because that which you will read herein was gathered over a period of years going back into the last century, yea even the last millennium, the source(s) of such have long disappeared into the sands of time. I may have included someone else's copyrighted material and if so, and proof of said copyrightedness is sent to me, I shall give the rightful owner proper credit due them in forthcoming editions of this book, should it last that far.

Should said rightful owners deign to afford me the privilege of continuing to use their work in this presentation, I shall render proper credit to them forthwith … fifthwith … and even sixthwith. As I'm sure they are well aware, no-one gets rich in aviation, either by publishing original materials or ~~stealing~~ … ahhh … ~~plagiarizing~~ … ummm … borrowing from others, to which I unabashedly plead guilty. Relying on the principle of it being easier to ask forgiveness than permission, I forged ahead and present this material as my own.

In words which will never be forgotten, I therefore quote the great Roman stentorian Gluteus Maximus: "Ipso Facto - Compost Heapo."

Drew Chitiea
Centennial, Colorado

INTRODUCTION

First off, if you are reading this book because you purchased and enjoyed the original *Aviator's Bathroom Reader*, then I thank you for enhancing this old pilots' paltry retirement income which then may afford a slightly better dining experience than "Frisky's" [dry kibble with milk and sugar is a great cereal substitute!]. Seriously though, I thank all of you who have read then loaned, given, or passed on the preceding book to friends and assorted aviation miscreants. The feedback I've received both in public comments and private communiques has been gratifying and frankly has been the impetus to produce the volume you are now holding.

Again, the stories, fables, whoppers, inspirationals and so forth are presented with tongue-in-cheek commentary by yours truly; occasionally the serious side of the topic is detailed in excruciating severity. This has been done as sometimes one needs to get the mules' attention via a firm smack on the forehead using a two-by-four [see: Law of Impact Education}.

I have also tied to many of these offerings' relevant quotations of the pertinent Federal Air Regulations [FARs] - you know, those pesky rules and legal admonitions you learned in flight training then promptly forgot since obtaining your certificates and/or ratings? Yeah, those. Well, part of this books purpose is to, using humor and such, assist the aviator who hasn't cracked the FAR's since the Clinton Administration or the flying ingénue who hasn't dusted off the *Pilot's Handbook of Aeronautical Knowledge [P-HAK]* since obtaining her certificate to refresh in their minds some of the 'rules of the air'.

It's been a proven educational fact knowledge - and skill, for that matter - decline with time after the point of examination. Since all who fly CANNOT and MUST NOT fly below the standards of the certificate(s) held, it behooves us to thoroughly review, renew, and refresh our knowledge and skills. No-one knows everything, and those who think they know it all are particularly offensive to those of us who do.

Enjoy this book, offered in a spirit of the fun side of aviation. Pay attention though, young Skywalker, to the serious nature of what we do up there in the sky. We've never left one up there yet; something we all can be proud of. But that means they've all returned to terra firma in an astonishingly high number of ... ahhh ... 'creative ways'. Only ONE of those myriad number of ways is correct. It's up to us, Pilots in Command, to insure we all return to ground with an airplane we may use again without major maintenance [the definition of a 'Great Landing'].

Following the rules, regulations, and the Precepts of Safety is everyone's responsibility, business, and duty. This book exists because I want all of you reading this book, and its predecessor, to be around to buy and enjoy *The Aviator's Bathroom Reader - 16.* When it is published sometime in the future.

Blue Skies and Tailwinds!

Drew Chitiea, DPE
Master CFI Emeritus

From his ~~lair~~, ~~hideout~~, ~~mancave~~, abode somewhere in Colorado, USA, Western Hemisphere, Planet Earth, Sol System, Milky Way Galaxy.

WHAT THIS BOOK IS ABOUT

Since this second volume is essentially a continuation of that found in the first, the rationale, focus and purpose of ABR #2 is the same as the original volume. The stories, poems, top-10 lists, etc. are all new and improved. The discerning reader may question how something can be both new AND improved? Well, delve deeper and discover for yourself: This second volume continues to present factors relating to aviation safety as its prime 'raison d'etre' [reason for being] through easy-to-recall examples of a bad idea when sometime aboard your airplane some 'pilot' says to his passengers, "Hey people, watch this!"

Drew Chitiea
Centennial, Colorado
2022

And now, without further ado... Enjoy!

A WORD FROM OUR SPONSOR

As a (now retired) FAA Designated Pilot Examiner [DPE] I have seen many ... shall we say 'creative' ... endorsements given by flight instructors which may - usually may not - state the essence of what privilege(s) the CFI is intending to convey to their student. See the example below; this was written in an applicant's logbook; I have redacted any identifying data of the unfortunate applicant.

"I certify I have given Mr. XXXX, holder of certificate # XXXX, the spin flight/ground training required by FAR 61.187(1)(i) and find him competent in <u>any and all matters related to spins and stalls</u>. This training was completed on (date).
CFI name CFI # CFI Expiration date

The underlined portion of this endorsement is what got my attention.

I recall looking at the trembling applicant and reading this out loud to him. I then asked him what the technique was to recover from an inverted spin. The 'deer in the headlights' look I got in return gave me his answer. I then made a joke about those who think they know everything are particularly repugnant to those of us who do. I placed the applicant at ease and called the instructor over and guided him through entering a much more precise and more carefully worded - and correct - endorsement in the hapless applicant's logbook.

If you are an active CFI, you better know that no job is completed until the paperwork is done - and done CORRECTLY! Paperwork is the bane of every CFI's existence, but it MUST be done right!

"FAR 61.193 Flight Instructor Privileges
(a) A person who holds a flight instructor certificate is authorized within the limits of that person's flight instructor certificate and ratings to train and issue endorsements that are required for:

[the regulation further details the certificates/ratings allowed depending on CFI authorizations]

There are two places to obtain suggested FAA wording for properly endorsing your students; first is Advisory Circular 91-67 available for downloading from www.FAA.gov. The second place is a book an enterprising CFI/DPE created 'way back in 1998 when the FAA rewrote FAR Part 61 and there was zero guidance for correctly wording endorsements for almost two years afterwards.

The book this enterprising CFI/DPE wrote not only has properly worded endorsements organized into sections relating to the certificate and/or rating applied for, but also includes CFI Notes and Guidance for what and when to use each and every endorsement a CFI could make. There are also several sections guiding the CFI through the TSA requirements and using IACRA - very handy if you are new to instructing. There are also sections in the back to comply with the CFI Records Rules for FAR Part 61 & 141 training [FAR 61.189] but also for those instructing Light Sport students [FAR 61.423].

You can securely order this great tool from:

www.Coloradoskymaster.com

Click on 'Products' & Publications'. If requested, the author will even autograph the book and add a pithy aviation salutation. Dealer inquiries are welcomed; volume discounts are available.

And now back to our regularly scheduled program ...

TABLE OF CONTENTS

TO MY READERS 17
ACKNOWLEDGEMENTS 18
UNDERSTANDING 20
& FORGIVENESS 20
INTRODUCTION 21
WHAT THIS BOOK IS ABOUT 23
A PAIR OF SILVER WINGS 33
AFTER-HOURS MEMORIES I 35
AFTER-HOURS MEMORIES II 37
AFTER-HOURS MEMORIES III 40
AFTER-HOURS MEMORIES IV 42
AFTER-HOURS MEMORIES V 44
AFTER-HOURS MEMORIES VI 47
AFTER-HOURS MEMORIES VII 49
ALASKA HUNT 52
AN AIRMAN'S GRACE 55
AN ODE TO THOSE WHO FLY 56
AREA 51 FOLLIES 58
AT THE AME'S 61
AUSSIE COMPLETE FABRICATION 65
AVIATION'S ANCILLARY LAWS 70
BEER, WINE & SPIRITS 74

BOUNCED LANDING 92
BUZZ JOB 93
C-130 OVER IRAQ 104
CAPTAIN DOUGHNUT HOLE 108
CELESTIAL FLIGHT 110
CFI DRESS CODE 113
PILOTS GUIDE TO DISCIPLING UNRULY CHILDREN 115
COLD WEATHER AHEAD 117
CONFIDENCE DEFINED 120
CROP-DUSTER FOLLIES 122
CROSS-COUNTRY NOTES 127
DIFFERENCES BETWEEN MILITARY AVIATORS 135
DPE JOB DESCRIPTION 137
EUROPEAN ALERT STAGES 141
EVERYONE SHOULD HAVE A GUIDE DOG 143
A FARM KID WRITES HOME AFTER JOINING THE MARINES 145
FEMALE QUARTERS REGULATIONS 148
THE FINAL INSPECTION 150
FISHING 152
FITREP FOR A MARINE CORP PILOT 154
FLATULENT PASSENGER FORCES EMERGENCY LANDING 157
FLIGHT COMPANY PERSONEL 159
FLIGHT INSTRUCTOR WISDOM 160
FLYBOY OLYMPICS 162

FLYING WEST	166
FLYING WITH THE BLUE ANGELS	168
FOOD FOR THOUGHT	173
FREIGHTDOGS	175
GOT TURBULENCE?	179
GRANDPA FLEW PHANTOMS	183
GREATEST AVIATION LIES PART 2	188
HISTORICAL MILITARY WEBSITES	191
HISTORY – MORE OR LESS- OF THE 'MILE HIGH CLUB'	193
HOW NOT TO START AN AIRPLANE	198
HOW TO *FAIL* AS A FLIGHT INSTRUCTOR	201
I LEARNED ABOUT FLYING FROM THAT	205
IDEAL AIRPLANES	211
INNER PEACE & THE ATTAINMENT THEREOF	213
LIFE EXPLAINED	214
MECHANIC-SPEAK	217
MECHANIC'S HARDWARE CHART	219
MECHANICS PROBLEM SOLVING FLOWCHART	220
AFTER-ACTION REPORT FROM ANNUAL MEDICAL EXAM	221
MORE RULES OF AVIATION	224
MORE B.S. ABOUT HELICOPTERS	227
MYSTERY P-51 PILOT	233
NOT 'RULES' MORE LIKE GUIDELINES	237
NOTES FOR PILOTS -1	240
NOTES FOR PILOTS - 2	247

NOTES FOR PILOTS - 3 253
NOW, AT LAST, THE STORY CAN BE TOLD...........................259
THE OLD MAN WITH THE BUCKET OF SHRIMP 262
'PEANUTS' PHILOSOPHY 267
PILOT APTITUDE TEST 269
POLITICALLY CORRECT COCKPIT COMMUNICATION 271
POSITIVE ATTITUDE 275
QUESTIONS FROM STUDENT PILOTS OR CONFUSION IS THE FIRST STEP TOWARDS NOWLEDGE 277
REAL SUPERHEROES 280
REGARDING HELICOPTER PILOTS 286
REMEMBER 'DEAD BUG'? 293
REMEMBER THE GOOD THINGS ABOUT BEING A 'FREIGHT DOG'?..297
REPLY LETTER FROM NASA 300
RULES OF THE AIR: HOW TO FLY YOUR MACHINE - I.........303
RULES OF THE AIR: HOW TO FLY YOUR MACHINE - II........308
SANTA'S RAMP CHECK...313
SAY YOUR LAST KNOWN POSITION? 316
SECRET TO A LONG MARRIAGE 319
SERVICE RULES OF ENGAGEMENT [ROE'S] 321
"SHIT-HOLE" DEPLOYMENTS 326
SHOT DOWN BY A W-2 329
SIX TYPES OF MAJORS ONE MEETS IN THE MILITARY 333
SOUTHERNERS ARE SO POLITE 341
THANKSGIVING ON THE 'HIGH LINE' 343

THE FIVE TYPES OF AIRLINE PILOTS	348
THE RIGHT CAP	354
THE RULES AS PERTAINING TO FLIGHT – EXCEPT HELICOPTERS	358
THE RULES AS PERTAINING TO HELICOPTER FLIGHT	361
TOP 10 REASONS TO FLY AT AURORA AIRPARK	366
THINKING OUTSIDE THE BOX	368
TO ALL CO-PILOTS	370
UAL TO STOP HIRING NAVY & MARINE CORP PILOTS	373
URBAN LEGEND… OR?	377
WHAT WE HAVE HERE IS FAILURE TO COMMUNICATE	380
WHEN MEN WERE MEN	386
WHEN NATURE CALLS IN THE COCKPIT	389
WHEN THE MUSIC STOPPED	392
WHERE AIRPLANE PILOTS COME FROM	395
WHERE HELICOPTER PILOTS COME FROM	398
A WOMAN'S BEST FRIEND	400
WINGLESS PLANE AT THE PUB – CRIKEY MATE!	401
ZEN TEACHINGS FOR PILOTS	404
ZULU – CHARLIE: THE PAYOFF	407
END PIECE & AFTERWORD	414
APPENDIX	416
ABR Pithy One-Liners	417
Miscellaneous Quotes That Didn't Make It To A Page Herein	429
Aviation Acronyms	436
Aviation Dictionary	454

Recommended Movies 476

Recommended Books 483

Request for Assistance 485

ABOUT COLORADO SKYMASTERS 486

ABOUT THE AUTHOR 488

HOW & WHERE TO ORDER MORE COPIES 490

PILOT'S TOASTS 491

A PAIR OF SILVER WINGS

I found this undated soliloquy in a pile of papers given to me by a fellow collector of wings, badges, and aviation insignia. Indicating it was penned during WWII by a Frank E. Ross, a staff writer for the Arizona Republic, a newspaper published in Phoenix, Arizona, it speaks of the many who have worn the silver wings in service to their country. In fairness I include the US Navy famous 'Wings of Gold' as equally honored by this piece.

I am a pair of silver wings over a young pilot's heart. Although I heft only 16 penny-weight, he is ever conscious of my presence. Not that I weigh heavily upon him, but because I am a source of continual and growing pride.

I measure only three inches from wing-tip to wing-tip, but because of the courage, skill, training, and daring which are wrapped up in me, all brought me to be affixed on this flyer's breast. I have spread my wings from Kobe to Burma, Kiska to Boulogne, Iceland to Saarbrucken, and from Port Moresby to Crete; never dishonored.

I represent not only man's conquest of the air, his ability to soar and swoop and dive and climb and wheel about in the freest of elements, but I also bear a proud American shield; for I am not merely wings but the wings of an eagle.

My dull silver may seem muted now, but I am eloquent with endless rich anthems - anthems of rare courage, of bountiful daring, and of the breath-taking tender beauties of an existence which none of the earth-bound will know.

Outspread for flight it may appear I am ever poised for combat; yet there is no war symbol which is also so tied to the treasure of peace, and the joys to which my wings may bring. Even if war had not made my attainment glorious in its symbolism, I have given glory, if only because I have brought one more soul from the poor restrictions of the earth to the limitless horizons of the sky.

I am the badge of an American pilot - but I am more than a badge; I am the fraternity pin of those who fly. It is apt that they made me of silver, for that is the metal which has been fluid coin of empires since before Cleopatra.

I am a pair of silver wings over a young pilot's heart.

It was with reason they stamped me "Sterling."

AFTER-HOURS MEMORIES I

One evening after a day-long session of 'butt-numbing smartness' mandated by our friends at the FAA, a bunch [gaggle?] of us found ourselves enjoying a 90-proof 'Safety Award' and recalling 'the olden days'. I had the presence of mind [amazing, ain't it?] to write these down as they arose from the deep, dark, dank, damp & dismal depths of our individual and collective memories. All of us had experienced most of these, or variations thereof. None of us has seen it all ... but all of us have seen a lot. We are the most fortunate group ... we are ALIVE to enjoy the memories another day. Enjoy, brothers and sisters! Presented in no particular order...

Formation takeoffs and landings in the rain ... or snow.

Flying close finger-tip formation in a flight of four.

Formation aerobatics

Flaming out while taxing back to the ramp after a mission.

[Notice how the first 4 begin with 'F"? Another 'F'-word ending in '-uck' ('Firetruck'?) was used when describing the less-glamourous aspects of these memories. – Ed]

Terminating afterburner at 2.2 Mach and experiencing deceleration so hard that you flew into the harness and had strap bruises on your body.

Pulling 9 "G's" and not blacking out. Pulling 3 negative "G's" and after removing your boots and socks, seeing the redness of your feet from burst blood vessels.

Being scrambled for takeoff from Alert ... from a sound sleep ... at night ... in the weather ... with hot guns and missiles.

Full afterburner takeoff in a clean fighter in below zero temperatures at night.

... Being #2 in this event.

Somehow, all the jetlag and other problems had some compensating balance!

Doing formation join-ups around big beautiful columns of Cumulus out of every fighter base.

Flying a ballet around clouds, through the holes, along the valleys, up the vertical cliffs.

Sunrises seen from the high flight levels that make the heart soar.

Multiple sunsets as you climb and descend in a large after burner loop.

The patchwork quilt of the great plains of the USA from 40,000' + on a day when you can see forever.

There a LOT more of these scattered throughout this book. Just look for variations of the title.

AFTER-HOURS MEMORIES II

Elsewhere in the book are sections of a "memories of aviators" compendium. Here is another part to that – I share this as all y'all have seen/done many of these - but no-one has done everything. From the individual and collective mind[s] of the "Brew Angels".

Cruising mere feet above a billiard-table-flat cloud deck at Mach .95, with your chin on the glare shield and your face as close as you can get to the windshield.

Knowing you got to land a fighter on a seven-thousand-foot runway, that is covered with hard packed snow, and no drag chute.

Punching out the top of a low overcast while climbing at max rate.

This maneuver is/was done strictly in communication with, and with the approval/clearance from, ATC. Why else do you think the following is universally known by all pilots?

> **FAR 91.155 Basic VFR Weather Minimums [look them up!]**
> *Every airspace in the CONUS requires aircraft be a minimum of 1,000' above the cloud tops [except, of course, with ATC approval/clearance]. Ideally, any high-performance aircraft climbing at 1,000 feet per minute will, when 'punching out of the cloud tops', will*

have one minute to see any other aircraft 1,000 feet above, and them to see you.

The majesty and grandeur of towering cumulus.

Rotating at VR and feeling 400,000 plus pounds of Airplane come "alive" as she lifts off.

The delicate threads of *St. Elmo's Fire* dancing on the windshield at night.

The twinkle of lights on the Japanese fishing fleet far below, on a night crossing of the North Pacific.

Cloud formations that are beautiful beyond description.

'Ice fog' in Europe on a cold winter morning.

Seeing the approach strobes appear through the fog on a 'must do' zero - zero approach when there is no other place to go.

Seeing geologic formations that no ground-pounder will ever see.

The chaotic, non-stop babble of radio transmissions in combat ... or at O'Hare during the afternoon rush.

The arcing lines of tracers approaching your aircraft ... and missing!

The quietness of center frequency at night during a

"Transcontinental flight", over the Atlantic, the Pacific ... or over the Amazon at any time.

The welcome view of approach lights appearing out of the mist just as you reach minimums.
[One of the greatest lies of aviation: "I broke out right at minimums." – Ed.]

Finding yourself in a thunderstorm with 12 x 750-pound bombs still hanging on your wings.

Lightning storms at night over the Midwest ... or Europe ... or Korea ... or Viet Nam.

Picking your way through a line of huge Thunderstorms that seemed to go all the way from Chicago to New Orleans.

My high school teacher told me no-one would pay me to gaze out the window. I've been flying now for over half a century - did I ever prove her wrong!

AFTER-HOURS MEMORIES III

More memories from the "Old Farts Flying Club": As you read these think on the beauty, wonders and miraculous sights you yourself have witnessed from aloft. Find a hard-covered journaling book and write them down – now! Add to them from time to time when the muse calls. Years from now you'll be glad you did – and the memories they will dredge up ... *whew!*

Watching a fellow pilot do an engine flameout approach and making it.

Seeing a "dumb" bomb you drop hit a target and knowing you had all the parameters right.

Watching 20-millimeter HEI cannon rounds sparkle around the target before it explodes

The lights of London or Paris or Munich or Buenos Aires or Quito at night from FL 350.

Landing at La Paz, Bolivia ... 13,300' msl elevation ... and taking off there from.

Squall lines that run as far left and right as you can see.

Exotic lands with exotic food ... and exotic women

Seeing Tokyo lights at night from thirty-five thousand feet stretching from horizon to horizon.

Maneuvering the airplane through day lit canyons between towering Cumulus Clouds.

The deep blue gray of the sky at FL 470. The deep black of the sky at noon at 70,000'.

The hustle and bustle of Hong Kong Harbor.

The softness of a touchdown on a snow-covered runway.

Hearing the nose wheel spin down against the snubber in the wheel well after takeoff - signaling that you were on your way!

Old Chinatown in Singapore before it was torn down, modernized, and sterilized.

Watching the lightning show while dodging thunderstorms at night.

Long-tail boats speeding along the klongs in Thailand.

The quietly turning paddle fans in the lobby of the "Raffles Hotel" in Singapore.

Dodging colored splotches of red and yellow light on the radar screen at night.

The sound of foreign accents on the radio.

Luxury hotels and royal service ... flea bag hotels and abusive service.

AFTER-HOURS MEMORIES IV

More memories of more adventures, courtesy of 'The Brew Angels'.

White picket fences in Auckland, New Zealand.

Trade winds.

White sandy beaches lined with swaying palms.

Double-decker buses in London.

The endless expanse of white on a Polar Crossing.

The "Star Ferry" in Hong Kong,

Bangkok after a tropical rain. A boat tour on the Chao Phya River

Mono Lake and the steep wall of the Sierra Nevada range when approached from the east.

The bus ride to Stanley ... on the upper deck front seat of the double-decker bus.

The "Long Bar" at the Raffles Hotel.

Heavy takeoffs from the "Cliff" runway at Guam.

Real low-level flights enroute to Konya Range in Turkey.

Landings in the B-767 when the only way you knew you had touched down was the movement of the spoiler handle.

Orsini's and Gorgat's in Aviano, Italy

The deafening sound of tropical raindrops slamming angrily against the windshield, accompanied by the hurried slap, slap, slap of the windshield wipers while landing in a torrential downpour in Manila.

Endless ripples of sand dunes across the trackless miles of the Sahara desert.

Miller's Pub in Chicago.

German beer and Oktoberfest.

The white cliffs of Dover.

Oom-pa-pa music at Meyer Gustels in 'Frankfurt'!

Norwegian fjords.

The aimless compass, not knowing where to point as you near the top of the world on a polar crossing.

The whiskey compass in a steep bank.

The old Charlie-Charlie NDB approach into Kai Tak.

Y'know? Whisky was invented to make aviation stories a lot more interesting.

AFTER-HOURS MEMORIES V

Doing a tail slide in a fighter at zero airspeed from a vertical climb and watching the fuel vent around the aircraft

Leak-checking your eyelids on a long flight.

["I hate waking up to find my co-pilot asleep!"]

Drinking your now melted frozen water bottle on the return of a night combat mission.

And, as one friend so perceptively pointed out, "Payday!"

Making an aural null range approach.

Venus coming up before the sun in the Eastern sky, giving the horizon a light show like no other!

Never envying any earth-bound person.

Recognizing that only TWO bad things can ever happen to a pilot:

You walk out to your aircraft knowing it is your last flight.

You walk out to your aircraft not knowing it is your last flight.

The soft, glow of the instrument panel in a dark cockpit.

Drinking numerous cups of bad coffee on international flights.

The dancing curtains of colored light of the "Aurora Borealis" on a winter-night "North Atlantic" crossing.'

Passing 30° West...

The taxiway names at O Hare before they were renamed: 'The Bridge', 'Lakeshore Drive', 'Old Scenic', 'New Scenic', 'Outer', 'The Bypass', 'Inner', 'Cargo', 'North-South', 'The Stub', and 'Hangar Alley'!

The majestic panorama of an entire mountain range stretched out beneath you from horizon to horizon.

Lenticular clouds over the Sierras. [AND the Colorado Rocky Mountains. – Ed.]

The brief, sad, yet tempting, glimpse of runway lights after you've already committed to the missed approach.

The Alps in winter on a clear day.

The South China Sea so smooth that you leave waves in the water from 75 feet above the sea as you fly over it.

FINALLY ...

Being able to turn a dull event into an exciting story for everyone's enjoyment.

[And often being accused of 'embellishment' by the rather emphatic use of the phrase "Bovine Feces!" or, as a friend of mine complains "It's when I have to say "That's incredible!" instead of the righteously accurate 'Bovine Feces!"]

Yabbut ... you've never really lived unless you've come close to dying. After that, life has a special flavor those who live safe and protected lives will never know.

AFTER-HOURS MEMORIES VI

To paraphrase the eloquent aviation writer, Ernie Gann, "The allure of the slit in a China girl's skirt."

Sunsets of every color imaginable. The "Green Flash" the instant the sun melts below the horizon.

The Grand Canyon flying below the rim. [Sadly can't do this no more. – Ed.]

We were vectored right over the Grand Canyon at 16,000'! - Photo by the author

The tantalizing glows of the flashing strobe lights just before you break out of the clouds on the approach.

Yosemite Valley from above.

The almost blindingly-brilliant-white of a towering cumulus cloud.

A cold San Miguel in Angeles City after a long day's flying.

The Diamond Horseshoe at Itazuke.

Ocean crossings and in-flight refueling.

Hearing every sound a single engine fighter makes at night over the open ocean.

 [These sounds occur only - and exclusively – when you are exactly at ocean's mid-point and/or the point of no return or over mountainous territory with any airport to which you can glide equally beyond gliding range, or… - Ed.]

The taxiway sentry (with his flag & machine gun) at the old Taipei (downtown) airport.

The bullet holes in the walls at Tempelhof Airport in Berlin

Eighty-thousand-foot + -high thunderstorm clouds in the tropics.

Sipping Pina Coladas in a hotel bar, while a Typhoon rages outside.

Chinese Junks bobbing in Aberdeen harbor.

The smell of spring kimchee in Korea.

Watching the latitude count down to zero on the INS, and seeing it switch from "N" to "S" as you cross the equator.

"Wake Island" at Sunrise.

Oslo Harbor at dusk.

Icebergs in the North Atlantic.

AFTER-HOURS MEMORIES VII

Brain bags crammed with charts to exotic places.

The Peak tram in Hong Kong.

Breaking out of the clouds on the IGS approach to Hong Kong's old runway 13 at Kai Tak and seeing a windshield full of checkerboard.

[https://www.youtube.com/watch?v=lx3Ccs5tKfw
You'll see the "Checkerboard" at 3:30 into the video. – Ed.]

An empty weight, max power takeoff in a B-757.

The bustle of Nathan Road on a summer day.

Sliding in over Crystal Springs reservoir for a visual approach and landing on 1R in SFO.

The smell of tropical blooms when you step off the plane in Fiji.

The rush of a full-speed-brakes descent at barber pole in a B-727.

Deadheading in First Class. Deadheading in the jump seat.

The Canarsie approach into JFK. The Bridge approach into SFO. Any instrument approach at minimums at Hahn AB

The Eiffel Tower lit up at night

Max Gross Weight Takeoffs in an airliner ... or with 18 x 500-pound bombs on a hot Asian afternoon

Crosswind landings at 30 kts/90 degrees ... or a landing with RCR of <10.

Good Co-pilots. Bad captains. Good wingmen. Bad Flight leads.

Man-sized rudder pedals as big as pie plates.

Contrails – from below and above.

Pago Harbor, framed by puffy cumulus clouds in the late afternoon.

The camaraderie of a good crew ... and good squadron.

Ferryboat races in Sydney Harbor. Samlar races in Viet Nam or Thailand.

Experiencing all the lines from the old Jo Stafford tune *:

> "See the pyramids along the Nile.

See the sunrise on a tropic isle.

See the marketplace in old Algiers.

Send home photographs and souvenirs.

Fly the ocean in a silver plane.

See the jungle when it's wet with rain."

* <u>You Belong to Me</u> (1952) – sung by Jo Stafford
[A great slow-dancing, romance-affirming song. – Ed.]

www.youtube.com/watch?v=zQfF84ackMM

And just WHY is there Braille on this sign?

There ain't no problem so large or complex that they can't find a way to always blame the pilot.

ALASKA HUNT

I spent three seasons [mid-May through-mid-September] as a bush pilot in Alaska; you'd be amazed at some of the shenanigans and ... ahhh ... loose interpretation of the regulations that go on up there. My first year there the Anchorage FSDO got all of us together in a school auditorium for a 'safety meeting' where we were made aware of airspace changes, procedural changes, and the like. The final word from on high went something like this:

"Fellas, I know what you're doing out there and I also know you're all a bunch of f***ing cowboys [and we were! – Ed.] but here's the deal: DO NOT MAKE PAPERWORK FOR US! If you make paperwork for us – and you're still alive – we're gonna make a LOT MORE of it for you and guess what? NEITHER ONE OF US IS GONNA BE HAPPY ABOUT IT! Got it?"

And that was the arrangement, sorta like "Let's not do anything which is going to reflect badly on us in the accident report, okay?"

Two friends, Bill L. and Dick J. get a pilot in Alaska to fly them out into the wilderness for a moose hunt ... they bag six.

As they start loading the plane for the return trip, the pilot says, "The plane can only take four of those."

The two object strongly. "Last year we shot six and the pilot let us put them all on board; he had the same plane as yours." Reluctantly, the pilot gives in and all six are loaded.

However, even with full power, the little plane can't handle the load and down it goes, crashing in the middle of nowhere.

A few moments later, climbing out of the wreckage, Dick asks Bill,

"Any idea where we are?"

"Pretty close to where we crashed last year, I think" says Bill.

FAR 91.323 Increased Maximum Certificated Weights for Certain Airplanes Operated

In Alaska

(A) ... the Administrator will approve ... an increase in the maximum certificated weight of an airplane ... operated within the State of Alaska by:

(1) A certificate holder conducting operations under part 121 or part 135 of this chapter …

(B) The maximum certificated weight approved under this section may not exceed –

(1) 12,500 pounds,

(2) 115 percent of the maximum weight listed in the FAA aircraft specifications,

So, here's a way to win a bar bet [see glossary for definition]:

Question: Is there any legal way to operate an aircraft in excess of its maximum certificated gross weight?

Answer: FAR 91.323 allows a 121 or 135 certificate holder in Alaska to increase the MCGW by 115%

[When I was there, we all knew it was an inadvertent oversight by the Feds that part 91 operations weren't included, but of course we obeyed all regulations. That's my story and I'm sticking to it. – Ed.]

Argentina Pilot.

AN AIRMAN'S GRACE

Lord of thunderhead and sky
Who places in man the will to fly?
Who taught his hand speed, skill, and grace?
To soar above man's dwelling place
You shared with him the eagle's view
The right to soar as eagles do
The right to call the clouds his home
And grateful, through your heavens roam
May all assembled here tonight
And all who love the thrill of flight
Recall with twofold gratitude
Your gift of wings. Your gift of food.

- Father John MacGillivary, RCAF

AN ODE TO THOSE WHO FLY

Elsewhere in this tome [a fancy word for 'chock'] are several listings of many things we pilots alone are privileged to witness and/or be a part of; experiences exclusively the domain of those who fly. And it doesn't matter where you are in the time-space continuum of aviation, be you a Cessna 152 Student Pilot or crusty old Skipper – there are times in almost every flight where one can relax [just a little bit] for a few seconds, gaze out at the glorious sky from however high above the earth you are and realize "I'm the luckiest guy/gal in the world right now." Why is that? It is because we fly ...

"Once the wings go on, they never come off whether they can be seen or not. It fuses to the soul through adversity, fear and adrenaline, and no one who has ever worn them with pride, integrity and guts can ever sleep through the 'call of the wild' that wafts through bedroom windows in the deep of the night.

When a good flyer leaves the 'job' and retires, many are jealous, some are pleased and yet others, who may have already retired, wonder. We wonder if he knows what he is leaving behind because we already know.

We know, for example, that after a lifetime of camaraderie that few experience, it will remain as a longing for those past times. We know in the world of flying, there is a fellowship which lasts long after the uniforms are hung up in the back of the closet. We know even if he throws them away, they will be on him with every step and breath that remains in his life.

We also know how the very bearing of the man speaks of what he was and, in his heart, still is.

Because we flew, we envy no man on earth."

~Author Unknown

The older I get, the better I used to fly.

Communist Romania 1948 - 1989

AREA 51  FOLLIES

Area 51 is 'located' northwest of Nellis Air Force Base, Las Vegas and was affectionately known as "Dreamland" [If you look on the Las Vegas sectional chart, you'll find Groom Lake up there but no other indication there's a base adjacent]. Flying over or even near this invisible auxiliary airfield was taboo. Pilots who did were met by the secret police guys after landing and were not seen again for at least 24 hours. The big secret we all knew was this was the place where the USAF kept and flew all the Soviet Block aircraft. All generations of MIG 15's, 17's, 19's, 21's plus other secret Soviet stuff. This was in the days before satellite cameras. Since then there are pictures available taken from space, but its existence is still denied. Rumor had it that the Stealth fighters/bombers were tested from there [at night, natch!] and it is the repository for all the space alien bodies and debris collected by 'da guvmint' over the years. Very hush-hush – I'm probably taking my life in my hands by including the story in this book.

Late one afternoon, the Air Force folks out at Area 51 were very surprised to see a Cessna 152 landing at their "secret" base. They immediately impounded the aircraft and hauled the pilot into an interrogation room. The pilot's story was that he took off from Vegas, got lost, and spotted the base just as he was about to run out of fuel. The Air Force started a full FBI background check on the pilot and held him overnight during the investigation. By the next day they were finally convinced that the pilot really was lost and not a spy.

They gassed up his airplane, gave him a terrifying "you-did-not-see-a-base" briefing complete with threats of spending the rest of his life in prison, told him Las Vegas was that-a-way on such-and-such a heading, and sent him on his way.

The next day to the total disbelief of the Air Force the same Cessna showed up again. Once again, the MP's surrounded the plane. Only this time there were two people on the plane.

The same pilot jumped out and said, "Do anything you want with me, but my wife is in the plane, and you have to tell her where the hell I was last night!"

Groom Lake, aka 'Area 51', is located in R-4808N. Per the AIM 3 - 4 - 3, Restricted airspace ... "while not wholly prohibited, is subject to restrictions." These published areas ... "denote the existence of unusual, often invisible, hazards to aircraft such as artillery firing, aerial gunnery, or guided missiles." "Penetration of restricted areas without authorization ... may be extremely hazardous to the aircraft and its occupants."

No kidding, Sherlock! Being hauled out of an airplane by strong men, with mean tempers, bad attitudes, and carrying automatic weapons is most certainly an 'in-flight hazard' in my book! Then, there's the ... ahhh ... ~~inquisition~~ questioning by those secret police guys. That's hazardous as well. Then, there's all that anal probing by the aliens kept there. Nope - not for me, that's for sure!

He's the kind of pilot who navigates using a sundial, a rotary telephone and a Howard Johnson placemat.

AT THE AME'S

It has been said that the medical field is the natural enemy of aviation; that being said I am grouping medical stories in one place such as is presented in the "Beer, Wine and Spirits" section. Pilots of virtually all flying machines – save those listed in FAR 61.23 (b) & (c) – must hold a medical certificate when exercising flight privileges AND in between the dates of their medical examination, self-certify they are fit to fly. Referring to the AIM, section 8-1-1 presents areas of personal health to consider prior to committing aviation, summed up in paragraph (h) Personal Checklist. This is the "IM SAFE" checklist usually [hint] addressed during flightchecks, flight reviews and other qualification exercises.

I – Illness

M – Medications

S – Stress

A – Alcohol

F – Fatigue

E – Eating [& hydration], Emotional state

During his physical, the doctor asked a pilot about his daily activity level. The old Captain described a typical day this way:

"Well, yesterday afternoon, I waded along the edge of a lake, drank eight beers, escaped from wild dogs in the heavy brush, jumped away from an aggressive rattlesnake, marched up and down several rocky hills, stood in a patch of poison ivy, crawled out of quicksand and took four leaks behind big trees."

Inspired by the story, the doctor said, "You must be one hell of an outdoorsman!"

"Naw", he replied, "I'm just a shitty golfer."

AME Q & A:

Q: Doc, I've heard that cardiovascular exercise can prolong my life. Is that true?

A: Heart only good for so many beats and that's it. Don't waste them on exercise. Everything wears out eventually - speeding up heart doesn't make you live longer; it's like saying you can extend your cars life by driving faster. You want to live longer? Take a nap.

Q: Should I reduce my alcohol intake?

A: Oh, no. Wine is made from fruit; brandy is distilled wine which means they take water out of fruity bit, so you get even more goodness. Beer and whisky are made from grain. Bottoms up!

Q: How do I calculate my body to fat ratio?

A: Well, if you have one body and you have fat, your ratio is one-to-one. If you have two bodies then your ratio is two-to-one.

Q: What are the advantages of a regular exercise program?

A: Can't think of a single one, sorry. My philosophy: no pain = good!

Q: Aren't fried foods bad for me?

A: YOU'RE NOT LISTENING! Food is fried in VEGETABLE OIL! How can getting more vegetable be bad?

Q: Will doing sit-ups keep me from getting soft around the middle?

A: Oh, no! When you exercise muscle, it gets bigger. You should only do sit-ups if you want a bigger stomach.

Q: Is chocolate bad for me?

A: Are you crazy? Hell-ooo! Chocolate comes from a bean - another vegetable! It's the best feel-good food around!

Q: Is swimming good for me?

A: If swimming is good for figure, explain whale to me.

Q: Is 'getting in shape' important for my lifestyle?

A: Hey! Round is a shape!

Life should NOT be a journey to the grave with the intention of arriving safely in an attractive, good-looking, and well-preserved body; rather one should come to one's end skidding in sideways - a whisky in one hand and cigar in the other - totally worn out and yelling "WOO-HOO! What a ride!"

The Key to a Long Life:

The inventor of the treadmill died at age 54.
The inventor of gymnastics died at age 57.
The world bodybuilding champion died at age 41.
The best football player in the world *[in the US, that's called 'soccer']*, Diego Maradona, died at age 60.

HOWEVER ...

Colonel Sanders, of Kentucky Fried Chicken fame, died at 90.
Inventor of Nutella [chocolate spread] died at 88.
Cigarette maker Winston died at 102.
The inventor of opium died at age 116 ... in an earthquake.
Milton S. Hershey *[you know - the chocolate bar king]*, died at 88.

Just HOW in the WORLD did doctors conclude that exercise prolongs life?

The rabbit is a hyper little animal always jumping around, but its lifespan is only about two years *[if a predator doesn't get to it first]*. The land tortoise is a slow mover and doesn't raise its heartbeat above dirge speed, and it lives 400 years!

So ... have a drink and take a nap.
And if you are fortunate enough to awaken, have some bacon and eggs!

AUSSIE COMPLETE FABRICATION

In the first volume of <u>The Aviator's Bathroom Reader</u> *there was the rendition of an Australian pilot's experience with a representation from the CAB – Civil Aviation Board – the Aussie equivalent of the FAA in the United States. My Australian counterpart 'Down Under' swears on a stack of Kangaroo-skin covered Bibles each AND EVERY word was true. He has since sent me the report below which, he also swears, is a true and faithful report of the events as they happened. He claims he was not the Captain involved but, as there are ~~a few~~, ~~some~~, ~~many~~, a lot of details which would only be known by the ~~perpetrators~~ ... ahhh, participants ... I surmise the truth does not lie with him.*

To: Chief Pilot, Quantas Airlines

Sir,

In your icy, indeed hostile, telephone call of yesterday, you requested a report about the alleged proceedings involving my crew at the Qantas 90th Birthday celebration at an overseas airport. As the reports from the local authorities and the head of the Australian legation were undoubtedly a complete fabrication, I must take this opportunity to put the truth of the matter on file. Qantas management's kind offer to "buy a round of drinks" was taken on board by the crew who decided to upgrade the event to its correct status, so appropriate quantities of libation and food were purchased, with festivities being held in my hotel suite.

An enjoyable evening ensued but a sufficient supply of comestibles had not been obtained, so several members of the crew left for further purchases at a local bar. In a truly magnanimous gesture, ten bar girls from that establishment helped carry the beer back to the hotel. To demonstrate our appreciation of their assistance, we served them some cool drink. They then offered to show us some local culture, and, in order not to offend, we allowed them to dance some local 'exotic' dances {I must commend to you the 'Dance of the Seven Lotus Flowers' as a most excellent example of native pulchritude].

The banging on the walls of my room had, by now, quite honestly, become invasive, and it was disturbing the dancers, so we arranged an amusing little deterrent. S/O Brown's impersonation of the Police Officer was excellent! In full Qantas uniform, with an aluminum rubbish bin upside down on his head, he goose-stepped to each room and harangued the occupants with a very witty diatribe about disturbing hotel guests. I personally heard nothing of his alleged threats of life in Alcatraz or the Gulags as claimed by the sister of the Minister of Police whose room was, unfortunately, next door.

I have no doubt that this woman was the sneak who called security and hotel management and I absolutely refute that the shout "Look out, here come the Indians! Circle the wagons!" was made. The simple coincidence of security arriving just as we stood the double bed on its side across the door to make the dance floor bigger is obvious. The major damage to the room occurred when a group of gate crashers, whom we could not know were hotel security, forced their way in just as most of us happened to be leaning against the bed watching the dancing.

The subsequent events in the foyer of the hotel are an equally vicious distortion of the facts. I was explaining the importance of the 90th Birthday to the General Manager of the hotel and noting that other guests were fabricating stories of noise, drinking and singing at the celebration, when F/O Smith (ex-SAS*) and several other keep-fit enthusiasts, in keeping with their almost monastic pursuit of health, organized the race up the drapes which hang along the foyer wall. It says nothing for the workmanship of some of these nations that the fittings were torn from the wall before most of the crew was even halfway up.

At this stage, in an amazing display of international posturing, the Governor of the city, who was attending the National Day cocktail party in the foyer, cast some denigrating remarks about Australian culture. Although he misunderstood our gestures of greeting, female Flight Attendant Williams rescued the situation with her in depth of knowledge of local culture. Her rendition of the Fertility Dancing Maiden in the foyer's 'Pool of Remembrance' was nothing short of breathtaking. Normally this dance is performed wearing just a sarong skirt so F/A Williams' extra step to nature was a bold step forward.

Unfortunately, during one intricate step, F/A Williams slipped and fell beneath the fountain, so we were lucky that S/O Brown, who had the great presence of mind to strip to avoid getting his uniform wet, leapt in to help. That the tiles of the pool were slippery is beyond dispute, as it took nearly ten minutes of thrashing about before S/O Brown could actually complete his rescue. Such concern was there for these two exemplary crew member's safeties that the rest of the crew were forced to assist, and I deny that this massed altruistic rescue attempt could be construed as a 'Water Polo' game! This slanderous accusation was first put to me by the Chief of the Riot Squad, whose storm troopers had apparently been called by some overzealous Fascists at the cocktail party.

Order had nearly been restored when the fire started. I prefer F/O Smith's version of events that the drapes had caught fire from being against a light fitting, and that he dropped his cigarette lighter whilst trying to escape the flames. Had host management fulfilled their responsibilities and used fire retardant material instead of velvet, the fire would not have spread to the rest of the hotel.

The responsible attitude shown by my crew in assisting the bar staff to carry out drinks from the cocktail party is to be commended, not condemned, and the attempt by male members of the crew to extinguish pockets of fire using natural means has been totally misrepresented in some quarters. I cannot overstate how strongly I resent the assertions made in the Chief Fire Officer's Report.

I made an official protest about these matters when the head of the Australian Legation visited us at the Police Station the next morning. However, not only did Ambassador Jones not attempt to refute the preposterous allegations made against me and my crew, but also by failing to secure our release immediately, caused the subsequent aircraft delay.

I did not know Her Majesty was to be aboard our aircraft, but I am sure that her enforced 12- hour visit to that country was appreciated by local dignitaries and probably HRH herself. (I must mention that the local manager is far too obsequious - Smarmy!

Smarmy! You should have seen him bowing and scraping. Never make a Prime Minister, that chap!)

Finally, I note that not since the motion picture 'Rainman' has Qantas been mentioned in so many newspapers. (Some people in Qantas would die for coverage like that.) The main newspaper at the slip port coincidentally mentioned Qantas 90 times on its front page alone, although some of the coupled epithets can only be described as the worst journalistic excesses of the gutter press.

I trust that now I have outlined the correct version of events; we may allow ourselves a discreet smile as to the lack of social sophistication of some of these developing nations and put all this behind us. As far as I am concerned, the crew carried on the finest Qantas traditions.

Regards,

Captain (redacted)

P.S. I checked amongst the language qualified members of the crew, but no one was up to speed on Latin. Can you recommend anyone in the International Department who could translate 'Persona Non Grata'?

---

* - SAS = Special Air Service: Equivalent to a cross between SWAT Teams and Navy SEALS in the USA.

USAAC Pre-WWII Flight Engineer wings (prototype).

AVIATION'S ANCILLARY LAWS

As aviators we all have been exposed to Bernoulli's Law of aerodynamics which many students quote as the reason an airplane can fly. Sadly they are mistaken*. That being said, there are many other 'laws' which can affect the life, operations, and activities of a pilot. I gather and present them here for the first time in a public forum as a service to my many reader.

Law of Mechanical Repair:
After your hands become covered in grease your nose will itch, and you'll need to go pee.

Law of Gravity:
Any tool, nut, bolt, or screw will, when dropped, roll to the least accessible corner of the hangar.

Law of Probability:
The probability of being watched is directly proportional to the stupidity of your act.
> Corollary - the quality of the landing is inversely proportional to the number and importance of the people watching, experiencing it.

Law of Random Numbers:
If you dial a wrong number, you will never get a busy signal; someone will always answer.

Law of Variation:
If you change the line [or traffic lane] you are currently in, the one you just left will always move faster than the one you're in now.

Law of the Bath [or shower]:
The moment you are fully immersed, the telephone will ring.

Law of Close Encounters:
The probability of running into someone you know increases dramatically when you are with someone you don't want to be seen with.

Law of Results:
When you attempt to prove to someone that something doesn't work - it will.
    Corollary - when attempting to demonstrate how something works - it won't.

Law of Biomechanics:
The severity of the itch is inversely proportional to one's reach.

Law of the Coffee Break:
As soon as you sit down to enjoy the first cup of coffee, someone will ask you to do something which will last until the coffee is cold.

Law of Lockers:
If there are only two people in the locker room, they will have adjacent lockers.

Law of Physical Surfaces:
The chances of a food item falling off a surface and landing face-down is directly correlated to the newness and cost of the carpet or rug.
    Corollary - any dropped food item will always land face-down

Law of Logical Arguments:
Anything is possible if you don't know what you're talking about.
    Corollary - the most well-explained logical argument will be wasted on someone incapable of understanding it.

Law of Physical Appearance:
If the clothes fit, they're ugly.

Law of Speaking Publicly:
A closed mouth gathers no foot.
    Corollary - Better to keep one's mouth shut and be thought a fool than to open it and remove all doubt.

Law of Health:
If one doesn't feel well, make an appointment to see the doctor. By the time you get there, you'll feel better. If you don't make the appointment, you'll stay sick for weeks.

Law of Theater and/or Sports Arenas:
The people whose seats are furthest from the aisle will always arrive last. They will leave their seats several times to fetch food, drinks or go to the bathroom. They will then always leave early before the end of the performance or game.
    Corollary - Those with aisle seats arrive early, never move once, have long gangly legs or big bellies, and always stay to the bitter end of the performance or game. They are usually very surly folks.

Law of Pessimism:
Anything which could go wrong but doesn't is waiting for a more critical time to go wrong.

*Bernoulli Principle:
In fluid dynamics, **Bernoulli's principle** states that for an inviscid flow, an increase in the speed of the fluid occurs simultaneously with a decrease in temperature and pressure.

This principle has erroneously been stated as the reason a wing creates 'lift' and thus the reason an airplane 'flies'. The real principle required to be in effect for an airplane to fly is stated simply as "Have plenty of money." Just wanted to clear that up so you can pass the aerodynamics portion of your next flightcheck. - Ed.

BEER, WINE & SPIRITS

Okay, you drunken derelicts – instead of interspersing alcohol-related pages randomly throughout this book, I decided to make it easier for you to find them and thus enjoy them collectively. But first ... the sermon – There's enough written about booze and flying to, well, fill a book. The only book that matters in this regard is 14 CFR, Part 91.17:

91.17 ALCOHOL OR DRUGS
(A) No person may act or attempt to act as a crewmember of a civil aircraft –
    (1) Within 8 hours after the consumption of any alcoholic beverage.
    (2) While under the influence of alcohol.
    (3) While using any drug that affects a person's faculties in any way contrary to safety; or
    (4) While having an alcohol concentration of 0.04 or greater in a blood or breath specimen

[There's a lot more to this regulation than what is presented above; mostly, what one must do when asked for a breath or blood sample by law enforcement and how soon the results must be reported to the FAA. It behooves a pilot to read this regulation in its entirety not only for familiarities sake but to also to impress upon self how serious a matter this is. Folks, the Feds have NO [none, zero, nichts, nada] sense of humor about this and haven't for a long, long time.]

I cannot stress highly enough, boys and girls, how important it is – REALLY IMPORTANT – that one NEVER mix alcohol and flying and [for those living on the Left Coast and other 'progressive' states] the mixing of marijuana and flying. There is no problem with alcohol <u>when used in moderation</u>; the Blood-Alcohol Concentration [BAC] ratio goes down quickly by the time the proverbial "Eight hours between bottle and throttle" is up and impairment should be negligible. Marijuana stays in the system for a long time and while currently there is no field sobriety test for pot, I have heard of several outfits working on this.

Are your certificates and privileges worth the risk?

And a DUI/DWI is equally catastrophic; you're looking at a minimum expense of $15,000 for court and lawyers' fees, the fact you've been convicted of this offense MUST be declared on every medical application <u>for the rest of time</u> and this alerts the FAA to the fact you might not be making the right decisions with/about your life and they could very easily suspend and/or revoke your certificates. Now what are you gonna do? Sell encyclopedias?

A friend of mine had a DUI when he was young – he straightened up and finished his career as a captain for a major airline. Five years [5 years!] after retirement he decided to return to General Aviation so applied for a medical certificate <u>forgetting to mention</u> he had a DUI back in the early 1970's! He received a certified, return-receipt requested letter from the FAA – "Emergency Revocation of Medical Privileges" - as they alleged, he lied on the form by not stating he had a DUI! It took him a year – over one year – to appeal and fight that denial!

People, the feds have a long memory, and they have little inclination to listen to reason, appeals or excuses – "I just forgot" is NOT in their lexicon. Exercise the highest level of discretion and judgement whenever mind-altering substances are involved [or, for that matter, marriage. But that's a sermon for another time and place].

Suggestion when out on the town: Use a 'social camouflage' technique of having ONE beer from a colored bottle then for the rest of the night refilling the bottle with soda or water. You'll always be seen with a 'drink' in your hand – thus blending in with the crowd – and yet never getting close to blowing over the BAC limit. This has worked for me for years; with slow consumption you can make one beer last a long time, can't you? Your certificates, your employment, your spouse, your family, and your life may very well depend on it.

That being said, if we were to meet someday, I will be more than happy to allow you to buy the first [and only] round. This is my vice of choice:

My taste is simple – I prefer only the best!
Put another way: Life is too short to drink bad whisky!

A conversation between a man and his new girlfriend

Woman:	Do you drink beer?
Man:	Yes
Woman:	How many beers a day?
Man:	Usually about three
Woman:	How much do you pay per beer?
Man:	$5.00 which includes a tip
Woman:	And how long have you been drinking?
Man:	About 20 years, I suppose
Woman:	So, a beer costs $5 and you have three beers a day which puts your spending each month at $450. In one year, it would be approximately $5,400. Correct?
Man:	Correct
Woman:	If in 1 year you spend $5400, not accounting for inflation, the past 20 years puts your spending at $108,000 correct?
Man:	Correct
Woman:	Do you know how much that would be worth today if you didn't drink so much beer?
Man:	No
Woman:	You could have put that money in an interest savings account.
Man:	And?
Woman:	After accounting for compound interest for the past 20 years, you could have now bought your own private airplane?

Pregnant pause ...

Man:	Do you drink beer?
Woman:	No.
Man:	Where's your airplane?

A couple were out shopping together; after placing two cases of beer in the cart, they found themselves at the cosmetics counter where the woman lingered for some time.

Man: Why are you buying so much of this stuff?
Woman: To help me look beautiful. Why do you buy so much beer?

Man: Same reason.

... and then the fight began ...

WARNING: The consumption of alcohol may cause you to believe you can make reasonable decisions!

Whisky was invented to make pilots' stories more interesting.

Beer and the Old Fighter Pilot

Yesterday morning an old fighter pilot bought two six packs of beer on sale at the Liquor Store.

He placed them on the front seat of the car and headed back home. He stopped at the service station where a drop-dead gorgeous, almost blonde was filling up her car at the next pump.

It was very warm, and she was wearing tight shorts and a light top which was wide open.

She glanced at the beer, bent over and knocked on his passenger window.

With her bra-less breasts almost falling out of her skimpy top she said, in a sexy voice, "I'm a big believer in barter, old fellow, would you be interested in trading sex for beer?"

He thought for a few seconds and then asked, "What kind of beer you got?"

This soliloquy came from an episode of the sit-com "Cheers" of [now] a few decades ago. It's a rare event when natural history, survival of the fittest and beer can be used in the same instance, but here it is in all its truthful glory:

"Well, ya see, Norm, it's like this. A herd of buffalo can only move as fast as the slowest buffalo. And when the herd is hunted, it is the slowest and weakest ones at the back which are killed first. This natural selection is good for the herd as a whole, because the general speed and health of the whole group keeps improving by the regular killing of the weakest members. In much the same way, the human brain can operate only as fast as the slowest brain cells. Excessive intake of alcohol, as we know, kills brain cells. But naturally, it attacks the slowest and weakest brain cells first. In this way, regular consumption of beer eliminates the weaker brain cells, making the brain a faster and more efficient machine. That's why you always feel smarter after a few beers."

Priorities of Revolutionary War Sailors

While definitely NOT an aviation-related story, this DOES show the 'Founding Fathers' and the budding US Navy had their priorities straight. One cannot help but wonder, though, that at 6 pounds per gallon, the water carried on board [291,600 pounds = 145.8 tons] could have been replaced by other, more useful cargo...like more rum.

The U.S.S. Constitution (Old Ironsides), as a combat vessel, carried 48,600 gallons of fresh water for her crew of 475 officers and men. This was sufficient to last six months of sustained operations at sea. She carried no evaporators (i.e. freshwater distillers); however, let it be noted that according to her ship's log,

"On July 27, 1798, the U.S.S. Constitution sailed from Boston with a full complement of 475 officers and men, 48,600 gallons of fresh water, 7,400 cannon shot, 11,600 pounds of black powder and 79,400 gallons of rum."

Her mission: "To destroy and harass English shipping."

Making Jamaica on 6 October, she took on 826 pounds of flour and 68,300 gallons of rum. She then headed for the Azores, arriving there 12 November. She provisioned with 550 pounds of beef and 64,300 gallons of Portuguese wine. On 18 November, she set sail for England. In the ensuing days she defeated five British men-of-war and captured and scuttled 12 English merchant ships, salvaging only the rum aboard each.

By 26 January, her powder and shot were exhausted. Nevertheless, although unarmed she made a night raid up the Firth of Clyde in Scotland. Her landing party captured a whisky distillery and transferred 40,000 gallons of single malt Scotch aboard by dawn. Then she headed home.

The U.S.S. Constitution arrived in Boston on 20 February 1799, with no cannon shot, no food, no powder, no rum, no wine, no whisky, and 38,600 gallons of water.

GO NAVY!

105-Year-Old Describes Keys to Longevity
"For better digestion – I drink beer.
In case of loss of appetite, I drink white wine.
In case of low blood pressure, I drink red wine.
In case of high blood pressure, I drink Scotch whisky.
When I have a cold, I drink Schnapps."
"When do you drink water?"
"I've never been that sick."

Giving up Drinking & Flying

A man was walking down the street when he was accosted by a particularly dirty and shabby-looking man wearing on old pilot's suit coat who asked him for a few dollars for dinner.

The man took out his wallet, extracted fifty dollars and asked, "If I give you this money, will you buy alcohol with it instead of dinner?"

"No, I had to stop drinking years ago," the old pilot retiree replied.

"Will you spend this on flying airplanes instead of food?" the man asked.

"Are you NUTS?" replied the homeless man. "I haven't flown in over 15 years!"

"Well," said the man, "I'm not going to give you money. Instead, I'm going to take you home for a shower and a terrific dinner cooked by my wife."

The homeless man was astounded.

"Won't your wife be furious with you for doing that?"

The man replied, "That's okay. It's important for her to see what happens to a man after giving up drinking and flying!"

Words which are Difficult to Say When Drunk

When the police pull someone over under suspicion of drunk driving, there are several 'road-side sobriety tests' which can be expected by the pull-overee. There may be a heel-toe walking exercise, a 'so-many-steps' this – a - way and 'so-many-steps' that – a - way, a close your eyes and touch the tip of your nose with your index finger test, and so forth. As a public service, I submit to you a test which, when performed only with a trusted ~~accomplice~~ friend, may avert certain disaster, embarrassment and/or financial loss.

Difficult Words to say when one has been drinking:

1. Innovative
2. Preliminary
3. Proliferation
4. Cinnamon

Words which are extremely difficult to say when drunk:

1. Specificity
2. Onomatopoeia
3. Anti - disestablishmentarianism
4. Transubstantiate

Words which are downright impossible to say when really, really drunk:

1. I know all the words and sound just like Elvis
2. No thanks, I'm married.
3. Nope, no more booze for me!
4. Sorry, but you're really not my type.
5. No thanks, I'm not hungry.

6. I'm not interested in fighting you.
7. Thank you, but I won't make any attempt to dance. I have no coordination and would hate to make a total fool of myself.
8. Oh no, I must be going home now as I must work in the morning.
9. No, you are too young and beautiful for me to ask to go home with me.

When was this elixir from heaven first discovered? That is covered by the mists of time gone by, but we might give thanks to those denizens of the outer isles of what is now Great Britain, Ireland and Scotland for their industriousness and creativity:

Writing of whisky in his Chronicles of England, Scotland and Ireland in 1577, Raphael Holinshed observed that – "Being moderately taken it cutteth fleume, it lighteneth the mynd, it quickeneth the spirits, it cureth the hydropsie, it pounceth the stone, it repelleth gravel, it puffeth away ventositie, it kepyth and preserveth the eyes drom dazelying, the tongue from lispying, the teeth from chatterying, the throte from rattlying, the weasan from stieflying, the stomach from womblying, the harte from swellying, the bellie from wirtching, the guts from rumblying, the hands from shivering, the sinews from shrinkying, the veynes from crumplying, the bones from akying, the marrow from soakying, and truly it is a sovereign liquor if it be orderlie taken".

Peru Pilot

Miscellaneous Quotes on the Subject:
"I think I promised to have 3 beers and be home by 10. I always get those two mixed up."

"Tell me what brand of whisky Grant drinks. I would like to send a barrel of it to my other generals" - Abraham Lincoln

"Never delay kissing a pretty girl or opening a bottle of whisky" - Ernest Hemingway

"Happiness is having a rare steak, a bottle of whisky and a dog to eat the rare steak." - Johnny Carson

"I'm here to drink whisky and kick ass and Pilgrim, I'm all out of whisky." - John Wayne

"If I cannot drink whisky and smoke cigars in Heaven then I shall not go." - Mark Twain

"Too much of anything is bad, but too much whisky is barely enough." - Mark Twain

"I always carry a flask of whisky in case of snakebite; furthermore I always carry a small snake." - W.C. Fields

"Whisky has killed more men than bullets, but most men would rather be full of whisky than bullets." - Winston Churchill

"There is no bad whisky. There are only some whisky's that aren't as good as others." -Raymond Chandler

"Whisky is liquid sunshine." - George Bernard Shaw

"Does love make the world go 'round? Well, yes; but whisky makes it go 'round twice as fast." - James Hauenstein

"Sitting on a bar stool and sipping a shot of whisky washed down by a cold beer is an impeccable routine. I cannot think of a finer ritual." - John E. Quinlan

"Whisky, the drink which enables a man to magnify his joy and his happiness." - Emily Arata

"The water was not fit to drink. To make it palatable we had to add whisky. By diligent effort I learned to like it." - Winston Churchill

"I never should have switched from scotch [whisky] to martinis." - Humphrey Bogart

"I spent 90% of my pay on good times, women and whisky. The rest I just wasted." - Tug McGraw

"In those days the best painkiller was ice; it wasn't addictive and was particularly effective if you poured some whisky over it." - George Burns

"My life is 50% wondering if it's too late to drink coffee and 50% wondering if it's too early to drink whisky."

"Then I tried whisky; if you get hooked on whisky then everything else just tastes wrong." - Ron White

"Lord, give me coffee to change the things I can and whisky to accept the ones I cannot." - Yourse Trooly

"I wish to live to be 150 years old, but the day I die I wish it to be with a good cigar in one hand and a glass of good whisky in the other." - Yourse Trooly

"The problem with some people is when they're not drunk, they're sober." - W.B. Yeats

---

Whiskey, aka 'Whisky'

"Some of my friends are for it and some of my friends are against it. I intend to stick with my friends."

The quote above, and the definition below, exactly, and thoroughly describes my view, attitude and respect for the afore-mentioned adult beverage – notably as a 'Safety Award' after the flying machine has been cleaned, prepared and rendered 'Flight Ready' for the next foray into the 'wild blue yonder'.

In 1952, Armon M. Sweat, Jr., a member of the Texas House of Representatives was asked about his position on whisky. What follows is his exact answer (taken from the Political Archives of Texas):

"If, by 'whiskey', you mean whiskey, the devil's brew, the poisonous scourge, the bloody monster that defiles innocence, dethrones reason, destroys the home, creates misery and poverty, yea, literally takes the bread from the mouths of little children; if you mean that evil drink that topples Christian men and women from the pinnacles of righteous and gracious living into the bottomless pit of degradation, shame, despair, helplessness, and hopelessness, then, my friend, I am opposed to it with every fiber of my being.

If, however, by whiskey you mean the lubricant of conversation, the philosophic juice, the elixir of life, the liquid that is consumed when good fellows get together, that puts a song in their hearts and the warm glow of contentment in their eyes; if you mean Christmas cheer, the stimulating sip that puts a little spring in the step of an elderly gentleman on a frosty morning; if you mean that drink that enables man to magnify his joy, and to forget life's great tragedies and heartbreaks and sorrow; if you mean that drink the sale of which pours into Texas treasuries untold millions of dollars each year, that provides tender care for our little crippled children, our blind, our deaf, our dumb, our pitifully aged and infirm, to build the finest highways, hospitals, universities, and community colleges in this nation, then my friend, I am absolutely, unequivocally in favor of it.

This is my position, and as always, I refuse to compromise on matters of principle."

The Wine Tester

"I never let my schooling interfere with my education." - ed.

At a wine merchant's warehouse the regular taster died, and the director started looking for a new one to hire. He posted a sign at the entrance to the building... EXPERIENCED WINE TASTER NEEDED -- POSITION STARTS IMMEDIATELY.

A retired Army Aviator named "Ace," drunk and with a ragged dirty look and smelling of last night's rounds, strolled by the building and saw the sign. He went into the building to apply for the position.

Aghast at his appearance, the director wondered... how to send him away but, to be fair; he gave him a glass of wine to taste. The old Warrant 5 held the glass up to his left eye, tilted his head toward incoming sunlight and studied the contents looking through the glass. He then took a sip and said, "It's a Southern California Muscat, three years old, grown on a north slope, matured in steel containers. Somewhat low-grade but acceptable."

"That's correct," said the boss. Glancing at his assistant he said..."Another one, please." The old Army pilot took the goblet, full of a deep red liquid, stuck his nose into the glass, sniffed deeply and took a long slow sip ... rolling his eyeballs in a circle, he then looked at the director and said, "It's a Cabernet Sauvignon, eight years old, south-western slope, oak barrels, matured at eight degrees. Requires three more years for the finest results."
"Absolutely correct - a third glass," said the director.

Receiving another glass, again, the Army pilot eyed the crystal, took in a little bit of the aroma, and sipped very softly... "It's a Pinot Blanc champagne, very high grade and exclusive," said the pilot calmly.

The director was astonished and winked at his assistant to suggest something.

She left the room and came back in with a wine glass half-full of urine.
The old Army pilot eyed it suspiciously... a color he could not quite recall.
He took a sip, swishing it over his tongue and across his teeth, musing upward all the while.
"It's a blonde, 26 years old, three months pregnant, and if I don't get the job, I'll name the father."

And Finally – the "Written Breathalizer Test"

"It's when things are going just right that you'd better be suspicious. There you are; fat, dumb, and happy. The whole world is yours and you're the answer to the Wright Brothers' prayers. You say to yourself, "Nothing can go wrong ... all my trespasses are forgiven." Best you not believe it."
- Ernest K. Gann, "Advice from an old pelican" The Black Watch, 1989

BOUNCED LANDING

While monitoring traffic at KAPA, we overheard a Skyhawk pilot having a difficult day. Having gone around on his first attempt, he ended up safely on the ground on his second – if a bit long and far from gracefully.

Tower: "Skyhawk 123, you O.K. there?"

Skyhawk 123: "Yeah. We took a bounce there. *[Pause]* I hope it didn't look as bad as it felt."

Tower: "It did."

One of "Drew's Rules of Flying":

Never be so intent on landing that you're not prepared to immediately execute a go around.
The vehicle you're in was meant to fly – if you don't like what is going on, get back into the middle of the sky, and then sort out your options. It may be rough, turbulent and such, but you are away from where aircraft come to grief; namely the edges of the sky. The edges of the sky can be identified as where celestial objects such as moons, spacecraft and satellites can be found on the high side and on the low side, where the houses, trees and towers are. The latter are more likely to be encountered than the former.

BUZZ JOB

A bit of a longer read but worth the time: Don't know where or when I gathered this story from the dustbin of times-gone-by, but I defy any of todays' flyboys to match this story for inventive creativity and plain old 'honest' fun. A yearning for the good old days! [Wasn't there – didn't do it.]

My last tour in the Corps, I was flying the RF-4B Recon-Phantom. The mission and the plane were a flathatters' dream. Ninety percent of our mission was single lane, solo sorties. And we made our living "down in the dirt" We were about the only people left in the military that did low level, VFR Operations on almost a daily basis. A normal mission for us was to leave El Toro [in Southern California – Ed.], fly the standard instrument departure (SID) and upon crossing Saddleback Mountain heading for the Salton Sea, call Los Angeles Center, request descent to FL 180 and upon arrival cancel the instrument flight plan for the next 40 minutes and go VFR down into the desert. We'd usually fly pre-planned routes and take pictures of all kinds of targets. This was usually from no higher than five hundred feet and seldom at less than five hundred knots. You have no idea what real speed feels like until you've been 1.1 Mach, at less than 100 feet! What a rush!

On occasion targets of opportunity would pop up in the desert and the hunt was on. The only worry we usually had was who was in the back seat; most guys in the squadron knew within a month who the players were compared to the passengers and if you had a good guy back there you could have a lot of fun. Things were a little loose then, most of us had been to Vietnam and we were a pretty salty bunch. The kids flying in the military today couldn't imagine the freedom we had and the limits we could stretch it to. My secondary MOS was as a Maintenance Officer: I was also a post maintenance check pilot and, as such, used to fly most of my functional flight tests over the Salton Sea. I hated the idea that if I ever had to shuck the bird (ejecting) of coming down in the cold waters in Warning Area [offshore ocean]. The desert: from the Salton Sea east to the Gila Bend Range and south to the Mexican border and north to Hoover Dam was our playground ... Got to know to know the area like the back of my hand. About a month before the fateful day... one of the Twidgets from the electronics shop came up to me and said, "Boss, the next time you're out in the desert have the backseater crank this frequency into the HF Radio and see what happens."

Now my family's Coat of Arms bears a Latin inscription that roughly translates "Beware of those bearing gifts". Heritage and experience made me alert - and suspicious (This bunch had already gotten me once when they submitted, and I approved, a requisition chit for fallopian tubes). I looked this young stud right in the eye and said, "What is it"? He was coy and evasive at first but finally said, "I don't know if it'll work in the airplane but in the shop with a dummy load on the antenna and on the lower sideband we can talk to the truckers up and down the freeway out here". He went on to say he thought it might be fun. I took the frequency, put it into my survival vest and promptly forgot about it.

About a month later, Denny Fitz and I and our two backseaters set out to make a parts run over to Hill AFB. Hill was the Air Force Supply Depot for F-4 parts and I had made the acquaintance of an Air Force MSgt. there who with adequate priming, could produce any hard to get part RFI regardless of the paperwork! Since the Marine Corps was always sucking hind teat when it came to parts, this Air Force MSgt. became an irreplaceable cog in my maintenance management plan. In plain English - it was easier to steal the shit from the Air Force than get it through our own supply system! The Sgt. was our inside man who made all things possible. We had the forward camera bay of Denny's airplane loaded with two inop parts (CSD generators), which we would turn in for new ones and two bottles of Jack Daniels (primer fluid). We had a 0600 brief and by 0700 were on our way out to the aircraft.

It was a beautiful day; the stars and moon were in all the right places - the air was crisp, and I was about to leave the surly bonds of earth once again. I used to love these early morning takeoffs! The lights were still bright and the nine to fivers were just getting up. Looking down on them, you couldn't help but feel superior; the drones were just getting up to service the queen bee and here I was high above them, seeing what they could only dream about and I was getting paid to do it! Life was good.

In the brief, I was to lead going over and Denny would lead coming back. At the end of the runway, we did our run-ups, nozzle checks, controls, gauges, and I looked over at Denny and he gave me a thumb's up "Show Time Rock and Roll"! I absolutely loved the acceleration of the Phantom, it was awesome. After I rotated and got airborne, I came out of burner at 350 knots and let the good times roll. A few seconds later, Denny radios, "Two's up" and I looked down on him as he joined up and slid into position.

The Phantom was an airplane that could look so different from various angles; from the side, it could look sleek and fast, especially the RF with its' long slender nose. But if you looked down on top of the aircraft in flight it looked fat and brutish, like a down lineman in football ugly and not something you'd want to **** with. From below, the way the wings melded with the fuselage it once again looked rakish. The RF-4 looked like and was the thoroughbred of the species. Like a young stallion it just wanted to run; there was not a fighter on the west coast that could stay with us in basic engine or burner. We probably had the last true Mach II birds left in the fleet - time and weight had slowed all the other F-4's down. At the top end, only the Vigilante could give us a run for our money. Note: Lost a race to a Vigi one day; passing 1.8 he just walked off and left me. I asked the guy in the wardroom later "Just how fast is the son of a bitch"? With a twinkle in his eye he said, "Don't know never had enough gas to find out."

Back to paradise, we're climbing through about 23,000 feet when my aircraft gave a noticeable thump, lurch and the "Master Caution" light came on. I looked down at the telelight panel and saw the right generator had dropped offline and the buss tie had stayed open. I already knew that from the plane's actions, and I'd started losing some of the associated equipment: I reset the generator, and all seemed well for about two minutes when it failed again. Hmmm, not looking good. I called Denny on the radio and explained what was going on.

Now flying on one generator was no big deal but taking off with only one was forbidden. If I continued to Hill AFB and landed, I'd be stuck there until the thing was fixed. We talked it over and decided the best course of action was for Denny to go on and I'd RTB (return to base) to El Toro. I called LA Center on the radio and made arrangements to split the flight with Denny proceeding as planned and me returning to El Toro. That settled, I kissed Denny off and turned back to the southwest. 'Hooters' was my backseater that day (so named because his wife had the biggest set of all the wives in the squadron). As soon as I set course, I tried to re-set the generator once again voila, it worked. I looked down and we were approaching the town of Thermal, near the north end of the Salton Sea and I still had almost a full bag of gas - 13,000 lbs. internal and still had some fuel in my drop tank. I decided it would be a shame to waste all that gas by dumping in order to land so I called LA Center and asked for a descent to FL 180 and canceled my IFR flight plan and told them I would do a pickup in 45 minutes. Center approved and upon reaching 180 we canceled instruments.

Now Marines can get pretty creative, especially living on the edge as we were in those days and we generally flew on hot mike that way we didn't have to key the mike in order to have a conversation. I asked Hooters if there was any place he wanted to see. "Naw, let's just cruise around". After circling the Salton Sea we were bored. Then I remembered the note in my survival vest! I then said, "Hey, Hoots - crank up the HF radio." A little explanation here; The RF-4 was the only Phantom that had the HF installed as far as I know. It was so we could communicate while over "Indian territory" (North Vietnam) and out of UHF range. The frequency control box for the radio was in the rear cockpit and only the backseater could set frequencies. However, the pilot could, once the frequency was set, take control of the radio in the front cockpit by simply flipping a switch (a feature obviously designed by a pilot).

The radio itself was a boomer 300 watts output and the whole tail of the aircraft was the antenna and of course whatever altitude you were at (in this case about 17,000 feet) that was the height of the antenna. Plainly put we were a 300-watt, mobile radio transceiver with a 17,000-foot antenna. We had a lot of range! Hoots then asked me if I wanted to make a phone patch through NORAD. "Nope" I replied, "I got a new frequency for you to try". Hoots plugged in the frequency and tried to load the antenna which in Marine parlance meant he blew and whistled into the radio mike - No go. The antenna was not responding (actually this was common procedure with HF radios, base or mobile). I then said, "Let me try". I took control of the radio and I blew into the mike and almost instantly we started hearing "Breaker, breaker one nine" and all kinds of other gibberish. Reading my mind (not hard in those days); Hoots says, "You're Not"! I said "F***in' A! This is too good to pass up"!

For the next minute or so, we carried on the last rational and sane conversation that would emanate from the cockpit for the next half hour. "Shadow [my callsign], you know how many watts we put out"? "Yeah, 300; now shut up and let me find one close". "Do you know what the average CB radio puts out"? "No - listen". "It's about 6 watts max". (****in' backseaters they were always so anal-retentive and tech oriented) "So what"? "Well I was just thinkin' - If you do this, you may fry a few radios". "Naw, ain't gonna happen". No sooner had I said that, then we hear loud and clear "Breaker, breaker one nine ... any station, this is Georgia Boy. How do you hear me, over?" The thought then occurred to me, that great moments in life can be preceded by the simplest of statements! Before Hoots could throw water on this great opportunity, I keyed the mike and said, "Georgia Boy This is Recon 05, I hear you loud and clear. How me, over?"

Immediately he came back "Ooh-weee man"! "What kind of radio is that? You just about blew me outta my cab! Hell Bubba I'm illegal and you pegged my needles! You a base station or something?" "Nope", says me "I'm mobile". "Mobile my ass! You must be on some mountaintop around here. You better shut that thing down, Bubba, before the Feds are on you like stink on poo!" "Georgia Boy, I assure you I'm mobile." "Yeah, right". At this moment I had a stroke of pure genius if I do say so myself; I had turned back toward Thermal, I keyed the radio and said, "Georgia Boy Where are you? I'll prove to you I'm mobile."

He replied. "I'm near Thermal east bound, and just passed Desert Center; I got my pedal pegged to the metal and I ain't stopping until I gets to Phoenix, Arizona!" "I'll catch you before you get to Blythe and prove to you I'm mobile" says I. "Ooh-weee, Shit, man you ain't fooling me. You in Thermal! You got to be a base station on a mountain top". "I assure you I'm mobile"! I said. He then said something that was too good to be true: "Recon - Old Georgia Boy is east bound and down, you ain't catching me 'lessen you in a Rocket ship"! Hoots says, "Aww **** Why'd he have to go and say that"?

This was going to be one of those cherished little moments in life. By now, I knew he was on Interstate 10 between Desert Center and Blythe. We had to be just southwest of him about fifty miles away. Now if the genies of fate didn't urinate on the best of intentions of man this was gonna be one for the ages! I brought the power up and started downhill! One of the marvels of the desert is that on a clear day from altitude you could literally see forever for miles and miles and miles. My mind went tactical: I knew he still believed I was really stationary but just in case I figured he would be checking his rear-view mirrors. My plan was to come from the southwest ... the desert. He wouldn't be expecting me to come from there. Hoots then chimes up "You gonna boom 'em"? You're .98 and accelerating". (Sometimes I think the only reason those guys were back there was to bring an extra conscience along in case your own went into fail mode of which mine was fast approaching) "No, don't think I wanna do that". (But my mind was saying Great f***ing idea though!)

With both consciences in order, I backed off about 3%. Going supersonic was now off the table so I had to think of something else. In a nano-second it came to me A few of us had discovered that if you get fast enough and low enough out in the desert you can leave a dust trail about a quarter of a mile behind you from your shock wave and wing vortices! (Before you say bullshit, I have plenty of others who can back me up on this. You also need to understand: Low and Fast was where we had to live in order to survive our mission. Some of us just liked to go a little lower and a little faster than others.)

Glenn Hyde saw it first-hand one day when he tried to follow me down in the weeds in a straight F-4 (he was supposed to be flying chase at 5,000 feet) his backseater later accused both of us of trying to kill him. Glenn tried to follow me up the contour of a mountain and then through a saddle in a ridge line where he hit my jet wake, which flipped him upside down at less than 100 feet AGL and at over 580 knots! Glenn had been a crop duster before joining the Marines and kept his cool, pushed forward on the stick and climbed inverted until he had enough altitude to roll upright. His backseater was still shaking over an hour later during the debriefing. By the way, Glenn's call sign was "Crazy" - obviously a well-deserved tribute. Back to Georgia Boy ... after less than five minutes I was now down to about a thousand feet, holding .98 Mach and could see the back of a white truck about 10 miles just northeast of me I keyed the radio and asked "Georgia Boy, what color is the back of your truck"? "It's white like my Georgia Cracker ass!"

As he answered, I saw the truck ahead do a little wiggle in the road ... he was obviously clearing his six! I saw no other traffic on the road in either direction for over ten miles (even the car Gods were co-operating). I told Hoots over the ICS "Man, we're getting' down in the dirt - it's Show Time! I dropped down as low as I dared and timed the merge for me to be in the center divider (it is very wide in that part of the desert) just as we would pass abeam Georgia Boy. About a half mile in trail Hoots confirmed a dust trail behind us as I moved into the center divider, keyed the radio and said: "GEORGIA BOY, LOOK OUT YOUR LEFT WINDOW!"

At this point and at those speeds and low altitude, everything is usually a blur in your peripheral vision if you're not looking sideways; all I remember seeing was the two biggest white eyes I ever saw - looked like goose eggs! I didn't see much else 'cause I was soo low and soo fast. As the cab passed my peripheral vision I stroked both engines into afterburner and pulled up at about 5 G's When the nose reached 60 degrees I unloaded and did two full deflection rolls ... Simultaneous with this I hear two voices: "Holy ... Sweet ... Joseph and Mary ... he swapped lanes!" Hoots exclaimed. "Oh my Gawd! You were in a ****ing Rocket Ship!" yelled out Georgia Boy.

That my friends, as they say in the commercial, was priceless and worth whatever price there was to pay, short of losing ones' wings. Then Hoots says "Holy Shit You almost blew him off the road. Man, he swapped lanes two times"! I continued out ahead for about 2 or 3 miles and pulled up through the vertical over the top and started downhill for another merge ... this time head on! As I rolled upright Georgia Boy could see me and he read my mind ..."Oh God No... Don't do that!" "Puh-leeeze, don't do that!"

Passing through about 5,000 feet I regained my senses and I leveled off and made a wide sweeping turn around the truck. Now relieved of another attack Georgia Boy gets diarrhea of the mouth. "Hot damn! Nobody's gonna believe this! Nobody will believe I got run off the road by a Rocket Ship! Recon, give me your phone number! I'm gonna win some money at the bar tonight! Shit-fire, this is unbelievable!" Even Hoots was laughing now: I happened to look up into the side mirror and noticed the crow's feet around my eyes that the oxygen mask caused from my smiling. This was a wonderful moment one you'll never forget.

I finally came back to reality and saw I was below 7,500 pounds of fuel; I called him on the radio and said "Georgia Boy, we'd love to stay around and play but I'm running out of gas. We're gonna have to break it off and head back to base". If I'd had one ounce of gray matter still working instead of operating on pure adrenaline, I wouldn't have said another word, but whoever said Marines were smart? Now I didn't want some Redneck calling my house in the middle of the night drunk and trying to settle a bar bet; I wasn't about to give him my home phone number. But my mouth engaged before my brain reacted and I said, "Hey, here's the Ready Room phone number; call me there and I'll back you up". What a stupid son of a bitch I was!

The rest of the flight was uneventful: The generator stayed online, I picked up my clearance, flew back to El Toro, landed and as I signed the Maintenance forms. Phil Seward my Maintenance Chief said "Boss, don't know what you did but the CO, XO and OPS-O are waiting for you in the Ready Room"! Euphoria was about to turn into HACQ (House Arrest, Confined to Quarters): I'll spare you the details - I got a butt chewing and thought I was toast until the XO smiled when he said I had to answer all these damn phones calls from all over the West Coast (Oregon, Idaho, Nevada, Arizona and California). 300 watts does indeed go a long way: One poor old lady who heard my next to last radio transmission and was sure I was running out of gas out in the desert, said someone needs to go "Help that Boy". He then said, "What freq were you using"? I handed him the note from the Twidget, and he smiled and tore it up. When word got around the squadron, I enjoyed new status with the troops, but I had to "check six" for a long time, especially around the standard F-4's.

But you want to know the truth?

I ENJOYED EVERY FREAKIN' SECOND OF IT!

One of Newton's Laws: That which goes up must perforce come down.

One of the Squadron CO's Laws: That which comes down better be able to go up again.

C-130 OVER IRAQ

This could only be written by a combat pilot, and one who must have taken a 'creative writing' class as an elective whilst obtaining a degree. Many creative mixed metaphors are presented herein as well as some descriptions which, when visualized, just elicit a shaking of the head by the reader. 'Course, you who have been there/done that will yawn and flip the page.

There I was at six thousand feet over central Iraq; two hundred eighty knots and we're dropping faster than Paris Hilton's panties.

It's a typical September evening in the Persian Gulf; hotter than a rectal thermometer and I'm sweating like a priest at a Cub Scout meeting. But that's neither here nor there. The night is moonless over Baghdad tonight, and blacker than a Steven King novel. But it's 2006, folks, and I'm sporting the latest in night-combat technology - namely, hand-me-down night vision goggles (NVGs) thrown out by the fighter boys.

Additionally, my 1962 Lockheed C-130E Hercules is equipped with an obsolete, yet, semi-effective missile warning system (MWS). The MWS conveniently makes a nice soothing tone in your headset just before the missile explodes into your airplane. Who says you can't polish a turd? At any rate, the NVGs are illuminating Baghdad International Airport like the Las Vegas Strip during a Mike Tyson fight. These NVGs are the cat's ass. But I've digressed.

The preferred method of approach tonight is the random shallow. This tactical maneuver allows the pilot to ingress the landing zone in an unpredictable manner, thus exploiting the supposedly secured perimeter of the airfield in an attempt to avoid enemy surface-to-air-missiles and small arms fire. Personally, I wouldn't bet my pink ass on that theory, but the approach is fun as hell and that's the real reason we fly it.

We get a visual on the runway at three miles out, drop down to one thousand feet above the ground, still maintaining two hundred eighty knots. Now the fun starts. It's pilot appreciation time as I descend the mighty Herc to six hundred feet and smoothly, yet very deliberately, yank into a sixty-degree left bank, turning the aircraft ninety degrees offset from runway heading. As soon as we roll out of the turn, I reverse turn to the right a full two hundred seventy degrees in order to roll out aligned with the runway.

Some aeronautical genius coined this maneuver the "Ninety/Two-Seventy." Chopping the power during the turn, I pull back on the yoke just to the point my nether regions start to sag, bleeding off energy to configure the pig for landing. "Flaps Fifty! Landing Gear Down! Before Landing Checklist!" I look over at the copilot and he's shaking like a cat shitting on a sheet of ice.

Looking further back at the navigator, and even through the Nags, I can clearly see the wet spot spreading around his crotch. Finally, I glance at my steely eyed flight engineer. His eyebrows rise in unison as a grin forms on his face. I can tell he's thinking the same thing I am - "Where do we find such fine young men?" "Flaps One Hundred!" I bark at the shaking cat.

Now it's all aim-point and airspeed. Aviation 101, with the exception there are no lights, I'm on NVGs, in Baghdad, and now tracers are starting to crisscross the black sky. Naturally, and not at all surprisingly, I grease the Goodyear's on brick-one of runway 33 left, bring the throttles to ground idle and then force the props to full reverse pitch. Tonight, the sound of freedom is my four Hamilton Standard propellers chewing through the thick, putrid, Baghdad air. The huge, one hundred thirty-thousand-pound, lumbering whisper pig comes to a lurching stop in less than two thousand feet. Let's see a Viper do that!

We exit the runway to a welcoming committee of government issued Army grunts. It's time to download their beans and bullets and letters from their sweethearts, look for war booty, and of course, urinate on Saddam's home. Walking down the crew entry steps with my lowest-bidder, Beretta 92F 9-millimeter strapped smartly to my side, look around and thank God, not Allah, I'm an American and I'm on the winning team. Then I thank God I'm not in the Army.

Knowing once again I've cheated death, I ask myself, "What in the hell am I doing in this mess?" Is it Duty, Honor, and Country? You bet your ass. Or could it possibly be for the glory, the swag, and not to mention, chicks dig the Air Medal. There's probably some truth there, too. But now is not the time to derive the complexities of the superior, cerebral properties of the human portion of the aviator-man-machine model.

It is, however, time to get out of this hole. Hey copilot how's 'bout the 'Before Starting Engines Checklist." God, I love this job!!!!

CAPTAIN DOUGHNUT HOLE

I was forced to write this and include it in the book by the co-pilot involved [who shall remain anonymous by request] as proof that NO Captain –even and especially Captain Yorse Trooly - is exempt from occasionally making a fool of himself. Okay ... okay ... so ONCE in my life I did something dumb ... and was caught at it. That's my story and I'm sticking to it.

During the first cross-country flight with a lady friend (also a pilot), we were heading to Southern California from Colorado and flying directly into the face of 40 - 50 knot headwinds. Normally truing out at .21 Mach <G>, that day we were seeing groundspeeds somewhere between that of a Nash Rambler in second gear *[You must be a certain age to remember that song. – Ed.]* and the average freeway speed found in Los Angeles on a Friday afternoon at 1600 local; I didn't mind so much the cars and trucks on the highway passing us, but the guy on the bicycle really hacked me off! With such glacial speeds and the long distances between ARTCC sectors, there was a lot of time going by when nothing was heard on frequency. Fortunately my co-pilot had thoughtfully provided some in-flight delectables, one of which was a bag of doughnut holes. As I was fading from boredom, I asked her to break them out. She said, "You know, the moment you put one in your mouth, ATC is going to call."

"Oh, c'mon. What are the odds of that happening? Gimme one!"

She says "Oh Kaayyyy..." No sooner had she squashed an entire donut hole into my mouth when the radio suddenly comes alive: "Centurion One Two Kilo, I've got an amendment to your routing; advise ready to copy."

I'm pretty sure "Mphm thzes futph pffm!!!" is not in the ATC-approved lexicon, so I'm pointing to the radio and looking at my trusty co-pilot, hoping she'll handle the reply. Her reaction was exactly what one should envision when using the phrase 'incapacitated by paroxysms of laughter'. She was doubled up in her seat roaring with laughter, my mouth was completely full of mashed doughnut hole and it took a second call by ATC before I was able to mumble out any kind of clear answer.

After copying the new route, it took the next half-hour to clean the instrument panel and headset mic of sticky little donut bits. No help of course from my co-pilot ... she was chuckling over the whole thing in a very self-satisfied 'toldyaso' manner - and hasn't yet allowed me to forget about it, either!

Mistakes are inevitable in aviation, especially when one is still learning new things. The trick is to not make a mistake that will kill you.
- Stephen Coonts, naval aviator and author

Bolivia Pilot.

CELESTIAL FLIGHT

by Elizabeth MacKethan

Elizabeth MacKethan was a member of the WASPs during WWII. For those who are unfamiliar, the WASPs were the <u>Women's Airforce Service Pilots</u>, an auxiliary of the US Army Air Corps. This group was made up of over 1,000 women pilots who flew everything the USAAC inventory, conducting ferry flight missions within the US borders freeing up the male pilots for war duty. Near war's end they were disbanded as men returned to jobs held by these brave and courageous women; this country treated them shamefully, not according them veteran status and benefits until almost 40 years after the war when many had already 'gone west'. There are many books on the history of this storied group and I heartily recommend them for all pilots, especially the young women pilots coming along so they can understand and appreciate the courage of the pioneering women pilots who led the way for women to enter the cockpit.

Several WASPs gave their lives in the service of their country; Ms. MacKethan wrote the following poem after a friend of hers died flying for her country.

She is not dead - But only flying higher.
Higher than she's flown before
Where earthly limitations
Will hinder her no more.

There is no service ceiling
Or any fuel range,
And there's no anoxia*
Or need for engine change.

Thank God that now her flight can be
To heights her eyes have scanned
Where she can race with comets
And buzz the rainbows span.

For she now is universal
Like courage, love, and hope
And all free emotions
Of vast and Godly scope.

Understand a pilot's fate
Is not the thing she fears
But rather sadness left behind,
Your heartbreak and your tears.

So all you loved ones, dry your eyes.
Yes, it is wrong that you should grieve,
For she would love your courage more
And she would want you to believe

She is not dead.
You should have known
She is only flying higher -
Higher than she's ever flown.

The National WASP Museum is housed in an original WWII WASP hangar at Avenger Field, Sweetwater, Texas. It's worth the trip to learn about and honor those brave women. You can look them up at www.WaspMuseum.org and I strongly suggest sending a contribution to help the museum in their restoration process and ongoing viability.

"A pilot who says they have never been frightened in an airplane is, I'm afraid, lying."
- Louise Thaden, Pioneer lady pilot and charter '99's' member

CFI DRESS CODE

[This pertains to the state of 'professional attire' seen – and not seen – on 'professional' flight instructors at various flight schools I visit as a DPE. It should be considered a "word to the wise."]

My mother – as of the day of writing this, 95 years old and still able to command her 4 sons just by tone of voice – admonished me ~~once~~ ... ahhh ... ~~occasionally~~ ... ahhh ... ~~many times~~ ... ahhh ... constantly "You don't have a second chance to make a good first impression; therefore always dress like you were going to meet important people." This was bought home to me [in middle-life and beginning a new career] when, on 'Casual Friday' – something I do NOT believe in, BTW – I was asked to work on a project servicing a company client with whom I had no prior connection. Later, as I came to know him better, I asked why he chose me out of the lineup of many younger – and at that time more experienced – candidates. He responded, "Because you dressed the part of the person I needed."

So, any 'Young Skywalkers' who may read this – ALWAYS dress like the most important person for your future is about to come around the corner: One day soon, they will.

Many people have wondered, "Why did the British wear red coats in battle?"

A long time ago, Britain and France were at war. *(One of many times, BTW. – Ed.)*

During one battle, the French captured a British Colonel. They took him to their headquarters and the French General began to question him.

Finally, as an afterthought, the French General asked, "Why do you British officers all wear red coats? Don't you know the red material makes you easier targets for us to shoot at?"

In his casual, matter of fact way, the officer informed the General that the reason British officers wear red coats is if they are wounded, the blood won't show and the men they are leading won't panic.

That's why all flight instructors should wear dark brown pants.

USAAC 1920's - 1930's Pilot wings.

PILOTS GUIDE TO DISCIPLING UNRULY CHILDREN

I've also seen this picture posted under the heading of "Take Your Child to Work Day". In either case, this new and novel technique appears to have the desired effect of getting the child's full and focused attention.

Most people today think it improper to spank children, so I have tried other methods to control children when they have had one of 'those moments.' Since I'm a pilot, one method that I have found very effective is for me to just take the child for a short flight during which I say nothing and give the child the opportunity to reflect on his or her behavior.

 I don't know whether it's the steady vibration from the engines, or just the time away from any distractions such as TV, video games, computer, iPod, etc. Either way, the child usually calms down and stops misbehaving after our flight together.

I believe that eye to eye contact during these sessions is an important element in achieving the desired results. I've included a photo below of one of my sessions with one previously obnoxious child in case you would like to use the technique. Should work with grandkids too!

No children were physically harmed when taking this picture.

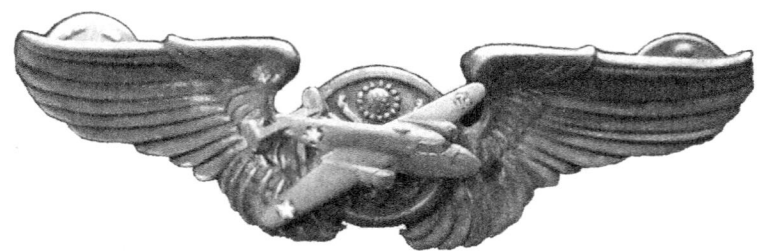

USAAC WWII B-25 wings (unauthorized).

COLD WEATHER AHEAD

In gathering weather information for a long cross-country, have you ever used the words "check your crystal ball" when talking to the FSS briefer? I have, and the person at the other end did not laugh or chuckle as that was, in essence, exactly what they were doing. Reporting current weather is factual, relating what is happening somewhere right then and therefore trustworthy. Any prognostications ['guessing']as to weather conditions five minutes or more later requires, well, a crystal ball. The science behind weather forecasting has come a long way, what with computer modeling and all, but it still takes human eyes on the information to make valid weather determinations with the experience and judgement gained over years. That's why, even with all the current digital wizardry available to pilots, I always speak with an FSS weather briefer [1-800-WXBRIEF] – I want another pair of human eyes on the information. They may catch something I missed which could materially affect my flight. And despite the demise of the Flight Watch service, I always like to give at least one pilot report [PIREP] per cross-country trip. Where do you think all the data for the computer models came from? It came from ground-based observers AND from pilots. So on the next cross-country flight you make, call up the closest FSS and tell them you'd like to make a PIREP; use the format below as that's what they'll be using. Speak each segment slowly, give a breath between each subject so they can type it up, and be as accurate as you can be. They, the weather data modelers and other pilots will be thankful for the information you've provided.

In late fall the Indians – Native Americans - on a remote reservation asked their new chief if the coming winter was going to be cold or mild. Since he was a college graduate and now chief in a modern society, he had never been taught the old ways. When he looked at the sky, he had no idea what the winter was going to be like. Nevertheless, to be on the safe side, he told his tribe that the winter was indeed going to be cold and that the members of the village should collect firewood to be prepared. Being a practical leader, after several days, he got an idea. He went to the phone booth, called the National Weather Service and asked, "Is the coming winter going to be cold?"

"It looks like this winter is going to be quite cold," the meteorologist at the weather service responded. So the chief went back to his people and told them to collect even more firewood in order to be prepared. A week later, he called the Weather Service again. "Does it still look like it is going to be a very cold winter?"

"Yes," the man at Weather Service again replied, "it's going to be a very cold winter." The chief again went back to his people and ordered them to collect every scrap of firewood they could find. Two weeks later, the chief called the Weather Service once again. "Are you absolutely sure that the winter is going to be very cold?"

"Absolutely," the man replied. "It's looking more and more like it is going to be one of the coldest winters we've ever seen." "How can you be so sure?" the chief asked.

The weatherman replied, "Well, the local Indians are collecting tons of firewood."

PIREP format: 1) Urgent or Routine PIREP 2) Location relative a NAVAID, airport, or route segment 3) Time 4) Altitude or Flight Level 5) Type of aircraft 6) Sky condition 7) Flight visibility 8) Precipitation type & intensity 9) Outside air temperature - Celsius 10) Turbulence type, intensity & altitude 11) Icing type, intensity & altitude 12) Other remarks - phenomena/wind shear/LLWS/etc.

CONFIDENCE DEFINED

Okay. Ladies ... I understand this may SEEM sexist and chauvinistic, but I'm actually doing you a favor by informing you one of the latest tactics to come to the attention of yours truly. NOT that I'd EVER try to use it – I'm an old, widowed guy without the time, inclination, or energy for games I used to play all those years ago [see: Trading Sex for Beer]. But just in case reincarnation is real and I get to come 'round this way again, I'm keeping this one in my hip pocket.

A fighter pilot walks into a bar and takes a seat next to a very attractive woman. He gives her a quick glance then casually looks at his watch for a moment.

The woman notices this and asks, "Is your date running late?"
"No," he replies, "I just got this state-of-the-art watch, and I was just testing it."

The intrigued woman says, "A state-of-the-art watch? What's so special about it?"
The pilot says, "It uses alpha waves to talk to me telepathically."

The lady says, "What's it telling you now?"
"Well, it says you're not wearing any panties."

The woman giggles and replies, "Well it must be broken because I am wearing panties!"

The pilot grimaces, taps his watch and says, "Damn thing's an hour fast."

And that, my friends ... is Confidence.

Prussia Early Pilot 1912 – 1914.

CROP-DUSTER FOLLIES

This was sent to me by a student of mine who eschewed the corporate/airline route to fame and glory, and went off to crop-duster school and, last I heard, was still plying his trade at 5' agl. I was the "unsuspecting CFI with a Decathlon" mentioned herein, this is indeed a true story. It is an excellent example of 'if it doesn't kill you outright, you should become smarter and wiser'. It was fortunate indeed we lived through the experience and came out the other side smarter and wiser.

Many years ago, early in my flying career, I had an experience indelibly imprinted in my feeble mind. I have never forgotten it, and while instructing, often cite it as an example of poor airmanship and inattention to detail. Upon passing my private pilot check ride I immediately found an unsuspecting CFI with a Decathlon and embarked on a program of taildragger and aerobatic training. Things progressed as well as they could for a 65 hour Top Gun, and before long we were spinning, looping, and rolling all over the sky.

During one training session, I was having a hard time completing a decent Cuban 8, so my suffering mentor took over and made a perfect demonstration. We then spent the next 5 minutes or so describing random climbs, descents, circles, steep turns, wingovers, and almost loops. I found this kind of fun but was unsure exactly what maneuver we were trying to accomplish and asked as much. The reply I received was amusing, enlightening, and disconcerting:

"I thought you were flying."

This, despite the fact that prior to every flight, we briefed thoroughly on proper procedures to exchange control: Pilot flying vigorously wiggles the stick, announces "I've got the airplane;" while the pilot not flying raises his hands (if the Guy in Front) so the GIB can see them, and announces "Your airplane." Somehow, we both thought we had made a smooth control transition, when in fact it was anything but. Despite having a good laugh over it, we recognized the potentially serious implications of our mistake and endeavored to never repeat it again.

As an agricultural aviator, almost all my airplane time since then has been in single seat, single control aircraft. I caught the Citabria bug early on and am currently happily flying my 3rd incarnation of that wonderful airplane. When a person decides he (or she) wants to become a crop-duster, one of the first things he needs to learn, other than the fact that he is probably not as hot a stick as he might think, and that there are books worth of knowledge to be absorbed that have nothing to do with operating an aircraft; is how to fly a taildragger. So with my trusty Citabria and CFII it frequently falls to me to help the hapless victim become familiar with the vagaries of rudder input, adverse yaw, p-factor, CG vs landing gear placement, directional control, reduced forward visibility, gross weight takeoffs, short unimproved runways, and so on.

 This is always an exciting prospect for me and one I approach with some trepidation. The front seat of the Citabria offers a pretty good view, but from the back seat forward visibility is a bit more "traditional taildragger," especially with a broad set of shoulders and a big, fat head in your way.

As I alluded to previously, tandem seating aircraft offer a different perspective on knowing "Who's on first?" During taildragger transition training so much time is spent in the pattern and close to the surface that it is imperative that both pilots positively understand what 's what, so I always relate my anecdote and make sure we both clearly understand who is flying when. As any CFI knows, one always walks a thin line between letting a student go too far, realize it, and then recover; versus taking over too soon and not allowing the student an opportunity for an "aha moment" and thus a powerful learning experience.

Now for a little joke: Two CFII's walk into a bar......No, that's not right......Two CFII's climb into a Citabria.

They're out screwing around, touching the wheels on tiny mesas too small on which to actually land, and looking for elk. The airplane is describing big looping climbing and descending circles when it starts downhill and the CFII in front (that would be me) starts thinking, "Sonovabitch. If he doesn't start pulling pretty quick, we're gonna stall into those pine trees."

The CFII in back is thinking, "I guess he must be doing some of his crop-duster stuff, but he's cutting it a bit close this time." After the little bump and appearance of ponderosa pine needles in the gear legs and even a few in the wing struts, they simultaneously say,

"I thought you were flying."

I guess that's a joke, but the more I think about it (always a bad idea) the less I'm laughing. I mean, here are two guys with close to 25,000 hours between them, one of 'em about grew up in the back seat of a T-38, the other one gets a nosebleed above 500' AGL, and they both just sat there and watched this [literally] go down!

It's not something I like to brag about, but in my line of work it can sometimes happen that you get into a situation where it might be possible to maybe run into something. So I know a little bit how different bumps might feel. And another nice thing about the Citabria is it's easy to look down and inspect the undercarriage. With a low wing it can be a bad feeling to pump the brakes and know you at least have pressure, but wonder if there's air in the tire. Or if the tire is there. So it was easy to see it was just a skimmer and no damage done, at least to the airplane. But we both knew at once the laughs we were having were a bit uneasy.

Being lucky enough to live in an area where there's still lots of places with nobody and nothing around, we were used to going out together and doing that sort of flying. Numerous times that flight we had taken turns and always been clear who was operating the machine. I thought we were clear this time, and so did he. When we banked over and started down the hill we both knew it wasn't right, but we both thought the other guy knew what he was doing; and the natural flying ability of the good old Citabria caused it to start pulling up on its own, just not quite enough. When we both gave it a little further tug, it was too late.

Every time I walk in the hangar now, I could swear it smells just like fresh piney woods and I shake my head and think, "You idiot. You are an even bigger moron than I thought possible." In an airplane, you're always a pilot. Just not as good as you thought you were.

Pay attention to where you are ... an always, first and foremost, fly the damn airplane.

As a matter of exacting protocol, when you are transferring control of the airplane to another, say "You have the flight controls." The receiving pilot should then say, "I have the flight controls." Then the first pilot will audibly and visually confirm this by saying "You have the flight controls." Saying "I have the airplane" can also mean "I 'have' the airplane - I see the airplane out there." *Use the words 'flight controls' and there is very little ambiguity is the message the flight controls are being transferred. - Ed.*

"And if you screw up just this much, you'll be flying a cargo plane full of rubber dog shit out of Hong Kong!"
- Air Boss Johnson in the movie <u>Top Gun</u>

USAAS WWI Balloon Pilot.

CROSS-COUNTRY NOTES

These notes were lifted from the 1917 U.S. Army Flying Corps pamphlet "Rules of the Air: How to Fly Your Machine". The rules referred to and 'Notes for Pilots' are presented elsewhere in this book. The forward to this pamphlet states:

"It is enjoined upon all pilots to preserve a copy of these rules and notes for future reference. The following "rules of the air" will be strictly observed by all pilots. With several machines flying, there is great danger of collisions unless due care is exercised. It is mandatory that all pilots should observe the utmost vigilance."

The original 'notes' are printed in boldface:

1. Before starting a cross-country, be sure that the gas you carry in tanks can get to the motor. Make test and become acquainted with the system of getting gas to [the motor].
Once you have been trained in airplanes with a "Both" position on the fuel selector, you will upgrade to airplanes with multiple fuel tanks; knowing how to get fuel from those tanks to the engine will be of prime importance! For instance, the tanks at the end of the wings of a Cessna 310 are the "Main Tanks" and the tanks internal to the wing are the "Auxiliary Tanks" whereas the tip tanks in my Cessna P-210 are the

auxiliaries and the internal wing tanks are the "Mains". Do you KNOW how to get fuel from each and every tank? Can you draw fuel directly from each tank or must it be transferred? If your transfer pump is INOP, can you still get fuel from that tank? Many pilots have 'run out of fuel' only to be shown there was ample fuel on board, they just didn't know [or 'forgot' ... yeah, right!] how to get to it. Fuel is gallons [yep], weight [yeah] but most of all, fuel is TIME! KNOW your fuel system, every little thing about it! You'll be able to stay aloft until 1. The cows come home 2. Pigs fly, or 3. You run out of fuel, whichever occurs first. Let's guess which one of those will occur first.

By the way, below the instrument panel is the fuel system from the Spirit of St. Louis in which Charles Lindbergh first flew solo across the Atlantic Ocean in 1927. SEVEN tanks in all PLUS the requisite number of petcocks to keep fuel flowing to a thirsty engine – could YOU manage this after being awake 36 hours straight?

2. In cross-country work, never let gas run below 4 gallons. [With] 4 gallons you will have approximately one-half hour to find a landing place.

A prudent and professionally-minded pilot KNOWS their per-hour fuel burn, knows the regulatory requirements for fuel remaining upon landing and, if they are wise to the evil ways book estimations and engine fuel consumption numbers LIE [have you correctly leaned the fuel flow to the percentage of power desired AND adjusted power settings to those which are optimum to the flight?], the wise aviator will have personal fuel minimums greater than that required by regulations. My fuel minimums for GA aircraft is: I will be on short final to my fuel stop with one hour of fuel remaining OR quarter-tanks, whichever is greater. You ARE familiar with the FAR's concerning fuel, right?

FAR 91.151 Fuel Requirements – VFR
(A) No person may begin a flight in an airplane under VFR conditions unless (considering wind and forecast weather conditions) there is enough fuel to fly to the first point of intended landing and, assuming normal cruising speed –

> **(1) During the day, to fly after that for at least 30 minutes; or**
> **(2) At night, to fly after that for at least 45 minutes.**

So nothing has changed in aviation regarding this regulation in over 100 years! For those pilots flying under IFR and in IMC, and in airplanes or helicopters, the regulations for fuel are more explicit and demanding. Refresh your knowledge thereof by reviewing FAR 91.167. Keep in mind no matter what you are flying and, in all conditions, the only time you have too much fuel on board is if you are on fire. At that point you've got more to concern yourself with than regulations.

3. All machines going cross-country will take the emergency set of tools.

For most of us nowadays there is little mechanical knowledge of how to repair; after all, that's the mechanics' job, right? But a multi-tool can be very handy in tightening loose cowling screws, untightening over-torqued oil dipsticks [remember guys – finger-tight, not wrenched down like you're the 'Incredible Hulk' or something] and a myriad number of things you're allowed to do. Refer to FAR 43, appendix A, section C for the approved list of things an owner/operator/pilot may perform in the areas of repair and/or preventative maintenance.

4. If motor trouble develops on a cross-country flight, select your field to land in and do not change unless a much better field presents itself. Vacillation on this point may cause an accident. A field you have passed over you should know more about than one you are approaching. Experience has proven that it is better to glide to a field you have passed over than to go forward to one you know nothing about.

This is a GREAT piece of advice! As you fly cross-country – or during any flight for that matter – are you aware of where you can go if/when the engine quits OR where you can make a precautionary landing should the need arise [decreasing oil pressure combined with increasing oil temperatures]? Flying over a vast urban wasteland such as the Los Angeles basin or inhospitable territory such as the Ozarks brings this into sharp focus – just where can you put down over these areas? AND are you at such an altitude so that:

FAR 91.119 Minimum Safe Altitudes: General
Except when necessary for takeoff or landing, no person may operate an aircraft below the following altitudes:

We all know the 500' rule over non-congested areas and 1,000' above the highest obstacle, but here's the 'gotcha':

(A) Anywhere: An altitude allowing if, a power unit fails an emergency landing without undue hazard to persons or property on the ground.
I flew Skywatch [traffic reporting] for a few years and my observer/reporter was always imploring me to "get lower" so he could see and report on the carnage during rush hour. In the center of town there was a minimum altitude I held to with religious fervor for if I had an engine failure the only place I could 'safely' go was into the river through town – and that was fraught with bridges, powerlines and riverbanks in close position to the water. Keep that in mind if you are traversing a congested area – you may be 1,000' above the highest obstacle but really, is it a safe altitude?

5. Before going on a cross-country flight, be sure the radiator is full of water, tanks contain enough gas for the flight, there are no leaks in manifolds or connections, there is sufficient oil in the motor for the flight, the motor tests out properly for speed and smoothness, barometer is set to zero, emergency tool kit is in the machine, you have blank telegrams, you have proper maps, the compass is functioning properly and you understand the gasoline feed system.

Sounds like "Do a thorough and complete preflight, doesn't it?

FAR 91.103 Preflight Action
Each pilot in command shall *[underlining added by editor]* **before beginning a flight, become familiar with all available information concerning that flight. This information must** *[underlining added by editor]* **include:**

Review this regulation yourself for there is much there which a prudent pilot in command will familiarize himself. One portion requires actions to be taken when "not in the vicinity of an airport"; I have challenged applicants for years to show me the official definition of the word 'vicinity'. Clue: The ONLY definition is in weather reporting when a station reports weather 'in the vicinity' – and THAT means within a 5 sm radius of the reporting station! Sooo ... anytime you are more than 5 sm distant from an airport you are NOT 'in the vicinity' and must accomplish those items required by 91.103. This just might be on your next flightcheck.

6. If you become lost, do not fly about aimlessly but land if possible and get your bearings. If no landing place is available, it may be possible to fly low enough to see the sign on a [train] station or some other sign that will give you the name of the place. If clouds interfere with seeing the ground, it is better to trust your motor and fly under them than to get far out to sea or far inland off your course.

I had to do this flying an old Birddog [O-1 E] to an airshow. A huge thunderstorm blocked my way and I had to divert literally off the chart. I paralleled my course when clear and then angled down to regain my course having zero clue where I was [had enough fuel, though!]. I'm sure the residents of

Enterprise, Kansas were astonished to see a fully-armed Birddog [Had USAF markings so they knew I was a 'friendly'] circling their water tower at *ahem* 500' agl but then I knew where I was and continued on to my destination. Of course, if you're a VFR-only pilot, don't get caught above a cloud layer or fly into IMC; you will NOT like the result(s).

7. Be sure to start your cross-country flight early enough to avoid landing at your destination in the dark.
Back then [1917!] there were no lights on landing fields and precious few anywhere else on the ground for that matter [these were the days prior to the country being electrified], so landing in the dark was fraught with peril. Axiom: If a forced landing must be made at night, turn on your landing light. If you don't like what you see, turn it off!

8. Test your compass before going cross-country. It may save you from getting lost if clouds come in underneath you.
For today's pilots with VOR navigation and the marvels of a GPS, how in the world can you get lost? Well, let me count the ways: not synchronizing your Heading Indicator EARLY & OFTEN with your Magnetic Direction Indicator [so named by FAA lawyers – pilots still call it a 'compass' and old-time pilots still call it a 'whisky compass']! Thinking you're flying a GPS course when the GPS is set on VLOC [VOR/Localizer].Thinking you're flying a VOR radial with your GPS set on GPS! BOTH of which will give you the wrong course guidance on your OBS [Omni-bearing Selector], both will get you lost AND all three will invite an issuance of the salmon-colored invitation for a recheck [Notice of Disapproval, otherwise known as a 'pink slip'] during a flightcheck. [Makes you wish for NDB's to come back, doesn't it?] At the USAF Academy and nearby Petersen

AFB I've seen pilots place their headset close to the compass so to witness a 'swing' of the indicator and then, after moving the headset away, witness a 'swing' back to the original heading. This is something I don't see at civilian flight schools and, since we're checking all our instruments, isn't this a required check as well? One of Drew's Rules of Flying: In God we trust – everything else we check and check again. Just a word to the wise ...

"Get rid at the outset the notion an airplane is only an air-going sort of automobile. It isn't. It may sound like one and smell like one, and it may have an interior decorated to look like one; but the difference is - it goes on wings."

- Wolfgang Langewiesche. The first words in his seminal work Stick and Rudder: An Explanation of the Art of Flying, 1944.
A recommended read to this day - Ed.

DIFFERENCES BETWEEN MILITARY AVIATORS

There is a lot of 'competition' between aviators of the various services, and this affords 'humorous' comparisons between same. In all honesty, no matter the service or the vehicle each pilot commands, those who devote their lives to serving the country [ours ... meaning the USA] in aerospace machines deserve the highest respect we, and this nation, can give them. Remember, it's a loooong way down to terra firma ... and we've never left one up there yet.

Naval Aviator

On a carrier, the Naval Aviator looks over to the Catapult Officer ("Shooter") who gives the run-up engines signal by rotating his finger above his head. The pilot pushes the throttle forward, verifies all flight  controls are operational, checks all gauges, and gives the Cat officer a brisk salute, continuing the Navy/Marine tradition of asking permission to leave the ship. The Cat officer drops to one knee while swooping his arm forward and pointing down deck, granting that permission. The pilot is immediately catapulted and becomes airborne.

Air Force Pilot

We've all seen Air Force pilots at the Air Force base look up just before taxiing for takeoff and the ground crew waits until the pilot's thumb is sticking straight up. The crew chief then confirms that he sees the thumb, salutes, and the Air Force pilot then takes off. This time-tested tradition is the last link in the Air Force safety net to confirm that the pilot does not have his thumb up his ass.

Army Aviator

If you've ever seen an Army helicopter pilot preparing for takeoff, you will note that the pilot gives the ground guy a thumbs up before he is given hover and takeoff signals. There are two theories about the origin of this gesture. One is that it is to show that the pilot has identified which of his fingers is the thumb so he will be able to properly operate his controls. The most compelling theory says that this is to show the ground crewman that the pilot indeed knows which direction is up.

DPE JOB DESCRIPTION

Since the FAA – in their infinite wisdom – awarded [?] me the title of Designated Pilot Examiner [DPE] I have administered several thousand flightchecks [not counting my time as Stan/Eval Officer] and I can honestly say it's been – for the most part – quite rewarding. Well, except for that one applicant who, when told of failure, curled into a fetal position in the left seat and broke into convulsive sobs ... [I had to fly the plane back and land it]. And the multi-engine applicant who stomped the wrong rudder when simulating an engine failure at 500' agl ... [I finished the roll he began]. And the applicant who entered the pattern at a non-towered airport ... at cruise airspeed ... going the wrong way ... intending to land on a runway with a 20-knot tailwind ... into the face of a departing corporate jet ... [ever see a twin perform a Chandelle ... from INSIDE the twin?]

And saving an untold number from landing gear up ... and ...

„Sitzen ist Arbeit? Ich will diesen Job."
(Sitting is work? I want that job.)

The 'sitzen' part includes meeting and greeting the Nervous Nugget, accomplishing the pre-qualification status check (applicant and airplane), looking at the application (hopefully the flight school computer was built in this century), determining the printer has paper and has an ink cartridge from the Bush administration [either one] or newer. Once "The test has begun" has been announced, one must objectively listen to the applicant spilling his/her guts out concerning the subject at hand*. This must take into account the discernment by the DPE between the Nuggets' knowledge of aeronautical fact and fiction, myth and reality, true facts versus old wives tales *[no insult to any old wives out there is intended by using this phrase]*, and what other ephemeral factoids and recently invented techniques pass for Standard Operating Procedures.

All this is prelude to arising, walking out to an airplane in which you may have, or more likely, have no experience therein. You then climb in next to a pilot wannabe with whom you have never flown before and have nothing but the instructors recommendation stating he is good to go. Then you watch calmly and objectively as said nugget flounders through the sky demonstrating 'mastery' of said aerospace vehicle by performing various operations *["Just what do you call that maneuver?"]* to ... ahhh ... 'flexible' performance interpretations.

Once alighted on terra firma *[it ain't over yet!]* said nugget then must demonstrate several 'controlled' impacts with the underlying planet. The complexities of these maneuvers being made more intricate and intense by the presence of an uncooperative wind [direction and velocity], nugget nerves *[or lack thereof]*, random appearances of other airplanes performing unexpected and unusual acts of airplane-runway interaction, complicated by the unintelligible ranting and raving of air traffic controllers over a scratchy and staticy radio turned up to the threshold of pain.

Asuming said Nugget passes, there is the matter of the 'Award Ceremony' which traditionally involves the topical administration of 90-proof dram of calming fluid [to the DPE] and a frameable small white piece of paper *[In case of emergency, break glass]* to the now-certificated Nugget. In case of a failure, repeat the above process as necessary *[incrimental certification]* until the DPE's patience and/or the applicant's bank account is exhausted.

Still want the job?
* "Okay, Lieutenant, what color is the sky?"
"Sir, {Nugget takes a big breath}... The-sky-is-blue-unless-there-are-clouds-in-the-sky-then-the-sky-is-blue-and-white-unless-the-clouds-are-overcast-then-the-sky-is-white-unless-the-clouds-are-thick-then-it's-mostly-dark-gray-and-if-you-see-green-in-the-clouds-you-don't-want-to-go-there and ... *gasp* ..." *[applicant takes first breath since beginning]*
"Lieutenant ... "
"Yessir?"
"What color is the sky?"
[Deer in the headlights look]
"Ahhh ... blue? ... Sir?"
"Thank you, Lieutnant"
Hint to test-takers: THINK about what the question was, then -

ANSWER EXACTLY AND ONLY THAT QUESTION!
Let the examiner do the digging - not you.
Another hint: **BE THE PILOT-IN-COMMAND!**

Do NOT ask the DPE if it's okay to do something. YOU are the PIC, solely responsible for the airplane, everythig it does, and the corner of the sky you're in; YOU are the decision-maker! You may ask questions regarding the flight check, however HOW you conductthat flight check is up to you.

FAR 61.47 Status of an Examiner ... Authorized to conduct Practical Tests

(a)   **An examiner represents the Administarator for the purpose of conducting practical tests ... and to <u>OBSERVE</u>** *[my underlining & all caps - ed.]* **an applicants ability to perform the areas of operations on the practical test.**

(b)   **The examiner is <u>NOT THE PILOT IN COMMAND</u>** *[my underlining & all caps - ed.]* **during the practical test unless ...**

© Michael & Stefan Strasser Used without permission

Mexico Pilot.

EUROPEAN ALERT STAGES

This submission is allegedly from the mind and pen of John Cleese, of Monty Python fame. It builds on some national stereotypes as viewed from the west side of the Atlantic Ocean and which, as a student of history, are not that far off – especially when viewing the Scots and Australians [with whom I lived for several years]. And YES, I KNOW Australia isn't a European country, but I didn't make this up, John Cleese did. So complain to him, okay?

The English are feeling the pinch in relation to recent events in the Middle East and therefore have raised their security level from "Miffed" to "Peeved." Soon, though, security levels may be raised yet again to "Irritated" or even "A Bit Cross." The English have not been "A Bit Cross" since the blitz in 1940 when tea supplies nearly ran out. Terrorists have been re-categorized from "Tiresome" to "A Bloody Nuisance." The last time the British issued a "Bloody Nuisance" warning level was in 1588, they were threatened by the Spanish Armada.

The Scots have raised their threat level from "Pissed Off" to "Let's get the Bastards." They don't have any other levels. This is the reason they have been used on the front line of the British army for the last 300 years.

The French government announced yesterday that it has raised its terror alert level from "Run" to "Hide." The only two higher levels in France are "Surrender" and "Collaborate." The rise was precipitated by a recent fire that destroyed France's white flag factory, effectively paralyzing the country's military capability.

Italy has increased the alert level from "Shout loudly and excitedly" to "Elaborate Military Posturing." Two more levels remain: "Ineffective Combat Operations" and "Change Sides."

The Germans have increased their alert state from "Disdainful Arrogance" to "Dress in Uniform and Sing Marching Songs." They also have two higher levels: "Invade a Neighbor" and "Lose."

Belgians, on the other hand, are all on holiday as usual; the only threat they are worried about is NATO pulling out of Brussels.

The Spanish are all excited to see their new submarines ready to deploy. These beautifully designed subs have glass bottoms so the new Spanish navy can get a really good look at the old Spanish navy.

Australia, meanwhile, has raised its security level from "No worries" to "She'll be right, Mate." Two more escalation levels remain: "Crikey! I think we'll need to cancel the Barbie this weekend!" and "The Barbie is cancelled." So far, no situation has ever warranted use of the final escalation level.

Regards,
John Cleese
British writer, actor, and tall person

[And as a final thought - Greece is collapsing, the Iranians are getting aggressive, and Rome is in disarray. Welcome back to 430 BC. – Ed.]

EVERYONE SHOULD HAVE A GUIDE DOG

I have not ascertained if this is true, an urban legend, or a put-on. But the picture speaks volumes.

During a flight from Seattle to San Francisco, the plane was diverted to Sacramento due to weather. The flight attendant explained that there would be a delay, and if the passengers wanted to get off the aircraft the plane would re-board in 50 minutes.

Everybody got off the plane except one lady who was blind. The flight attendant knew this as her guide dog lay quietly underneath the seat in front of her throughout the entire flight.

He could also tell she had flown this very flight before because the pilot approached her, and calling her by name, saying, *"Kathy, we are in Sacramento for almost an hour. Would you like to get off and stretch your legs?"*

The blind lady said, *"No thanks, but maybe Buddy Would like to stretch his legs."*

Picture this:

All the people in the gate area came to a complete stand still when they looked up and saw the pilot walk off the plane with a guide dog for the blind! Even worse, the pilot was wearing sunglasses! People scattered.

They not only tried to change planes, but they were trying to change airlines!

Captain's PA announcement after an 'arrival': "Ladies and Gentlemen, this is your captain speaking. This leg of the flight was commanded by the co-pilot, and he was at the controls during the landing you all just experienced. I have asked him to stand at the door as you deplane and receive your comments regarding his skills and performance today.

A FARM KID WRITES HOME AFTER JOINING THE MARINES

I'm sure this 'letter home' is a set-up, but there ARE a few elements of truth to it. I'm no slouch but there was one woman – a 'Lady' in all senses of the word - I knew who, at 5' 3" didn't look like much of a threat but could send you to the hospital seven ways to Sunday before you could say "I gi- ...!" She retired as a full bird Colonel if I recall correctly and is now a missionary to indigenous tribes in the worlds' hinterlands. I pity the fool headhunter who crosses her ...

Dear Ma and Pa –

I am well, hope y'all are too. Tell brothers Walt and Elmer the Marine Corps beats working for old man Minch by a mile! Tell them to get over here and join up before all the places are filled up. I was restless at first because you get to stay in bed until nearly 6 am but I am getting so I like to sleep in late. Tell Walt and Elmer all you gotta do before breakfast is smooth your cot and shine your shoes and some trinkets you wear on your Sunday-go-to-meeting uniform. No hogs to slop, feed to pitch, mash to mix, wood to split, fire to lay in – practically nothing!

The menfolk got to shave but it ain't so bad, they got hot water right out of the spigot. Breakfast is strong on trimmings like fruit juice, cereal, eggs, bacon, and such but thin on chops, potatoes, ham, steak, fried okra, pie, regular food and all. But tell Walt and Elmer you can always sit by the city boys that live on coffee – Your food plus theirs keeps you going until noon when you get fed again. It's no wonder these city boys can't walk much.

We go on strolls they call 'route marches' which the platoon sergeant says are long walks to harden us. If he thinks that's so it's not my place to tell him different. A 'route march' is about as long as from our house to town and even then, we get packs to stuff our possibles in instead of carrying all that by hand. Then them city boys get sore feet and we all ride back in trucks.

The sergeant is kinda like Miss Grundy the schoolmarm back home, he nags a lot but mostly at them city boys. Lieutenants got lots of book-learnin' but they're dumb as a box of rocks. The captain is sorta like the school board; majors and colonels just ride around and frown a lot; they don't bother you none.

This next part will kill Walt and Elmer with laughing – I keep getting medals for shooting! I don't know why – the bullseye is as big as a chipmunk's head and it don't move none. AND it ain't shooting back at you like them Higget boys back home. All you gotta do is lie there all comfortable and such and hit the target. You don't even have to reload your rifle, all the cartridges come packed in little boxes they call magazines.

Then there's this drill they call 'hand-to-hand combat training – I get to rassle with them city boys. I got to be real careful though, they break pretty easily. It's nothing like fighting that rangy old bull at the feed lot in Possum Holler. I'm about the best at this they got 'cept for Cotton McGill from two draws over from us at home. He joined up the same time as me and I beat him only once but I'm only 5'6" and 135 pounds and he's 6'2" and near 260 pounds dry.

Be sure to Tell Walt and Elmer to hurry on down and join up before other fellers figger out what a good deal this is and come stampeding in!

Your loving daughter,

Alice

Communist Czechoslovakia 1946 – 1992.

FEMALE QUARTERS REGULATIONS

Years ago the "Senior Officer – Women" did not care for her title abbreviation [S.O.W.] and complained loudly about it. Upon due consideration, her title was changed to "Commanding Officer – Women." That was the end of that little 'dust-up.'

The Pentagon has ordered that all military commanders provide female personnel with separate, private, "OFF LIMITS" quarters on all bases.

While addressing all personnel at Fort Hood, Texas, the Commanding General said, "Female sleeping quarters will be "out-of-bounds" for all males. Anyone caught breaking this rule will be fined $50 the first time."

The General continued, "Anyone caught breaking this rule the second time will be fined $150. Being caught a third time will cost you a fine of $500. Are there any questions?"

At this point, a Warrant Officer Helicopter pilot stood up in the crowd and inquired: "How much for a season pass?"

Thanks for this submission to
Robert "Brown" Cabell, CW5, US Army [ret.]
R.I.P   8 August 1950 – 4 August 2018

Remember, in the end gravity always wins.
Put another way - Obey gravity: It's the LAW!

THE FINAL INSPECTION

I include this in honor of my brothers and sisters who stepped forward, donned the uniform – it doesn't matter which service branch – and did their duty to the best of their ability.

The Soldier stood and faced God, which must always come to pass. He hoped his shoes were shining, just as brightly as his brass.

Step forward now, Soldier, how shall I deal with you?

Have you always turned the other cheek? To My Church have you been true?'

The soldier squared his shoulders and said, 'no, Lord, I guess I ain't. Because those of us who carry guns, can't always be a saint.

I've had to work most Sundays and at times my talk was tough.

And sometimes I've been violent, because the world is awfully rough.

But, I never took a penny that wasn't mine to keep

Though I worked a lot of overtime, when the bills just got too steep.

And I never passed a cry for help, though at times I shook with fear.

And sometimes, God, forgive me, I've wept unmanly tears.

I know I don't deserve a place among the people here.

They never wanted me around, except to calm their fears.

If you've a place for me here, Lord, it needn't be so grand.

I never expected or had too much; but if you don't, I'll understand.

Silence all around the throne where the saints had often trod, As the Soldier waited quietly for the judgment of his God.

Step forward now, you Soldier, you've borne your burdens well.

Walk peacefully on Heaven's streets: You've done your time in Hell.'

~Author Unknown~

Heaven is crowded with civilian pilots who neglected obtaining an instrument rating.

FISHING

While there's a LOT of inter-service rivalry providing LOTS of humor out there [when the CMS/CPO doesn't get wind of it - until after the fact], one has to admit the old hands had it best. Hell, lots of guys got away with murder – musta had eyes in the back of their heads and a sixth sense when there was incoming. The new guys/gals are too constrained by PC-dom to come up with the likes of fun we had. To wit:

The rain was pouring and there was a big puddle in front of the pub just outside the Air Force Base. A grizzled old retired Marine fighter pilot wearing a faded baseball cap emblazoned with a VMFA 224 squadron patch, his tatty leather flight jacket with many more squadron and aircraft carrier patches was standing near the edge with a fishing rod, his line in the puddle.

A curious young Air Force Second Lieutenant came over to him and asked what he was doing.

"Fishing," the old Marine simply said.

'Poor old fool, just another dumb Marine fighter pilot', the Air Force officer thought. So he invited the ragged old timer into the pub for a drink.

Sipping his semi-sweet white wine while watching the old Marine drinking a Johnny Walker Black Label whiskey, he felt he should start some conversation, so the haughty Air Force officer asked,

"So ... how many fish have you caught?"

"You're the eighth," the old Marine fighter pilot answered.

RIP: Glenn Endlsey, Centennial, CO

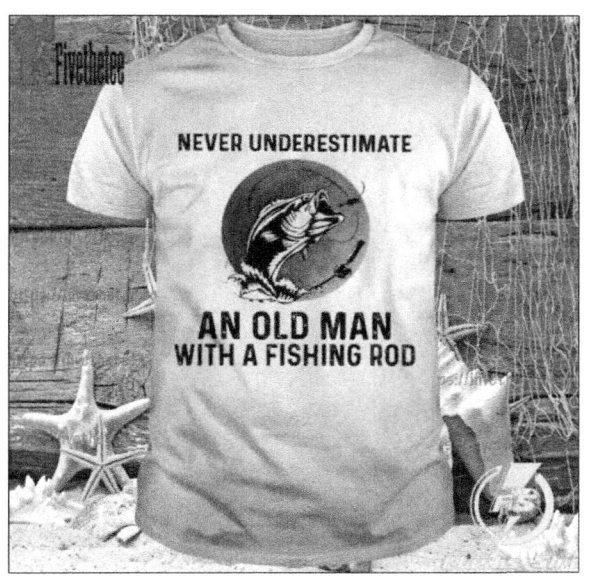

Italy - 1930's - Wings awarded to pilot setting Altitude record.

FITREP FOR A MARINE CORP PILOT

The following was - allegedly - obtained under the Freedom of Information Act by a Marine aviator who, in a fit of morbid curiosity, wanted to see what was in his last Fitness Report [FITREP]. It is published here as a guide to those who must write these with some degree of ... ahhh ... 'accuracy' and with a flair for creative writing. Whether or not the acts allegedly perpetrated by said aviator actually happened remains a closely guarded military secret.

1. Inclined to take excessive risks, even where none exist.

2. Appears to be chronically narcissistic and has high opinion of himself-for no apparent reason. One instructor's comment: Thinks he is God's gift to Naval Aviation."

3. Frequently displays lack of respect and deference to authority figures.

4. Believes that any landing approach he can walk away from is a good one.

5. Has a false and unsupported feeling of superiority, especially after consumption of alcohol.

6. Apparently has political ambitions, stating he aspires to be the Mayor of "Alongpoo".

7. Not well suited for any other career path, after F-8 squadron assignment; does not get along well with superiors, Black Shoes, Submariners, and shows only grudging respect for U.S. Marines - especially those who are Naval Aviators.

8. Overly aggressive; states he wants to have a full ordnance load, even while flying in CONUS on training missions. He once zoomed to 50,000 ft. and fired a Sidewinder at the sun, to see if he could hit it.

9. Resists complying with established Naval protocols and etiquette - once left a calling card in the tray at an admiral's home that said: C.J. Judkins, World`s Greatest Fighter Pilot

10. After receiving a poor Fitness Report, instead of promising to correct his deficiencies, pointed out to his CO several misspelled words in the report.

11. Fails to use proper decorum in wardroom or officers' mess. Instead of politely asking the senior officer at a table if he could be seated there, he grabbed a spoon and simulated a ship's bell on the Commander's water glass saying, "Fighter pilot arriving!"

12. When invited to join a senior officer's family for breakfast, he replied, "I've already had a Fighter Pilot's Breakfast: A puke and two aspirin. Thanks anyway."

13. When the interviewer inquired what he usually wore to bed, he replied, "Nothing but my G-suit and flight boots. You never know when you have to launch."

14. When asked what approach speed should be used in the F-8E, he replied, "Whatever is necessary."

15. According to his statements, he thinks night refueling is asking the O-Club bartender for another round.

BOARD CONCLUSION: This man is expendable, but highly qualified for an F-8 squadron.

"I enjoyed my service flying very much. That is where I learned the discipline of flying. In order to have freedom of flight You must have discipline. Discipline prevents crashes."

- Captain John Cook, British Airways Concorde Training Captain

FLATULENT PASSENGER FORCES EMERGENCY LANDING

"Tis far better to break ground and fly into the wind than the other way around."

From the "You can't make this s**t up" file:

A Dutch airliner was forced to make an emergency landing recently after a fight broke out due to a staple of low-brow comedy. Two women were sitting next to a man who apparently was unable to keep his flatulence in check. The passengers reportedly asked the man to stop, but he either couldn't or wouldn't. The two passengers then tried to enlist the flight attendants to help them out. They didn't - in fact the pilot issued a warning to the two ladies.

Soon enough, a fight broke out between the gaseous guest and another man and the pilot was forced to divert to Vienna. Upon landing, police boarded the planes with police dogs, removing the two men and the two women. Those women, sisters, claimed they were not involved in the fight and said they would sue the airline. "We had nothing to do with the disturbance, we distanced ourselves from all of that." The airline disputes their story, claiming the two were "knee-deep in the mayhem, taking part in the fight." All four were removed from the airplane and last word indicates all four have been banned for life from ever flying that airline again.

I'd love to offer up some insight to this event but it's difficult to do [amid the chuckles]; I guess you would have to have been there. Did Mr. SBD [Silent But Deadly] have any control over this ... ahhh ... function? Was there a medical condition causing this diversion of discommoded gas? If so, he should not have been flying as there is an 8,000' difference between normal sea-level pressure and that in flight - the difference certainly could cause uncontrolled gaseous emissions. That being said, a fistfight at altitude would not be the best way to resolve the issue where no good could come from any outcome: Unless you're on the ground reading about it.

FARTS
A fart can be a pleasant thing giving the belly ease.
It warms the bed in winter and suffocates the fleas.
A fart can be quiet, or it can be loud,
Some may leave a powerful poisonous cloud.
A fart can be short, or it can be long,
Some have been known to sound like a song.
A fart can create a most curious medley
Or it can be harmless or silent and deadly.
A fart may not smell while others are vile,
They may pass quickly or linger a while.
A fart can occur in a number of places
And leave everyone there with strange looks on their faces.
From wide-open prairie to small elevators
A fart will find all of us sooner or later.
Farts being all bad is simply not true.
We must never forget sweet old farts like you!

~ Anonymous

FLIGHT COMPANY PERSONEL

Sorta speaks for itself, don't it?

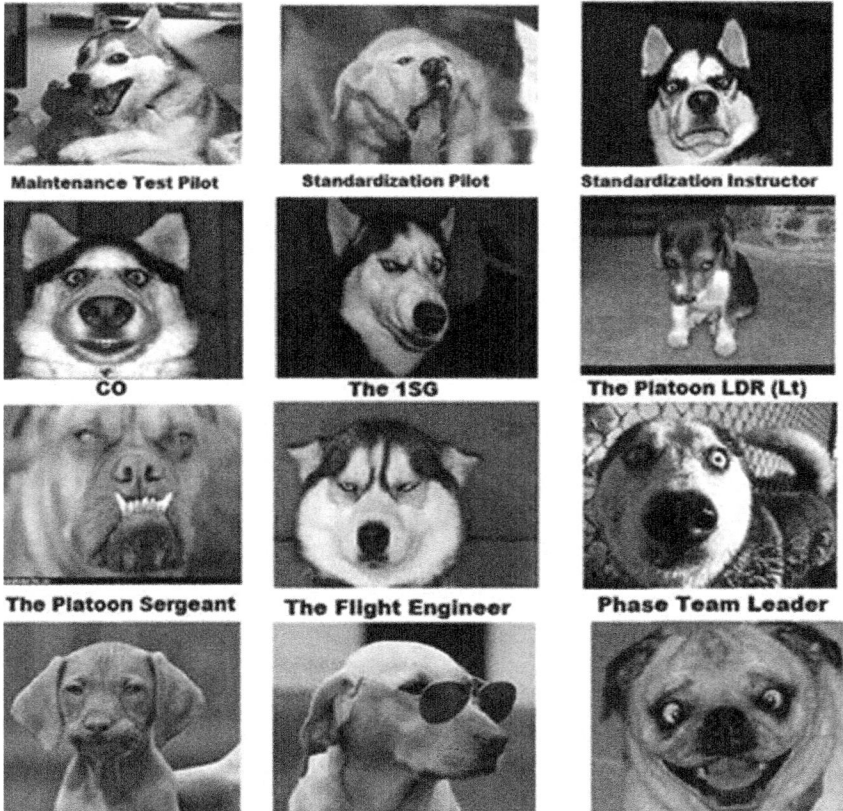

FLIGHT INSTRUCTOR WISDOM

I've spent some time as a CFI/IP and can say with a high degree of certitude that one will never learn so much about a subject until they are required to instruct. From strange questions coming from the 'back of the classroom' crowd to the truly thought-out question(s) from the hotshot you're trying to stay a step ahead of, it all requires effort on the instructors' part to return a true, useful, and legitimate answer to the questioner. And THEN comes the time when one must step into the aerospace vehicle du jour and allow them to put all that-there book-learning to use. While it has been said there are no atheists in the trenches, there are most assuredly no atheists in the rear [or right] seat of an aircraft.

1. You don't know what you don't know.
2. Much of what you think you know is wrong.
3. Together, we must discover why you don't know what you don't know.
4. Much of learning to fly is unlearning preconceived notions and habits.
5. Unlearning these preconceived notions and habits is a very necessary, and the most difficult, part of learning to fly.

6. We progress through repeated successes; we learn from our mistakes.
7. If you must make a mistake, make it a new one.
8. A mistake is evidence someone is trying to do something.

    If you don't try to do something, you'll never make a mistake ... but you'll never achieve anything either.

9. It is practice of the right kind that makes perfect.
10. You will never do well if you stop doing better.
11. The way you are taught and learn a procedure the first time is the way you will react in an emergency. It is important to learn it correctly the first time.
12. You learn according to what you bring to the class.

    Think long and hard about that one.

13. Given the choice, always go for the safest decision.
14. Trusting to luck alone will not be conducive to a long aviation career.

    Luck will do for skill occasionally, but not consistently.

15. Knowledge and good habits deteriorate over time.

    Reread rule # 9. A ballplayer was asked why he practices every day, good weather or bad. He answered, "The day I don't practice my opponent has; he will be the one who beats me."

16. What you know is not as important as what you do with that knowledge.

FLYBOY OLYMPICS
OR ....
WHAT PILOTS (used) TO DO AT THE BAR BESIDES DRINK

This appeared in the November 2019 issue of the QB BEAM, from which it has been unrepentedly and unabashedly lifted so I can present it to you all. Written by Jon Goldenbaum [QB #35223] the article ... well ... speaks for itself. "Those were the days, my friend ..." I've edited and condensed Jon's original article because the original would require two sittings ... and this IS a Bathroom reader, right?

In my twenty years as an Air Force fighter pilot, my best memories come from events that happened in the cockpit followed closely by the shenanigans in the bar. The bar is essential to military aviators; it is the place to unwind, review flights, laugh at [your and others'] mistakes, settle beefs, and teach young pilots how to get along in the world's most competitive culture. Recent political correctness has forced the most spirited bar activities underground, but they will never die: Military pilots are a special breed and their aggressive personalities are at the other end of the PC pole. I have had the good fortune to play in fighter bars all over Europe, the Pacific and Vietnam. Thus, I rubbed shoulders with the finest from our Air Force, Navy and Marines as well as great personalities from the

Royal air Force {Great Britain], the German Luftwaffe, Canadian Forces as well as Italian and French pilots. What follows are recollections of some of the best games we played in the bar.

SONGS:
Military bar songs have been around since The Great War [WWI]; the point is not the quality of the singing, but the camaraderie gained by belting out songs guaranteed to shock the uninitiated. The songs are always sarcastic, irreverent, and ridiculously ribald - they break out only after the singers are well-lubricated and usually delivered at the top of one's lungs by artists with zero talent for music. Many of those songs were very, very old; passed down in squadrons from generation to generation. For instance, many front-line fighter squadrons today still sing the WWI ditty "A Poor Aviator Lay Dying" with verses like "...take the pistons out of my kidneys, the crankshaft out of my brain, the spark plugs from out of my liver and assemble the engine again."

Consistently, the best of all bar singers are Royal Air Force pilots who delight in singing Nazi marching songs whenever they share a NATO bar with modern German Luftwaffe pilots: "The flag flies high on the masthead, we'll fight for glory to the Reich. So tonight, we fly against England, England's island shores, island shores. Sieg Heil!"

DICE GAMES:
Dice cups with at least three sets of dice are mandatory fliers' bar equipment. They are used to compete for drinks in a variety of games: "Horses", "4, 5, 6," and "Trips out" are classics. Best of all are the huge games where 30 or more will pass the dice cup, the loser buying a very expensive round for all participants. This led to the popular saying "You can't lose in a big game." Over the years this phrase was the last thing spoken to your comrades as you walked out for a perilous mission.

CRUD:
Originating at Canadian Air Force, Cold Lake, home of Maple Flag [the Canadian equivalent of Red Flag in the US], the game is played around a pool table by two competing teams [number of players on each team is ... ahhh ... variable]. No cue sticks are used, the object is for rotating shooters to throw the cue ball at a target ball hopefully knocking it into a corner pocket. The shooter ball must NEVER come to rest which leads to frantic running, blocking, checking and other full body contact between shooters and defenders. Hopefully at games' end the players will walk away with only bruises and minor concussions, nothing more serious. In recent years the game has been banned as aircrew losses and injuries playing this game can rival those of actual combat.

CARRIER LANDING:
Invented by Naval Aviators at Cubi Point, Philippines, during the Southeast Asia War Games [Vietnam]. It began with a chair on wheels then became more sophisticated when a half-scale mockup of an A-7 cockpit was built. The intent was to be pushed as fast as your comrades could, then deploy the tailhook before splashing into the pool. The USAF had no such equipment, so long tables were laid end-to-end and well-watered down with beer to allow the participant a frictionless slide. The goal here was to get a running start, belly-flop onto the table and slide along to then raise your legs at just the right moment to catch the '3-wire' [your 'buddies' arms extended across the table]. It was amazing how many 'cable-breaks' there were, and the participant went headlong off the end of the table.

NIGHT CARRIER LANDING:
Use your imagination on this one, people. - ed.

DEAD BUG:

Usually played at the bar but can be used in other venues as well. A simple game in which someone yells "DEAD BUG!" at the top of their voice. Upon hearing this siren call of the faithful, everyone dives for the floor, rolls over onto their backs and waves their arms and legs frantically to mimic a dying insect. This must be done with great enthusiasm and dispatch because anyone slow enough to be last buys the adult beverages. This game is MOST effective when done while the bar is filled with drinkers in dress uniforms at a formal event guaranteeing to ruin expensive dress uniforms and piss off wives and Colonels. It is less effective if the bar is populated with those just off a mission in sweat-stained flight suits; nevertheless, it is great fun especially if you don't break something personal diving for the floor.

I recall one night somewhere - probably Nellis, or perhaps Edwards, AFB O-Club - where we were dining in the club and there were about six older gentlemen and their wives at a table across from us. Someone had ratted us out to the server who, when she entered the room, yelled out that phrase. We all hit the floor dead bugging and as we got up the looks on the ladies' faces were priceless. The older men just laughed - seems they were some of the last of Doolittle's Raiders in to meet up with General Doolittle the next day. I was able to get the great man's signature in his autobiography; he passed away six months later. - ed.

China 1932 - 1945 Attributed Flying Tiger wings.

FLYING WEST

Unabashedly lifted from the QB Beam, © 2020. Used without permission.

By: Captain Michael J. Larkin, TWA (ret.)

I hope there's a place, 'way up in the sky where pilots can go when they have to die. A place where a guy can buy a cold beer for a friend and a comrade whose memory is dear. A place where no doctor or lawyer can tread, nor a management type would e'er be caught dead.

Just a quaint little place, kind of dark, full of smoke where the songs are sung loud, where they love a good joke. The kind of a place where a lady could go and feel safe and protected by the men she would know.

There must be a place where old pilots go when their wings become heavy and airspeed gets low. Where the whiskey is old, and the women are young and songs about flying and dying are sung.

Where you'd see all the fellows who'd flown west before and they'd call out your name as you came in the door. Who would buy you a drink if your thirst should be bad and relate to the others "He was quite a good lad!"

And there, through the mist, you'd spot an old guy you had not seen in years though he taught you to fly. He'd nod his old head and grin ear to ear saying "Welcome, my boy, I'm glad that you're here!"

For this is the place where true flyers come, when battles are over, and the wars have been won. They've come here, at least, to be safe and alone from the government clerks and the management clone,

Politicians and lawyers, the Feds, and the noise; where all hours are happy, and those good old boys can relax with a cool one and a well-deserved rest!

This is Heaven, my son - you've passed your last test.

FLYING WITH THE BLUE ANGELS
OR
BANANAS AND MILKDUDS

Below is an article allegedly written by Rick Reilly of Sports Illustrated ... [If indeed so then this story is ©Sports Illustrated and from whom I beg forgiveness for including it herein -Ed.] He details his experiences when given the opportunity to fly in an F-14 Tomcat... If you aren't laughing out loud by the time you get to 'Milk Duds', your sense of humor is seriously broken.

This message is for America's most famous athletes: Someday you may be invited to fly in the backseat of one of your country's most powerful fighter jets. Many of you already have; John Elway, John Stockton, Tiger Woods to name a few. If you get this opportunity, let me urge you, with the greatest sincerity....

Move to Guam.

Change your name.

Fake your own death!

Whatever you do – DO NOT GO!!!

I know.

The U.S. Navy invited me to try it. I was thrilled. I was pumped. I was toast! I should've known when they told me my pilot would be Chip (Biff) King of Fighter Squadron 213 at Naval Air Station Oceana in Virginia Beach. Whatever you're thinking a Top Gun named Chip (Biff) King looks like, triple it. He's about six-foot, tan, ice-blue eyes, wavy surfer hair, finger-crippling handshake -- the kind of man who wrestles dyspeptic alligators in his leisure time. If you see this man, run the other way. Fast.

Biff King was born to fly. His father, Jack King, was for years the voice of NASA missions. ('T-minus 15 seconds and counting'. Remember?) Chip would charge neighborhood kids a quarter each to hear his dad. Jack would wake up from naps surrounded by nine-year-old's waiting for him to say, 'We have lift off'.

Biff was to fly me in an F- 14D Tomcat, a ridiculously powerful $60 million weapon with nearly as much thrust as weight, not unlike

Colin Montgomerie. I was worried about getting airsick, so the night before the flight I asked Biff if there was something I should eat the next morning.

'Bananas,' he said.

'For the potassium?' I asked.

'No,' Biff said, 'because they taste about the same coming up as they do going down.'

The next morning, out on the tarmac, I had on my flight suit with my name sewn over the left breast. (No call sign -- like Crash or Sticky or Lead Foot. But, still, very cool.) I carried my helmet in the crook of my arm, as Biff had instructed. If ever in my life I had a chance to nail Nicole Kidman, this was it. A fighter pilot named Psycho gave me a safety briefing and then fastened me into my ejection seat, which, when employed, would 'egress' me out of the plane at such a velocity that I would be immediately knocked unconscious.

Just as I was thinking about aborting the flight, the canopy closed over me, and Biff gave the ground crew a thumbs-up. In minutes we were flying straight up at 600 mph. We leveled out and then canopy-rolled over another F-14. Those 20 minutes were the rush of my life. Unfortunately, the ride lasted 80. It was like being on the roller coaster at Six Flags Over Hell. Only - without rails. We did barrel rolls, snap rolls, loops, yanks, and banks. We dived, rose and dived again, sometimes with a vertical velocity of 10,000 feet per minute. We chased another F-14, and it chased us.

We broke the speed of sound. Sea was sky and sky was sea. Flying at 200 feet we did 90-degree turns at 550 mph, creating a G force of 6.5, which is to say I felt as if 6.5 times my body weight was smashing against me, thereby approximating life as Mrs. Colin Montgomerie.

And I egressed the bananas.

And I egressed the pizza from the night before.

And the lunch before that.

I egressed a box of Milk Duds from the sixth grade

I made Linda Blair* look polite. Because of the G's, I was egressing stuff that never thought would be egressed.

I went through not one airsick bag, but two.

Biff said I passed out; twice… I was coated in sweat. At one point, as we were coming in upside down in a banked curve on a mock bombing target and the G's were flattening me like a tortilla and I was in and out of consciousness, I realized I was the first person In history to throw down. I used to know 'cool'. Cool was Elway throwing a touchdown pass, or Norman making a five-iron bite. But now I really know 'cool'. Cool is guys like Biff, men with cast-iron stomachs and Freon nerves. I wouldn't go up there again for Derek Jeter's black book, but I'm glad Biff does every day, and for less a year than a rookie reliever makes in a home stand.

A week later, when the spins finally stopped, Biff called. He said he and the fighters had the perfect call sign for me. Said he'd send it on a patch for my flight suit.

What is it? I asked

'Two Bags.'

*For the uninitiated, or for those too young to remember, the mention of 'Linda Blair' was referring to that actress' performance in the movie "The Exorcist' [1973] in which a scene depicts the demonically possessed character 'egressing' stomach contents for miles around, thoroughly grossing out the audience who were thankful none of it got on them.

Communist Yugoslavia 1946 – 1992.

FOOD FOR THOUGHT

Once you read this, it may occur that the ending is pretty morbid - and just WHY was it included in an otherwise great and funny book? The reason I've included this is the price for screwing up in an automobile is usually bent metal, but screwing up in an airplane means someone's funeral, most likely the screwup-ee. A constant theme throughout this and the original Bathroom Reader was SAFETY. Learning from your mistakes, learning from the mistakes of others, and NOT making those mistakes again. I don't know about any of my readers, but I plan to die at the hands of a jealous husband when I am 100 years old having just spent my last dollar, and owing the electric bill - I do NOT plan on dying in an airplane. Sooo ...

Food for Thought

In days gone by I've proved my worth
By zooming low across the earth.
I've buzzed the valleys and the mountain ridges,
I dove my craft beneath the bridges.
I've looped and spun and rolled my wings,
I've sung the songs that pilots sing.
I've tried most stunts, it must be said
Yet never learned to use my head.
So here's a toast - to you and me,
But you drink both,
I'm dead ... you see.
~ Anonymous

"Great pilots are made, not born. A pilot may possess great eyesight, sensitive hands, and perfect coordination. The end result is only fashioned by good instruction, steady coaching, much practice, and experience."

- Air Vice Marshall J.E. 'Johnnie' Johnson, RAF

FREIGHTDOGS

Many, many of us cut our professional teeth flying freight, usually alone ... at night ... in bad weather ... in an airplane that was 'just barely' within weight and CG limits ... and 'just barely airworthy' ... carrying checks, auto parts or who knows what to locations that aren't even today listed on Google maps ... with no such thing as a GPS ... relying on VORs and NDB's ["Excuse me, sir. What's an NDB?"] and AM radio stations to find our destinations. Wouldn't take a million dollars for the experience ... and wouldn't give you a dollar to do it again.

To those who understand the world of flying.

You see them at airport terminals around the world. You see them in the morning early, though mostly at night.

They appear neatly uniformed and hatted, sleeves striped; wings over their left pocket; they show up looking fresh.

There's a brisk, young-old look of efficiency about them. They arrive fresh from home, from hotels, carrying suitcases, battered briefcases, bulging with a wealth of technical information, data, filled with regulations, rules.

They know the new, harsh sheen of Chicago's O'Hare. They know the cluttered approaches to Newark; they know the tricky shuttle that is Rio; they know but do not relish the intricate instrument approaches to various foreign airports; they know the volcanoes all around Guatemala.

They respect foggy San Francisco. They know the up-and-down walk to the gates at Dallas, the Texas sparseness of Abilene, the very narrow Berlin Corridor, New Orleans' sparkling terminal, the milling crowds at Washington. They know Butte, Boston, and Beirut. They appreciate Miami's perfect weather; they recognize the danger of an ice-slick runway at JFK.

They understand short runways, antiquated fire equipment, inadequate approach lighting, but there is one thing they will never comprehend: Complacency.

They marvel at the exquisite good taste of hot coffee in Anchorage and a cold beer in Guam. They vaguely remember the workhorse efficiency of the DC-3s, the reliability of the DC-4s and DC-6s, the trouble with the DC-7 and the propellers on Boeing 377s. They discuss the beauty of an old gal named Connie. They recognize the high shrill whine of a Viscount, the rumbling thrust of a DC-8 or 707 on a clearway takeoff from Haneda, and a Convair. The remoteness of the 747 cockpit. The roominess of the DC-10 and the snug fit of a 737. They speak a language unknown to Webster. *[The paragraph above would fit my time back in the last century and last millennium; today the 'dogs' may remember the last of the Twin Beech, Baron, Navaho and other 'second generation' aircraft far removed from the relics left over from WWII and the years leading up to the turn of the century. –ed.]*

They discuss ALPA, EPRs, fans, Mach and bogie swivels. And strangely, such things as bugs, thumpers, crickets, and CATs, but they are inclined to change the subject when the uninitiated approaches.

They have tasted the characteristic loneliness of the sky, and occasionally the adrenaline of danger. They respect the unseen thing called turbulence; they know what it means to fight for self-control, to discipline one's senses.

They buy life insurance, but make no concession to the possibility of complete disaster, for they have uncommon faith in themselves and what they are doing.

They concede the glamour is gone from flying. They deny a pilot is through at sixty. They know tomorrow, or the following night, something will come along they have never met before; they know flying requires perseverance and vigilance. They know they must practice, lest they retrograde.

They realize why some wit once quipped: "Flying is year after year of monotony punctuated by seconds of stark terror." As a group, they defy mortality tables, yet approach semi-annual physical examinations with trepidation. They are individualistic, yet bonded together. They are family people. They are reputedly overpaid, yet entrusted with equipment worth millions ... and entrusted with lives, countless lives.

At times they are reverent: They have watched the Pacific sky turn purple at dusk and the stark beauty of sunrise over Iceland at the end of a polar crossing. They know the twinkling, jeweled beauty of Los Angeles at night; they have seen snow on the Rockies.

They remember the vast unending mat of green Amazon jungle, the twisting silver road that is the father of waters, an ice cream cone called Fujiyama; the hump of Africa. Who can forget Everest from 100 miles away or the ice fog in Fairbanks in January?

They have watched a satellite streak across a starry sky, seen the clear, deep blue of the stratosphere, felt the incalculable force of the heavens. They have marveled at sun-streaked evenings, dappled earth, velvet night, spun silver clouds, sculptured cumulus: God's weather. They have viewed the Northern Lights, a wilderness of sky, a pilot's halo, a bomber's moon, horizontal rain, contrails and *St Elmo's Fire.*

Only an aviator experiences all these.

It is their world. And once was mine.

Forever missed.

Shouldn't the skydivers be on the other side to balance the asymmetrical lift? Just askin'.

"Just try and remember, I said slowly, if God had intended men to fly, He'd have given us wings*. So all flying is against the nature of things. It's unnatural, wicked, and stuffed with risks all the time. The secret to flying is learning to minimize the risks or - the secret to life is to choose your own risks.
- Gavin Lyall, 1966

GOT TURBULENCE?

Flying in the mid-teens from Santa Fe to Scottsdale in turbulent conditions, someone else on the frequency asked ATC a question. And NO, neither airplane mentioned herein was me!

Unidentified Pilot: "Is there anyone flying out there in this stuff?"

ATC: "Yes, one other aircraft."

Unidentified Pilot: "At what altitude?"

ATC: "Well, he's assigned 10,500, but he's anywhere between 9,000 and 12,500."

I'm sure many of us 'old greybeards' still committing aviation have heard the trembling voice of a low-time pilot reporting "severe turbulence" from within a Cessna 172. Admittedly, the turbulence experienced by this rookie is the worst he's ever been in, but an <u>accurate</u> estimation and description of this weather phenomenon is necessary for ATC to pass on truthful and meaningful weather information to other pilots. Make an accurate, estimable and meaningful report to ATC in a PIREP and other pilots will praise your name as a pilot's pilot. This Table comes from the Aeronautical Information Manual [AIM], Chapter 7 [Safety of Flight], Section 1 [Meteorology].

TBL 7-1-10
Turbulence Reporting Criteria Table

Intensity	Aircraft Reaction	Reaction Inside Aircraft	Reporting Term-Definition
Light	Turbulence that momentarily causes slight, erratic changes in altitude and/or attitude (pitch, roll, yaw). Report as **Light Turbulence:** [1] or Turbulence that causes slight, rapid and somewhat rhythmic bumpiness without appreciable changes in altitude or attitude. Report as **Light Chop.**	Occupants may feel a slight strain against seat belts or shoulder straps. Unsecured objects may be displaced slightly. Food service may be conducted and little or no difficulty is encountered in walking.	Occasional-Less than $1/3$ of the time. Intermittent- $1/3$ to $2/3$. Continuous-More than $2/3$.
Moderate	Turbulence that is similar to Light Turbulence but of greater intensity. Changes in altitude and/or attitude occur but the aircraft always remains in positive control. It usually causes variations in indicated airspeed. Report as **Moderate Turbulence:** [1]	Occupants feel definite strains against seat belts or shoulder straps. Unsecured objects are dislodged. Food service and walking are difficult.	NOTE 1. Pilots should report location(s), time (UTC), intensity, whether in or near clouds, altitude, type of aircraft and, when applicable, duration of turbulence.

	or Turbulence that is similar to Light Chop but of greater intensity. It causes rapid bumps or jolts without appreciable changes in aircraft altitude or attitude. Report as **Moderate Chop.** [1]		2. Duration may be based on time between two locations or over a single location. All locations should be readily identifiable.
Severe	Turbulence that causes large, abrupt changes in altitude and/or attitude. It usually causes large variations in indicated airspeed. Aircraft may be momentarily out of control. Report **as Severe Turbulence.** [1]	Occupants are forced violently against seat belts or shoulder straps. Unsecured objects are tossed about. Food Service and walking are impossible.	**EXAMPLES:** 1. Over Omaha. 1232Z, Moderate Turbulence, in cloud, Flight Level 310, B707.
Extreme	Turbulence in which the aircraft is violently tossed about and is practically impossible to control. It may cause structural damage. Report as **Extreme Turbulence.** [1]		b. From 50 miles south of Albuquerque to 30 miles north of Phoenix, 1210Z to 1250Z, occasional Moderate Chop, Flight Level 330, DC8.

[1] High level turbulence (normally above 15,000 feet ASL) not associated with cumuliform cloudiness, including thunderstorms, should be reported as CAT (clear air turbulence) preceded by the appropriate intensity, or light or moderate chop.

Being able to 'read sky' is an ability and skill developed to a razor's edge by using all available information accessible by a pilot, paying attention to the little details and clues in evidence from Mother Nature, and putting all that together in a meaningful way so the intrepid birdman knows just what he's getting into.

For example, below is a cloud formation seen from my back deck at 9,000' msl in Colorado indicating it's probably not a good day to go flying. BTW – it takes years and years of diligent study to become this good at weather recognition and avoidance.

[Brought to y'all as a public service by the author]

"Cloud-flying requires practice, even if you have every modern instrument, and unless one keeps calm and collected you will get into trouble after you have been in a real thick one for only a few minutes. In the very early days of aviation, 1912 to be exact, I emerged from a cloud upside-down much to my discomfort as I didn't know how to get right way up again. I found out, somehow, or I wouldn't be writing this."

- Charles Rumney Samson, <u>A Flight From Cairo to Cape Town and Back</u>, 1931

GRANDPA FLEW PHANTOMS

Found this on Ubon Vets FB. There's a lot of writer's "liberty" in here - but a fun read. I loved it.

PS. Not saying y'all are old, but ...

"Hey, Grandpa," the young lad said to me; "tell me a war story. What did you do in the war?" "I flew "Phantoms. Rhino. Big Ugly." Fascination and concern shone in his eyes. "Phantoms?" "Absolutely," I said, looking off into the wild blue yonder and the setting sun. "Tell me about the Phantoms, Grandpa." I thought for a moment about what to say. How much could he really understand? Not much, actually. But kids sure like airplanes, even big kids like Grandpa. I thought a little more about what to tell him:

Actually, they're called F-4s. The term, "F-4," is like a scientific definition for a giant wild animal that will level your 18-wheel truck if it feels like it. The Phantom was the biggest, loudest, meanest-looking, raw power fighting machine ever built. It was a Man's jet. Spectators' innards rumbled when Phantoms took off! Wide-eyed kids instantaneously decided they were going to be a fighter pilot just like me. They didn't understand about back-seaters and crew chiefs, but they did understand brute power and speed. You could point this airplane at the moon and for a while you thought you were going to get there. It went a mile per breath at high cruise. A mile per breath! *[True fact! - ed.]*

Phantom. The big leagues. Normal earth people never witness the splendor nor feel the terror of Big Ugly closing for guns. Over the years, my jet fought them all: Tomcats, Eagles, Falcons, Hornets, F-5s, F-106s, A-4s, A-7s, F-111s, Buffs, B-1s, U-2s, even the F-105. Yeah, my pilots lost some, but won plenty! Don't try to run from a Thud. To win with "Big Ugly," use power, altitude, vertical, surprise.

Don't get slow; speed is life. Cut across the circle. Don't bury the nose. Kill the bandit now. Take that slashing gunshot. Don't say the pilot cheated; he got the shot. You can't outrun the missile. That magnificent airplane remained a major player in our nation's defense for decades, despite sharing birthdays with early pocket calculators. Is anybody still driving a '65 Chevy? It's the people who bring this aircraft to life and provide the brainpower. A roomful of

Phantom crews sets a unique social environment. Seemingly insignificant behaviors and unusual events create career-spanning nicknames and legends. "Two Dogs" shot the tanker. "Tripod" kissed the colonel's dog. They remember forever! Don't believe the dreaded words, "Your secret is safe with me." Don't point fingers, for if you live by the sword, you will die by it.

It's a rare combination of he-man pilots whose egos, fangs, and foolishness are tempered by an inseparable conscience embodied in the blind, trusty WSO who almost equally share credit for the fabulous success of this durable-crew airplane. It's a 'we' airplane – not an 'I', not a 'me', but 'we' airplane. "We shot the drone. We didn't go out of our airspace – not us." The new stuff extends off duty as well. We were at the movies when the windows shattered. You get the idea.

Riding in the "pi", WSOs are among the bravest souls on earth, betting their lives and reputation on the driver up front who will take them who knows where at a moment's notice. The backseater lives by his cunning, competing against advanced technology with systems older than himself. His understanding of human thought processes makes great WSO'ing an art form. He must be ready for any eventuality and provide timely information in a logical, understandable sequence for the multitasked Phantom driver to digest in small pieces. The key is to make the driver, "Mr. Sometimes Macho," think it was his idea in the first place. The WSO must sense when his inputs have gone unheeded, yet never waste a second with unnecessary or mistimed information. He must find the target and get the front seater's eye on it. Then it's grunt time, fighting the Gs while the animal front seater maneuvers for the kill. No whimpering gents; we're riding a Rhino! Sometimes we become the Rhino!

A flight of F-4s paired against multiple bogies creates instant comm jamming when only half the crewmen are talking. Hit the merge and they're all start yakking away, like a gaggle of geese sorting out the variables. Phantoms somehow excel in defeating large numbers of superior aircraft under severe comm conditions. The more targets, the better. Rhinos charge the fight, shoot bogies, and accept a few losses. There's no way to recall everything that happened in a multi-ship merge, but each crewman brings back various recollections to defend vigorously at the debriefing. At the height of the discussion, several pilots talk at once while gesticulating hands "gun" each other. The WSOs nod approvingly. Somehow, most participants emerge from the debriefing with the positive notion that "we did fairly well...considering the circumstances."

Computers changed the flying professional, but an evolution of slippery Phantom tactics continued to confound the sometimes-embarrassed good pilots in modern machines. There was a lot of challenge. You were always up against supposedly better aircraft. Phantom crews shriek with delight, like the wide-eyed kid, when describing unobserved stern missile launches or tracking gunshots against a magic dream machine. Yet, satisfaction is rarely displayed in the presence of your opponent. The adversary must think that Phantoms gunning Hornets is fairly common, which it is, if you don't keep exact score.

Let's see now, 14 years and 2,500 hours flying Phantoms. No wars, only one engine problem, only one hydraulic failure (on the ground). Hot brakes once (my fault). Never lost a generator, no gear problems, never diverted, two fire lights (both false), no high-speed aborts, can't remember my last air abort (it's been years). Can't remember my last ground abort, either. Never had a compressor stall. Killed a horse once. Popped circuit breakers a few times (usually they reset). Took the cable once for antiskid (no big deal). What a great airplane! Dependable with a capital D. Weather? No problem. Ice? Wind? No problem. The F-4 has done the job as an all-weather, day/night fighter extraordinaire.

Big ugly. Been my friend. Never scared me, never hurt me. Knock on wood. I suppose we'll launch missiles at her at Tyndall – from some new magic jet. They'll miss; too bad. Or, Big ugly will drag them back home stuck in her sides like porcupine quills. And someday we'll look back at our Rhino pictures and remember her as we do steam locomotives. I never knew an engineer or assembler who built the Phantom, and probably never will. But thanks, folks! Helluva job! What a great airplane! It's been my everlasting pleasure and privilege to fly her. You just can't imagine.

"Hey, Grandpa," the little voice urges. "I thought you were going to tell me a war story. I began to tell. "So there we were, trying to dig this F-111 out of the canyon. We spot him flying along the cliff, fast and too low for a missile shot…" I swallowed hard and lost my voice there for a second. Kitchen clatter broke the silence with the distant call, "Food's ready!"

Okay, guy," I said quietly. "It's time to wash your hands. Your mom's calling for supper." "I didn't hear her," he claimed, with a twinkle in his eye and a knowing smile like my old buddies had. Food's ready tiger; wash up. I'll be along shortly." A couple of minutes slid by. Then I heard the voice from a distance. "Grandpa? Grandpa. You okay?" A tear plopped on the windowsill. "Yeah, yeah, be there in a minute. Just checking the moon."

Real airplanes require but a single stick to fly.
That is why helicopters - and bulldozers - need two.

GREATEST AVIATION LIES PART 2

Greatest Aviation lies, Part I appears in the original Bathroom Reader [you'll have to buy that book to find them, heh heh heh]; since then several of youse pilots have sent me others to add when the sequel book – now resting in your grubby mitts – comes out. So, without further ado [or adieu], I present words spoken by those, as is mentioned in scripture, where "truth does not abide within them."

1. I KNOW the gear was down.

2. Of course, I know where we are. *Well, I don't know <u>exactly</u> where we are ... but we're making great time.*

3. I have the traffic in sight.

4. I have the field in sight.

5. I thought YOU took care of that.

6. It just came out of maintenance – how could anything be wrong? *Mechanic holding a handful of hardware: "Take her up and see if you really need all this sh ... stuff."*

7. I fly every day – I don't need recurrent training.

8. Your plane will be there and ready by that time.

9. We'll be home by lunch [or dinner, or …].

10. If I can start it, I can fly it. *I can fly the box it came in.*

11. No need to look that up; I've got it memorized.

12. I have 5,000 hours – 3,200 actual IMC.

13. Oh, sure – no problem; I have plenty of time in that make & model.

14. We in aviation are underworked, overpaid, and well-respected. *The older I get, the better I flew.*

15. This plane out-performs the book by 20%.

16. All you need to do is follow the book.

17. That part was shipped yesterday.

18. A little lower and we'll see the approach lights.

19. I'm 22, got a 4-year degree, 6,000 hours with half of those in a Lear.

20. Don't worry about the weight … she'll fly.

21. The weather is going to be okay – its forecast VFR by the time we arrive.

22. I broke out right at minimums.

23. I only need glasses for reading.

24. Why yes, I AM a Mile-High Club member. *[See: origin of Mile-High Club elsewhere in this book]*

25. All that turbulence [or: that crosswind] spoiled my landing.

26. Of course, I fixed it by the book – it must have failed for some other reason.

27. I have no interest in flying for the airlines.

28. Pardon me, Miss – have you seen my Learjet keys?

29. We will be there on time, maybe early.

30. Me? Why, I've never busted minimums.

And to repeat the SECOND greatest lie in aviation:

"I'm from the FAA and I'm here to help you."

And to repeat the FIRST greatest lie in aviation, in reference to the second greatest lie:

"I'm SO happy to see you here."

"When asked why his nickname was 'Ace', Captain Ray Lancaster, USAAF, replied, "Because in World War II, I was responsible for the destruction of six airplanes. Fortunately, three of them were the enemy's"

HISTORICAL MILITARY WEBSITES

For those of you who have 'way too much time on your hands [and after all, how many times can you rearrange the kitchen utensil drawer without the wife's permission before she throws you out of the house?], a look-see through this list of websites should keep you busy for, oh, the next decade or so. I haven't checked on each and every site - had to get this book to the printer this year, dontchaknow? - so if one or several are not up anymore, a kind word to yours truly will get the list revised correctly. DO come up for air occasionally ... and remember to take out the trash.

* Aviation Pioneers   http://acepilots.com/pioneers.html
* World War I Aces   http://acepilots.com/wwi/main.html
* Hall of Fame of the Air   http://acepilots.com/wwi/hfa.html
* WW2 European Theater (ETO)
    http://acepilots.com/usaaf_eto_aces.html
* WW2 Pacific Theater (PTO)
    http://acepilots.com/usaaf_pto_aces.html
* WW2 US Marine Corps   http://acepilots.com/usmc_aces.html
* WW2 US Navy Aces<http://acepilots.com/usn_aces.html
* WW2 Mediterranean (MTO)
    http://acepilots.com/usaaf_mto_aces.html
* WW2 German Aces

http://acepilots.com/german/ger_aces.html
* Korean War Aces   http://acepilots.com/korea_aces.html
* Russian Aces   http://acepilots.com/russian/rus_aces.html
* Vietnam Era Aces   http://acepilots.com/vietnam/main.html
* Airplanes   http://acepilots.com/
* World War I Planes   http://acepilots.com/wwi/main.html
* 1930s Aircraft Photos
  http://acepilots.com/pioneer/air_photos.html
* WW2 Fighters
  http://acepilots.com/planes/main.html#fighters
* WW2 Bombers
  http://acepilots.com/planes/main.html#bombers
* WW2 German Planes   http://acepilots.com/german/main.html
* WW2 Airplane Pictures
  http://acepilots.com/archives/main.html
* History of Airplanes Blog   http://acepilots.com/airplanes/
* Nose Art   http://acepilots.com/planes/nose_art.html
* Postwar Jets   http://acepilots.com/jets/main.html
* World War Two   http://acepilots.com/
* WW2 Facts and Firsts   http://acepilots.com/misc_ww2.html
* WW2 Medals   http://acepilots.com/medals/main.html
* WW2 Museums   http://acepilots.com/ww2/museums.html
* WW2 Pictures   http://acepilots.com/ww2/pictures.html
* WW2 Ships   http://acepilots.com/ships/main.html
* WW2 Weapons   http://acepilots.com/ww2/weapons.html

"I was asked "How much money do I need to fly?"
The answer, of course, is: "All of it."
- Gordon Baxter

HISTORY – MORE OR LESS- OF THE 'MILE HIGH CLUB'

Claims made by pilots - usually male - about being [or becoming] a member of this ... ahhh ... 'prestigious' club can and should be considered with an exceptionally large shaker of salt. That is, with a generous amount of skepticism and, shall we say, 'discernment' as to the veracity of the claimant. These boasts are most difficult to confirm factually; usually the other party - female - will deny everything vehemently and will bring accusations as to the status of his parentage into question. There have been many documented events of this 'maneuver' being attempted in airliner restrooms, but in Cessnas and Pipers - where one of the participants should have been in charge of holding altitude and/or heading, the outcome can be an entirely different one. I recall reading an accident report wherein it was stated "...peculiar injuries to the pilot indicate he was receiving oral sex at the moment of impact."

A milestone in the history of aviation was celebrated in 2014: the debut, a century prior, of the autopilot. In June 1914, at a historic aeronautical-safety competition in Paris, a 21-year-old American daredevil pilot-inventor named Lawrence Burst Sperry stunned the aviation world by using the instrument to keep a biplane flying straight and level along the Seine. According to his biographer,

William Wyatt Davenport, Sperry stood on a wing as the plane, in effect, flew itself—a feat that won him the event's $10,000 prize.

By eliminating the need for taxing "hand-flying" on long journeys and thereby reducing pilot fatigue, Sperry's autopilot ultimately made flying much safer. But it had another, less obvious benefit. It freed up pilots to do other things with their hands—and bodies. The brilliant young Sperry himself soon grasped the possibilities. Legend has it that in late November 1916, while piloting a Curtiss Flying Boat C-2 some 500 feet above the coast of Long Island, he used his instrument to administer a novel kind of flying lesson to one Cynthia Polk (whose husband was driving an ambulance in war-torn France). During their airborne antics, however, the two unwittingly managed to bump and disengage the autopilot, sending their plane into Great South Bay, where they were rescued, both stark naked, by duck hunters. A gallant Sperry explained that the force of the crash had stripped both fliers of all their clothing, but that didn't stop a skeptical New York tabloid from running the famous headline "Aerial Petting Ends in Wetting." For his caper, Sperry is generally considered the founder of the Mile High Club, a distinction that loosely includes all those who have ever "done it" in flight *(though precisely what constitutes "it" remains a lurking definitional issue)*.

"Flying," the 1930s stunt pilot Pancho Barnes is often quoted as saying, "makes me feel like a sex maniac in a whorehouse with a stack of $20 bills." Today's overcrowded, underfed, overstressed airline passengers, consigned to travel in "just a bloody bus with wings" as Ryanair CEO Michael O'Leary puts it, are unlikely to share that enthusiasm. It's all the more remarkable, then, that airborne sex remains on the bucket list of plenty of passengers, at least male ones. A "Sex Census" published in 2011 by the condom maker Trojan found that 33 percent of American men aspire to have sex on an airplane. (The top locale for women: a beach.) Similarly, nearly a third of the Brits who responded to a 2010 TripAdvisor poll said they wanted to try in-flight sex.

A lot of U.S. fliers may have already acted out that fantasy. In a global survey of more than 300,000 adults conducted in 2005 by the condom maker Durex, 2 percent of respondents worldwide (and 4 percent of American respondents) claimed to have had sex on an airplane. A 2010 survey commissioned by Sensis Condoms (when did condom makers become avid pollsters?) found a similar incidence of in-flight sex (3 percent) among its respondents. Assuming that about 100 million Americans have traveled by air, and discounting for lying braggarts, if even only *1 percent* of them have indulged, then that's a million or so Mile-Highers.

Less-than-scientific anecdotes abound too. When Virgin Atlantic installed diaper-changing tables aboard its new Airbus A340-600 long-haul jets, in 2002, it wasn't just mothers and children who found them useful. Within weeks, according to the airline, the tables were destroyed by "those determined to join the Mile-High Club." That said, the airline's founder, the billionaire bad boy Sir Richard Branson, has waxed nostalgic about a tryst he had at age 19 in a Laker Airways lavatory ("It was every man's dream"). Almost 20 years ago, Singapore Airlines, for its part, reported that a third of its cases of "unruly behavior" involved in-flight sex.

For the airlines, the "sexy skies" are all about marketing the fantasy. Actual in-flight sex is the last thing they want to deal with, especially since 9/11, when the preferred cabin ambience has become no-fun, no-drama—a shift more self-protective than puritanical. Is it just love, or is that couple huddled together in their seats trying to ignite explosive-filled sneakers? Even a visit to the bathroom can trigger a full-bore fighter-jet scramble, as it did on the 10th anniversary of 9/11, when a pair of F-16s shadowed a Frontier flight until it landed in Detroit after two passengers made for the lavatory at the same time. Cabin crews working chock-full flights now also have no time, much less the inclination, to play chaperone.

Almost perversely, as the reality of today's air travel for the ordinary coach passenger moves from bearable to downright nasty, reviving the lost "romance" of flying makes marketing sense. Branson, the master marketer, beckons passengers to "get lucky" when they fly Virgin America jets outfitted with seat-back touch screens that let you send "an in-flight cocktail to that friendly stranger in seat 4A." After all, if you're busy punching your video screen to chat up some "friendly stranger," you're not griping about an airline's $7.50 snack pack. And when Singapore Airlines proudly unveiled for global media its super-jumbo double-decker Airbus A380 jet, the hype was all about the glories of its 12 ultra-costly first-class "suites." Combine two of the private pods (about $10,000 each for the round trip from New York to Frankfurt), and you can share a legit double bed, shown in publicity photos strewn with rose petals, alongside a gold tray holding an open bottle of Dom Pérignon and two half-full champagne flutes. What are you *supposed* to think? Then there's Air New Zealand's "Skycouch" (three adjacent coach seats that can be transformed into a flat, bed-like surface), popularly known as "cuddle class." It comes with the coy admonition to "just keep your clothes on thanks!"

Could we return to the good old days when travelers were "mad men" and flight attendants were "sexy stews," when the "sex sells seats" mantra drove some carriers to adorn "trolley dollies" in hot pants and go-go boots and to offer "executive" (men-only) flights between Chicago and New York? Not likely, at least in the United States, where women constitute more than 40 percent of frequent fliers and half of international air travelers and make most travel buying decisions. How many of these women are really looking to "get lucky" on their next flight? Being hit on by an unseen stranger while buckled into a seat at 35,000 feet, online commenters have complained, is at best "a little creepy" and at worst like being trapped in a "mile high stalker club."

For those moved by the marketing, or otherwise compelled to act out the mile-high fantasy (Freud posited that the fantasy of flight itself has "infantile erotic roots"), there's a better solution than flying commercial: your own plane. Think Playboy's *Big Bunny*, a 1970s-era DC-9 jet outfitted as a "party pit," complete with a fur-covered oval bed, a shower, and a discotheque, all presided over by flight attendants ("Jet Bunnies") in black-leather mini-jumpsuits: "Imagine Studio 54 with wings," enthused a *Playboy* feature. That particular icon supposedly now resides, dismantled, in a small city in Mexico, but some air-charter services offer hour-long jaunts for adventurous couples wanting to live out the dream, or at least spice up their relationships. These outfits come and go, with names like Erotic Airways and Flamingo Air, but typically they equip their small Pipers or Cessnas with a mattress (in lieu of the customary four or six seats), overfly scenic spots like Cincinnati or western Georgia, and throw in a bottle of not-quite-vintage bubbly, all for about $500.

The sheets—no joke—are yours to take home as souvenirs.

Beware of men on airplanes. The minute a man reaches 30,000 feet, he immediately becomes consumed by distasteful sexual fantasies which involve doing uncomfortable things in those tiny little toilets. These men should not be encouraged, their sexual fantasies are sadly low-rent and unimaginative. Affect a cool, aloof demeanor as soon as any man tries to draw you out.
Unless, of course, he's the pilot.
- ~~Stewar~~ ... ahhh ... unidentified female flight attendant

HOW NOT TO START AN AIRPLANE

This is one of those apocryphal stories illustrating one of the best reasons to NOT do something; sort of like being the good example of a bad technique. What helps get the point across here is there are pictures taken concerning this event (see below - with commentary). If anyone out there is contemplating hand-propping their airplane, they should 1) have a damn good reason for doing so and 2) know what the hell they are doing. This is NOT an activity for someone who thinks "Hey, I saw my instructor do this once, I think I remember how." Or for anyone not SPECIFICALLY trained in performing this EXTREMELY DANGEROUS task. There are better and safer alternatives, including spending the night somewhere in order for someone who KNOWS WHAT THEY'RE DOING to arrive.

I'm copying the report just I got it; it uses some disparaging remarks regarding the skills [lack of], intelligence [ditto] and decision-making ability [entirely deficient] of the person involved.

Pilot 'A' pushed his plane to the fuel island and refueled it. Knowing his battery was dead, he pushed the airplane back from the fuel pit, hopped in and primed the engine leaving the throttle one-half open, mags on and exited the ill-fated craft. He gave the propeller an exuberant swing and the engine fired right up ... right up to 1800 rpm, more or less [most likely more]. The plane began moving forward at an equally exuberant pace ... straight towards the fuel island.

Fortunately, the propeller hit the concrete-filled steel posts surrounding the fuel pit designed for this very situation; that of keeping idiots from running into the fuel tanks. Prop hits post; engine crankshaft shears in two; propeller/hub/spinner flies through the air [like you see in cartoons] landing on top of a hangar 150 yards away. Not being able to 'buff out the damage', Pilot 'A' *[can you guess what the 'A' stands for?]* sells the airplane on the spot for $400 and it was parted out on eBay.

With today's medical expertise, knowledge, and skills, much can be fixed - stupidity is not one of these things. Pilot 'A' had no insurance and was already in the crosshairs of the FAA for running another airplane out of fuel in flight. Hand-propping is sometimes called the

"Ernest Hemingway Maneuver" - one slip-up and it's 'Farewell to Arms.' *[or other personal parts]*.

I heard once that 80% of all General Aviation accidents/incidents are caused by 20% of the 'pilots.' Check out the pictures again - if these do not convince you of how serious this maneuver is, then KMAG YOYO. And make sure your insurance policy is paid up to date.

HOW TO *FAIL* AS A FLIGHT INSTRUCTOR

As a DPE I travel all over the state – and now the country - administering flightchecks to many individuals flying many different airplanes from many different airports. I have seen and heard a LOT administering those exams.

I have a special regard in my heart for FLIGHT INSTRUCTORS – those special pilots who will accept the responsibility for instructing the future of aviation. I have witnessed the good, the bad, and the ugly performing the duties of a Flight Instructor. As a pilot based at KCFO [in Denver, Colorado] and as a DPE, I submit these thoughts to focus your thoughts and actions while you are instructing the future of aviation.

© Chickenwingscomics [*Used without permission*]

TELL EVERYONE – you are just doing this until you get on with the airlines – however many years that may take. *[That will impress your students with your 'professional outlook' for your future]*

RELUCTANTLY – take on Private Pilot students. They are beneath you and it takes forever to get them through. *[Remember when you were one?]*

CHARGE LESS – than everyone else. *[After all, this really isn't a 'profession']*

BE EASY – on friends and acquaintances when they train with you. *[They will remember this 'courtesy' and tell everyone how ineffective you were/are as an instructor]*

THE COCKPIT IS A GREAT PLACE – to ask for a date from a student; if you get turned down you can just drop them. *[That will teach them!]*

DRESS CASUAL – clean and pressed shirt and trousers don't impress like a rock band t-shirt, cutoffs, and sandals. *[Neither does bathing and shaving]*

SKIRT THE TASKS WHICH MAKE YOU UNCOMFORTABLE – like stalls, spins, long cross-countries, hot days, long nights, Class B/C operations, etc. *[They'll pick up on this stuff later]*

SHARE NOTHING – with fellow CFI's and ask nothing of them. *[They will appreciate this more than you will]*

ATTEND NOTHING – that will offer new information, knowledge, skills, or awareness and do not expect your students to attend these either. *[Your 'wisdom' is all your student needs, right?]*

STAY AWAY FROM THE FAA – and any safety seminars, programs, or meetings they offer. *[After all, what can you learn from the enemy?]*

DO NOT ATTEND – any airshows, trade fairs, expos, or other gatherings of pilots, instructors, or airplanes. *[Why should you, you know it all anyway, right?]*

ADD NOTHING TO YOUR CERTIFICATE – your existence as a CFI is just temporary until the airlines call. *[And then it's autopilot and crew meals forever]*

DO LOTS OF FLIGHT REVIEWS AND IFR PROFICIENCY CHECKS – you can fly less, charge more and ride in a lot of neat airplanes you ordinarily wouldn't have the chance to ride in. *[You might even get a free meal out of it if the weather is bad]*

DO NOT TEACH GROUND SCHOOL – either organized classes or one-on-one with your students. They have the textbooks; they can look things up and learn that way. *[Besides, you don't want them to discover how much you really know, do you?]*

GRAB THE FLIGHT CONTROLS EVERY CHANCE YOU GET – if a student is about to make a mistake, take the airplane controls and show them how to do it, over and over again. *[They might not learn as much or as quickly, but it keeps you current]*

TAKE A LONG TIME BEFORE SOLOING THEM – if they crash or bang up the plane it will reflect badly on you.

STAY IN THE AIRPORT TRAFFIC PATTERN – for the first 20 – 30 hours. It's familiar territory for the student. *[And convenient for you if your cellphone/text goes off]*

TAKE YOUR CELLPHONE WITH YOU – every flight, leave it on and answer every call or text. *[That one just might be the airlines calling you]*

COINCIDE YOUR STUDENT CROSS-COUNTRY TRIPS – with airports where you have business and/or can deliver an application or resume. *[What the hell, its good use of time and the student needs the hours]*

CANCEL YOUR STUDENTS' FLIGHTS – every time you can and/or by making up a 'good' excuse.

CHANGE AIRPORTS AND/OR FLIGHT SCHOOLS OFTEN – after you have had the opportunity to make an impression on the student base, other instructors, management and local DPE's. *[Besides, the other CFI's have been stealing your students anyway. What in the world could cause this slump?]*

When you earned your Flight Instructors' certificate, you agreed to be a role model, an example of professionalism, and a TEACHER! Take charge of your destiny and JUST DO IT! While you are earning your way up the aviation ladder as a flight instructor, BE THE BEST YOU CAN BE! The world will beat a path to your door – I guarantee it.

Drew Chitiea, DPE
Master Instructor Emeritus

"Let's get one thing straight: there's a big difference between being a pilot and being an aviator. The former is a technician, the latter an artist in love with flight and the sky."
 - Elrey Jeppesen   inventor of instrument approach charts

I LEARNED ABOUT FLYING FROM THAT

I wrote this for a flying magazine which has a column of the same name as the title of this article; since it wasn't published I include it here for general instructional purposes and 'bragging rights' that I can do something stupid and live through it.

I rolled the "Magic Carpet" – my 1979 Cessna P-210 - from its hangar in Denver, Colorado intending a flight to Georgetown, Texas, just north of Austin to work with a client. Friends heard I was flying that way and offered to contribute to the fuel fund if I would drop them off in San Angelo, about an hour's flying west-northwest of Austin then pick them up on my return flight. Grateful for the companionship and contribution, I agreed. The flight to KSJT then KGTU was uneventful.

I worked with my client for three days, all the while watching a tropical storm build in the Gulf of Mexico which began moving towards the gulf coast my last day there. The morning of my departure found Georgetown with 500' overcast, 5 miles visibility in light rain; San Angelo about the same. With my client departing (by car) the next day "I have to get out of here today" I said to myself, "Or else I'll be stuck here for days." Any time you hear yourself beginning a sentence with "I have to ..." in aviation it should be a warning to yourself. So, strike one on me.

I departed into the clag settling down for a quick hop to San Angelo: I'll get my friends on board and we're off – should be home a little after noon. Twenty minutes out of KSJT I noticed my Low Voltage light illuminate; not good. A quick glance at the ammeter showed the needle buried in the discharge mode. {Expletive deleted} I turned off non-essential electrical users, checked the circuit breakers and cycled the alternator switch to no avail. A double-check of the emergency checklist showed nothing else to be done. I was losing electrons, protons or morons from the battery and still was in solid IMC. Strike two.

Sidenote: An aircraft battery may be advertised as a 30 amp-hour battery. Meaning it should be able to provide 30 amps of current for an hour. *Don't you believe it!* As it turned out, my battery was able to provide maybe 15 amps for maybe15 minutes ... maybe.

I declared an emergency to SJT approach; they immediately provided vectors to the ILS. I descended to vectoring altitude still in solid IMC, and I thought that perhaps I didn't want to be low to the ground, in the clag, hand flying (autopilot was off by now) having to manually extend the gear by pumping the emergency gear handle those 476 times it takes to get the gear down. I elected to use a few electrons to get the landing gear extended which fortunately did get down and locked. That friendly little green light glowed in a comforting manner: Score one for the good guys.

The next few things occurred in far less time than it takes to read, so bear with me. With the gear down and locked I took an intercept vector to the ILS which was displayed on the Garmin 530. I noted I was on a 5-mile scale; estimating I was three miles from joining the localizer and perhaps five miles from the outer marker. The ATIS, which I heard just prior to the low voltage light illuminating, still presented 500' overcast six miles in light rain. My autopilot was off as I was hand-flying by now and I was praying {"Hello, God. It's yer ole buddy Drewster here again."}I had enough electricity left for the approach. My iPad, with which I was just becoming familiar, was on the floor between the seats – not at all a good place for it – as I had been too busy dealing with the problem and managing the approach to pull it out. Strike three. I knew exactly where my hand-held back-up radio was, too; in the charger on my workbench in the hangar back home. Strike four.

And then everything on the panel went dark.

Expletive deleted squared

No HSI, no flight director, no turn coordinator, no electrical back-up attitude indicator, no GPS, no secondary nav radio, no ability to communicate, no autopilot, no systems gauges, no flaps. Strikes five, six, seven, and so on. Talk about being up the proverbial creek of tribulation without any means of propulsion! However, I indeed had two ideas: the first being if I couldn't find the ground in a safe and sane manner I would climb up to the Off Route Obstacle Clearance Altitude [OROCA] keeping wings level with my vacuum-driven Attitude Indicator, maneuver so the magnetic compass read 'N' then fly about 100 miles to where VFR was said to exist.

The second plan – which became 'Plan A' for the time being – was to keep the approach-level airspeed where it was – 90 knots. Since I figured {using the 'TLAR Method': That Looks About Right} I was three miles from joining the localizer all I had to do was fly the intercept heading for two minutes so I would be approximately where I would join said localizer. I also 'TLARed' I would then be about four miles from the outer marker. I would turn to hold the localizer heading for three minutes putting me inside the OM where I could gingerly begin my descent. The land around SJT is pretty flat – I don't recall any towers and/or obstructions on the final approach course – so I would slowly descend to localizer approach minimums looking for signs of the planet underneath me.

As I neared the localizer approach MDA the clouds swirled away revealing the welcome sight of the ground far enough below me so I didn't have to concern myself with tying the record for low flying. I broke out under a flat overcast to see the airport at twelve-thirty and four miles: Now, what does a steady green light from the tower mean? Heck, y'all clear the area 'cause I'm a-landing! Flashing green gave me permission to taxi and I cruised over to where I was to meet my friends. Nothing a pro couldn't handle, right? I sure wish that pro was along with me!

As it turns out, my alternator belt had broken causing the alternator to cease production. The battery – remember the battery? – had just enough poop in it to give me an idea where the localizer, outer marker and airport was located. If this had occurred five minutes sooner I would have been out of luck and would have ended up in Lubbock. Certainly not a bad place to be considering the situation, but then an entirely new set of challenges would have been presented.

So, what did I learn from this?

First: On a workbench in the hangar is exactly the wrong place for one's back-up emergency hand-held radio to be. It should have been – and will be forevermore when I fly – within easy reach inside the cockpit.

Second: I usually begin briefing my arrivals about an hour from my destination amending my plans as circumstances dictate. As soon as I got into the cruise mode on a leg of this short duration I should have had the iPad out, plugged in and displaying all the pertinent data, charts and information so I could achieve and maintain good situational awareness. The day after this 'adventure, the iPad is out, alive, programmed and ready for action prior to engine start

Third: When planning an IFR trip, "Plan A" is when everything works as it should; there are no challenges, glitches or untoward circumstances arising. "Plan B" is how Plan A can be achieved when a weather issue, malfunction or emergency occurs during the flight. "Plan C" is what must be done when and if it all goes to hell in a handbasket? What will I do if the old vacuum pump fails? How about a complete and total electrical failure? Where's the nearest VFR? What will I do if I'm down to the old 'needle, ball and ripcord' mode of instrument flight? The time and place to sort out the answers to these questions is the night before the flight sitting at one's desk in a calm, thoughtful manner.

Fourth: When something untoward does occur, stay calm; focus and deal with the highest priority item first. Then go down the list of tasks in order of their importance. Remember, the job to do right now is to fly the airplane. Be scared later – do your duty as Pilot-in-Command NOW.

Fifth: I'm glad I practice emergency procedures. Practice dealing with situations which could rarely but still probably happen. I jump into a simulator every chance I get. I get an Instrument Proficiency Check every three months no matter the state of my being current per the regulations {'current' does not necessarily mean 'proficient'}. Practice and drill; drill and practice. The time to prepare for these eventualities is when one can control the circumstances, not in flight when your adrenaline to red-blood-cell ratio is climbing past 20 to 1.

"Prepare for the unknown, the unexpected, and the inconceivable. After fifty years of flying I'm still learning something every time I go up."
-Gene Cernan, astronaut. Last man to walk on the moon

"You've got to expect things are going to go wrong. And we always need to prepare ourselves for handling the unexpected."
-Neil Armstrong, astronaut. First man to walk on the moon

IDEAL AIRPLANES

As mentioned somewhere else in this tome, airplanes are designed by PhD's, tested by Masters', flown by Bachelors', maintained by High Schoolers, and built by the lowest bidder. What possibly could go wrong? Well, here's a glance at that possibility - and do NOT tell me "If I can start it, I can fly it." I challenge you to even find where the ignition key is inserted.

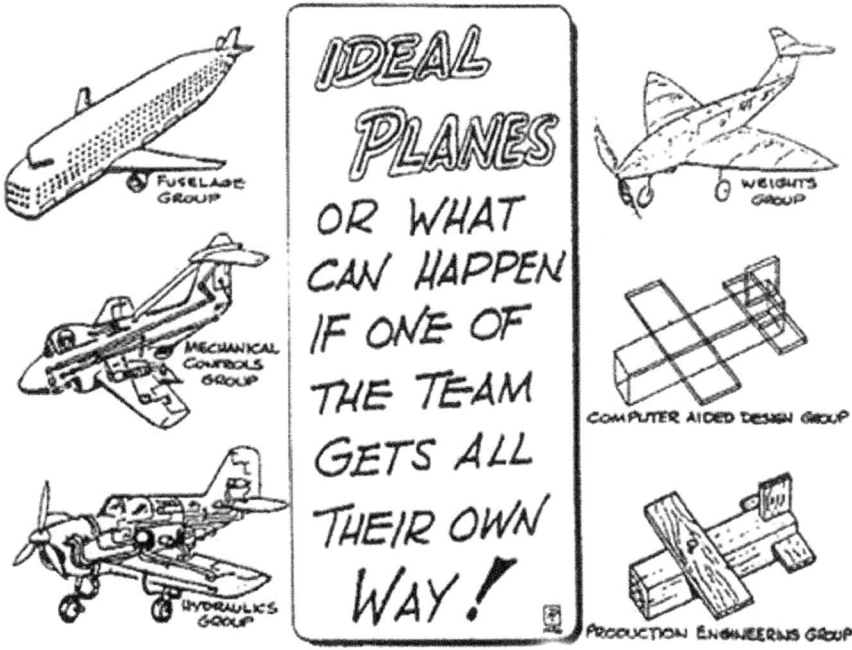

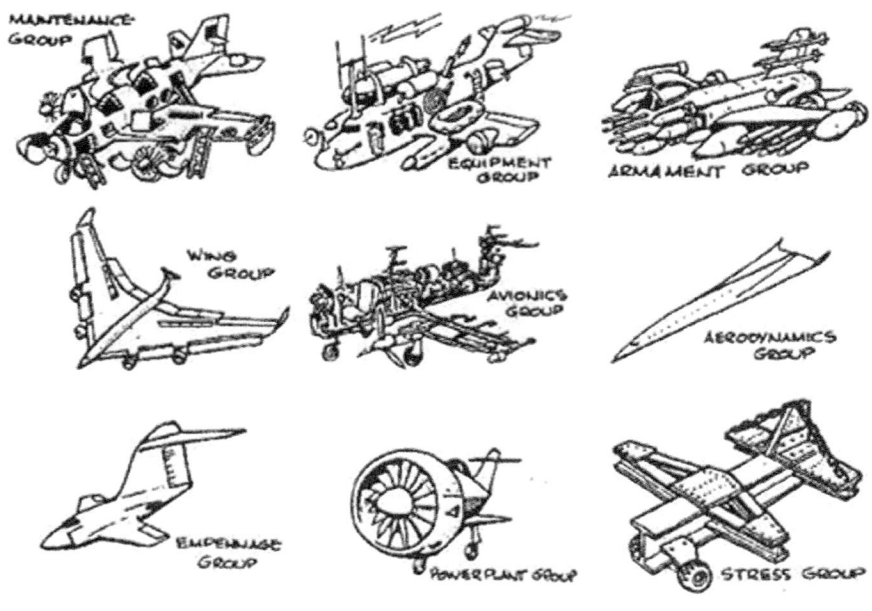

"If you are in trouble anywhere in the world, an airplane can fly over and drop flowers, but a helicopter can land and save your life.
- Igor Sikorsky, 1947

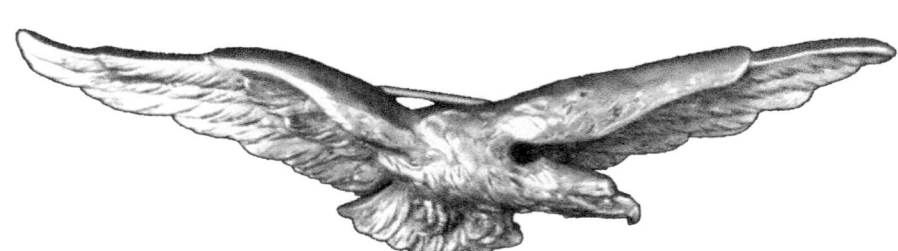

USAAS WWI Lafayette Escadrille pilot wings.

INNER PEACE & THE ATTAINMENT THEREOF

What with demands of work, the pressures of life and the damage stress can wreak on our bio-rhythms, circadian cycles and such, I offer the following as ' alternative therapy'. It is much less expensive than psychotherapy, works well and lasts a relatively long time – well, long enough to forget the immediate causal reasons for the time being.

I'm passing this on as a public service ... no need thanking me.

A doctor on TV said that in order to have inner peace in our lives, we should always finish things that we start. Since we all could use more calm in our lives, I looked around my house to find things I had started & had not finished.

As a result, I finished a bottle of Merlot, a bottle of Chardonnay, a bodle of Sotch, a butle of wum, tha mainder of Valiuminun scriptins, an a box a choclutz.

Yu has no idr how fablus I fele rite now.

Sned this to all ur frenz who need inner piss.

An telum u luvum.

LIFE EXPLAINED

While not an aviation-specific submission, many of us pilots sitting there in our reverie at cruise altitude & airspeed have had the time and/or inclination to take a moment and ponder the meaning of life. Often this approaches either the maudlin, ridiculous, unrealistic and/or plain old crazy. These introspections usually begin with the phrase "How in the world did I ..." [You can fill in the rest: ... deserve this? ... get in this deep? ...end up here? ...miss that promotion? - and so forth]

All-in-all, I will fall back on a passage in Genesis where God, after creating the world and all its denizens and inhabitants, hangs up His hat and set his flight case in the corner [God's a pilot after all, right?], puts his feet up and says [paraphrased] "Yep, pretty good for a first try, if I do say so myself."

On the first day, God created the dog and said, "Sit all day by the door of your house and bark at anyone who comes in or walks past. For this I will give you a life span of twenty years." The dog said, "That's a long time to be barking. How about only ten years and I'll give you back the other ten?"

And God said that it was good.

On the second day, God created the monkey and said, "Entertain people, do tricks, and make them laugh ... for this, I'll give you a twenty-year life span." The monkey said, "Monkey tricks for twenty years? That's a long time to perform. How about I give you back ten like the dog did?"

And God again said that it was good

On the third day, God created the cow and said, "You must go into the field with the farmer all day long and suffer under the sun, have calves and give milk to support the farmer's family. For this, I will give you a life span of sixty years." The cow said, "That's kind of a tough life you want me to live for sixty years. How about twenty and I'll give back the other forty?"

And God agreed it was good.

On the fourth day, God created humans and said, "Eat, sleep, play, marry and enjoy your life ... for this, I'll give you twenty years." But the human said, "Only twenty years? Could you possibly give me my twenty, the forty the cow gave back, the ten the monkey gave back, and the ten the dog gave back; that makes eighty, okay?"

"Okay," said God, "You asked for it"

So that is why for our first twenty years, we eat, sleep, play and enjoy ourselves.

For the next forty years, we slave in the sun to support our family.

For the next ten years, we do monkey tricks to entertain the grandchildren.

And for the last ten years, we sit on the front porch and bark at everyone.

Life has now been explained to you. There is no need to thank me for this valuable information. I'm doing it as a public service.

If you are looking for me, I will be on the front porch.

God may not subtract from a person's life those hours spent flying, however harsh penalties are exacted for those who do not learn to land properly.

Phillipines Pilot.

MECHANIC-SPEAK

As I mention to those wishing to become Flight Instructors [CFI's and IP's], one of the most important tasks for which they are responsible is to teach aviation-specific language. Every endeavor of humankind has a specific language - medicine, engineering, law, etc. So does aviation; instructors have the responsibility to instruct using proper aviation terminology, NOT slang, jargon or 'cool-speak' - the student will pick all that up later, but NOT from the instructor pilot. That being said, being able to describe clearly and accurately to mechanics the conditions, problems and operations in specific aircraft components is crucial to a speedy return to airworthiness of said aerospace vehicle. Therefore the wise pilot should be able to describe what is going on with the following VIAPOs [Very Important Aircraft Parts & Operations].

- Levitators [small, medium and large]
- Tachynator units
- Corelian Obfuscator
- Radalt Transmogrifier
- Thermoplumes and the Thermoplume modus adjuster
- Autodefumigator
- Knot marshalling management
- Cryogenic tendencies of the temperature modulator

- Hyper - and Hypo-spanner *[the difference between the two is important!]*
- The mechanical Swear Index
- Installation, location, and operation of the Anti-Groundloop Switch *[exclusive to tailwheel airplanes]*
- Navigational guidance reflexation
- Missile Wave Guidance Theory
  https://www.youtube.com/watch?v=T85PQe8L1r4
- Turbo Encabulator
  https://www.youtube.com/watch?v=Ac7G7xOG2Ag

... and to modify this into the aviation field

- https://www.youtube.com/watch?v=bOV0v1Uq5CY

If Leonardo Da Vinci had used mechanics for models:

MECHANIC'S HARDWARE CHART

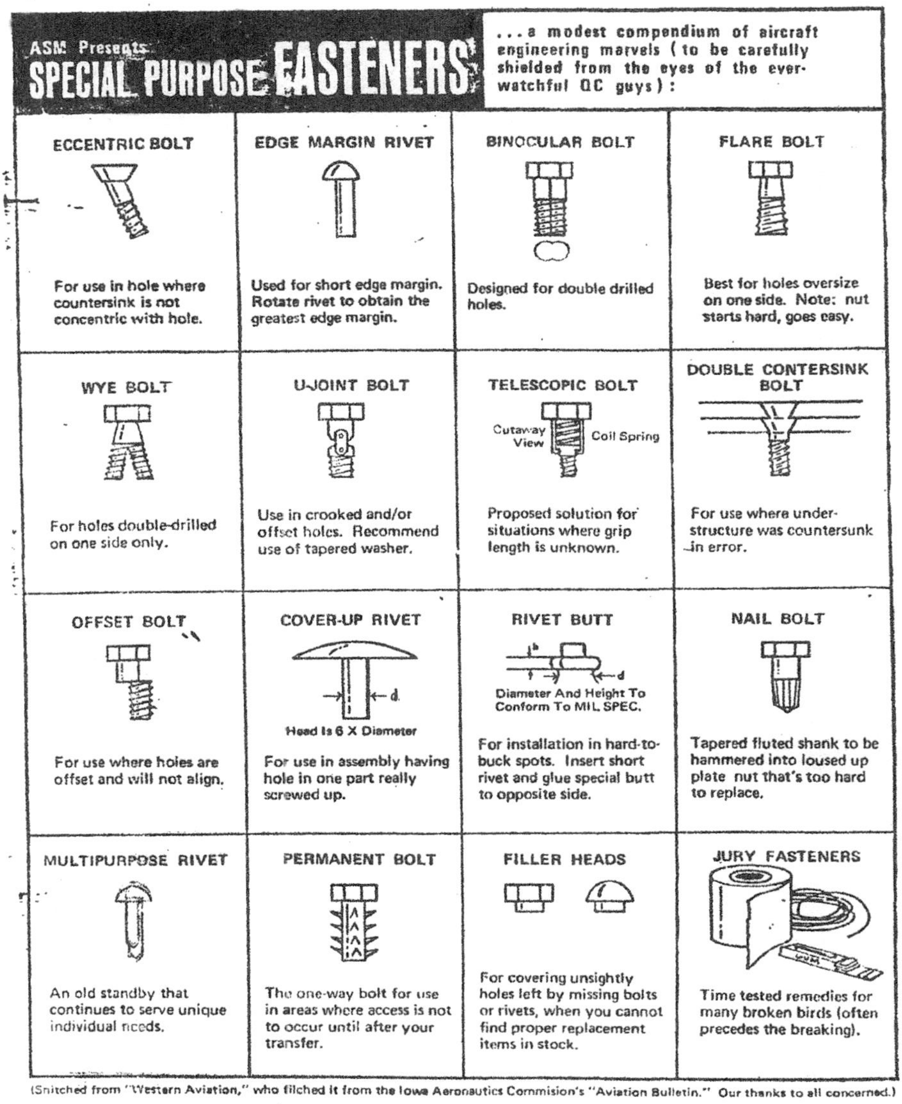

ASM Presents: SPECIAL PURPOSE FASTENERS

...a modest compendium of aircraft engineering marvels (to be carefully shielded from the eyes of the ever-watchful QC guys):

ECCENTRIC BOLT	EDGE MARGIN RIVET	BINOCULAR BOLT	FLARE BOLT
For use in hole where countersink is not concentric with hole.	Used for short edge margin. Rotate rivet to obtain the greatest edge margin.	Designed for double drilled holes.	Best for holes oversize on one side. Note: nut starts hard, goes easy.
WYE BOLT	**U-JOINT BOLT**	**TELESCOPIC BOLT** (Cutaway View, Coil Spring)	**DOUBLE COUNTERSINK BOLT**
For holes double-drilled on one side only.	Use in crooked and/or offset holes. Recommend use of tapered washer.	Proposed solution for situations where grip length is unknown.	For use where understructure was countersunk in error.
OFFSET BOLT	**COVER-UP RIVET** (Head Is 6 X Diameter)	**RIVET BUTT** (Diameter And Height To Conform To MIL SPEC.)	**NAIL BOLT**
For use where holes are offset and will not align.	For use in assembly having hole in one part really screwed up.	For installation in hard-to-buck spots. Insert short rivet and glue special butt to opposite side.	Tapered fluted shank to be hammered into loused up plate nut that's too hard to replace.
MULTIPURPOSE RIVET	**PERMANENT BOLT**	**FILLER HEADS**	**JURY FASTENERS**
An old standby that continues to serve unique individual needs.	The one-way bolt for use in areas where access is not to occur until after your transfer.	For covering unsightly holes left by missing bolts or rivets, when you cannot find proper replacement items in stock.	Time tested remedies for many broken birds (often precedes the breaking).

(Snitched from "Western Aviation," who filched it from the Iowa Aeronautics Commision's "Aviation Bulletin." Our thanks to all concerned.)

MECHANICS PROBLEM SOLVING FLOWCHART

Somewhat related to the "Pilot's Problem-solving Flow Chart" [Detailed in the original Aviator's Bathroom Reader], the chart below sussinctly details two of the four items a pilot needs today in their airplanes tool kit, the other items being a multi-head Phillips screwdriver with #1 and #2 bits and a set of pliers, preferrably channel-locks usefull for loosening oil caps over-torqued down by the last gorilla to fly that rental plane.

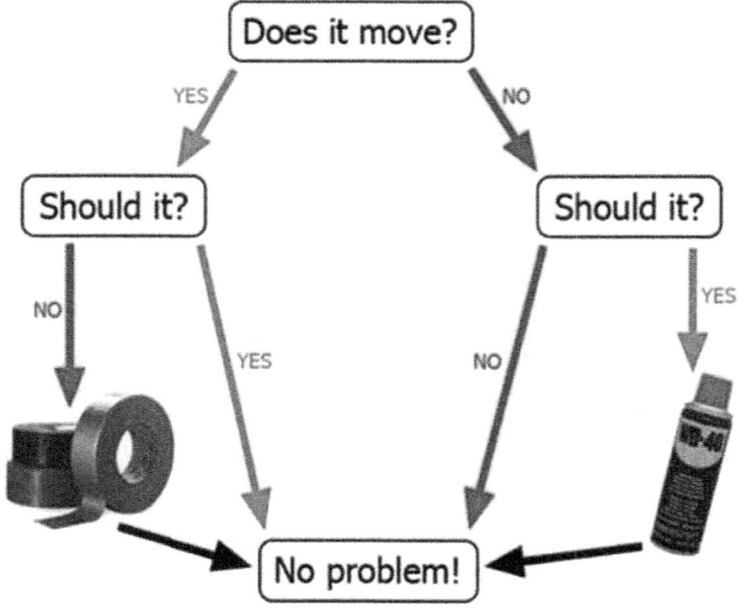

AFTER-ACTION REPORT FROM ANNUAL MEDICAL EXAM

The following report was submitted by me to the FAA (I wish) in preparation for completion of an annual flight review required by said 'Alphabet Agency' of the applicant. Notwithstanding that said applicant was well into the high 80's of solar circumnavigations, his life of aviation adventurism covers a multitude of ... ahhh ... 'course corrections' a lifetime of aeronautical adventurisms can require and/or provide.

Al -

While the alleged 'accomplishments' cited in your most recent FITREP appear, on the surface, commendable [they were mostly sub-surface, complete with finger wave], I cannot help but wonder if the medical report was based merely on Color Exam Criteria (CEC), which is to say "Red blood plus green money = you pass." Don't forget the additional brown finger exam for someone your age. A discernable heartbeat and commensurate evidence of a respiratory cycle only adds to the compounding evidentiary documentation of ambulatory capability. Certainly more tests are needed. Knocking over the optical test equipment because "you didn't see it there in the corner" is an exact example of what I'm addressing here.

The alleged accomplishment of a Flight Review, IPC and annual recurrency check could all be managed by "there is no financial reason in the world why you cannot pass your next (fill in the blank) test". I will warn you however, that suspicions arise when the claimant alleges all these required flights were accomplished during one sortie. After four hours, not having in-flight refueling capability, we do have to land to refuel. The relief of the undersigned Stan/Eval Officer after multiple near-misses with the planet below did allow him to walk away from your aerospace vehicle physically unscathed (yet mentally a quivering pool of goo), which could have easily resulted in him signing anything, including his life, away. Certainly a retest by a more impartial check pilot is warranted - NO, I do NOT volunteer for this duty and if assigned by the Commanding Officer I shall resign any and all commissions immediately forthwith, fifthwith and even sixthwith.

In addition to bragging, crowing and otherwise self-inflating ones ego at having, at your advanced years, once again passing the required medical exam required of today's aeronauts; the tooting of one's own horn (even for cause) brings said tooter dangerously close to the realm of being required to buy all present in the O-club a suitable adult beverage for the remainder of the evening. For that I will attend - and invite everyone above the rank of 2nd Lieutenant on the base to also attend. Your argument the horn-tooting was required by the three different insurance companies with which you allege having a business relationship is categorically spurious. We all know it's the FAA, not insurance companies, which govern aviation operations of the type you perform; despite the previously mentioned FITREP being forwarded on to them.

Finally, I must congratulate you on being able to pass yet again the stringent mental, emotional, physical, and psychological standards required to dance amongst the clouds. I and my few remaining minions will await your arrival in the O-club drinking lemonade and soft drinks until we are graced by your presence

> when you can regale us on how you can continue, year after year, to fool all the people all the time ... except me, of course.

And then later - woe betide all those in the same Area of Operation - I receive this:

> His Most Exalted Airworthiness - Captain Drew Chitiea, BFD, AFU, EIEIO:
>
> It gives me great pleasure to apprise you that on (date redacted) I was thoroughly examined by (Name redacted), MD., a senior aerospace Medical Examiner and airplane pilot par excellence of some repute himself in these parts and once again - probably to the great dismay of several student pilots around this here locale - was found qualified for reissuance of my FAA Medical Certificate -First Class.
>
> Furthermore, on the morning of (date redacted) I did present myself prostrate on the ramp of (Name redacted) AFB in a position of worshipful adoration and obedience to one Captain (Name redacted) who immediately thereafter engulfed me with annual recurrency training, a flight review and Instrument Proficiency Check in one Beechcraft model BE-60 airplane (N-number redacted). In witness whereof I have hereto attached copies of the appropriate certificates, documentations, forms, correspondence, and endorsements required as evidence.
>
> Your obedient (if not disrespectful) servant,
>
> Al Uhalt, Colonel, USAF (ret.)
>
> Boy Airplane Pilot

MORE RULES OF AVIATION

Yeah, yeah – I know ... there are rules, more rules about rules; then there are exceptions to the rules, regulations relating to the rules, and then those rules which are more like guidelines. None the less, these rules didn't become rules just as a matter of someone's invention; something had to happen for these rules to come about starting with what we in the USA call "WW I" and the rest of Europe calls 'The Great War for Civilization'. The 1919 Rules of the Air cab be found elsewhere in this book.

1. Every takeoff is optional. Every landing is mandatory.
2. If you push the stick forward, the houses get bigger; if you pull the stick back the houses get smaller. That is, unless you pull the stick all the way back and keep it there, then the houses get bigger again going 'round and 'round. *["House-barn-house-barn" etc.]*
1. Flying isn't dangerous – crashing is dangerous.
2. It's always better to be down here wishing you were up there than up there wishing you were down here.
3. When in doubt, hold altitude; no-one ever collided with the sky.
4. A 'good' landing is one you can walk away from; a 'great' landing is when you can use the airplane again without major maintenance.

5. Learn from the mistakes of others – you won't live long enough to make them all yourself.

6. The probability of survival is inversely proportional to the angle of arrival. High angle of arrival = low probability of survival. Low angle of arrival = high probability of survival.

7. The key to a long life is keeping the number of landings equal to the number of takeoffs.

8. There are three simple rules for making a good landing – unfortunately no one knows what they are. *[The key to a good landing is a good (stabilized) approach. The key to a good approach is good procedures]*.

9. Stay out of clouds: the silver lining everyone talks about could be another airplane going in the opposite direction. Reliable sources also report that mountains have been known to lurk in clouds.

[Cloud type: Cumulo-Granitus ... a cloud with a mountain inside of it]

10. If all you can see is ground going 'round and 'round and all you can hear is a commotion coming from the rear of the airplane – things are not as they should be.

11. In the ongoing battle between objects made of aluminum going hundreds of miles per hour and the ground going zero miles per hour, the ground has yet to lose.

12. It is always a good thing to keep the pointy end of an airplane going forward and the greasy side down.

13. Keep looking around – there's always something you may have missed.

14. Remember, gravity is not just a good idea, it's the law. And it's not subject to repeal anytime soon.

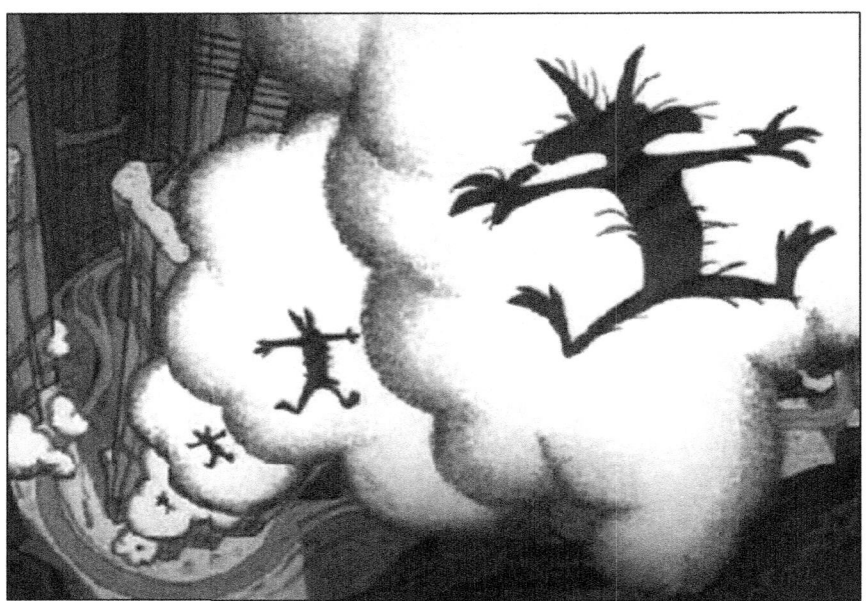
The "Wile E Coyote Patented Vertical Descent" © Warner Brothers

15. The most useless things to a pilot are:
    - Altitude above you
    - Runway behind you
    - Airspeed you don't have
    - Fuel in the truck *[air in the fuel tanks]*
    - A tenth of a second ago

16. Never let the airplane get to a point in the air where your brain hasn't arrived there first.

17. Good judgement comes from experience – experience comes from bad judgement.

MORE B.S. ABOUT HELICOPTERS

Hey, a helicopter DOES rise into the heavenly firmament and the pilot MAY "put out his hand and touch the face of God" - albeit very briefly. You don't want to let go of anything for too long if you're 'flying' a helicopter. For all that, I've seen people pay good money for an 'exciting' helicopter ride at airshows. Hell, EVERY flight I made was 'exciting' - you won't stay bored for too long in a helicopter. And if you are, you are far behind the 'aerospace vehicle'!

"According to aerodynamic law, the bumble-bee cannot fly. Its body weight is not in the correct proportion to its wingspan and ability to create lift. Ignoring these laws and precepts, the bee flies anyway." - M. Sainte-Lague, early 1900's mathematician

[The same may be said of rotary-winged aircraft. - Ed.]

Helicopter 'High Flight'

Oh, I've slipped the surly bonds of Earth and hovered out of ground-effect

On semi-rigid blades.

Earthward I've auto'ed and met the rising brush of non-paved terrain

And done a thousand things you'd never care to name

Skidded and dropped and flared low in the heat-soaked roar.

Confined there, I've chased the earth-bound traffic

And lost the race to insignificant headwinds.

Forward and up - a little - in ground effect I've topped the General's hedge

With drooping turns where neither Phantom nor even Mustang flew.

Shaking and pulling collective I've lumbered

The low, untrespassed halls of airways,

Put out my hand and touched ...

A tree!

A true story [I'm told]:

While ferrying workers back from an offshore rig, the helicopter lost power and began to descend. Fortunately, it landed safely in the ocean; the pilot tells the passengers to remain seated and keep the doors closed as, in a water landing, the craft is designed to stay afloat. Struggling to exit the craft, one oil worker tore off his seatbelt, inflated his life vest and was yanking on the door handle.

"Don't jump out!" the pilot yelled, "This helicopter is supposed to float!"

As the worker opened the door, he was heard to yell back "Yeah, and it's supposed to fly, too, and look how good that turned out!"

Airplane pilots 'land' and then they try like hell to stop.

Helicopter pilots 'stop' and then … when they're good and ready, they land.

Helicopter's 10 Commandments:

> He who inspecteth not his craft giveth his guardian angel cause to concern him
>
> Hallowed be thy airflow across thy rotating disc restoring thine Translational Lift.
>
> Let infinite discretion govern thy movement near the ground, for vast and myriad are the areas of destruction.
>
> Blessed is he who strives to retain his skills and standards, for without them he shall surely come to grief.
>
> Thou shalt maintain thy airspeed betwixt ten and four hundred feet above the firmament lest the firmament rise up and smite thee.
>
> Thou shalt not make trial of thy centre of gravity limits lest thou shalt dash thy foot against the firmament.
>
> Thou shalt not allow thy confidence to exceed thy abilities, for broad is the way to destruction.

He that performeth an approach yet alloweth the wind to turn behind him shalt surely needeth the ministrations of yon insurance broker.

He that alloweth his tail rotor to catch the thorns curseth his children's children.

When thy craft ceases communication with thee and goeth quiet ... just like women ... 'tis not a good sign.

... and the 11th commandment ...

Observeth thou these admonitions lest on the morrow other aviators avail themselves of the opportunity to comfort thy grieving widow.

This was told to me by a graduate of the "Mother Rucker" school for failed fixed-wing pilots.

"Mother Rucker" is the polite and affectionate name for Fort Rucker, Alabama, home of US Army Aviation. From the fact a Huey Cobra is mentioned tells you how long ago this was purported to happen.

Practicing auto-rotations during a night military training exercise, the helicopter landed tail-low and hit the tail rotor, tearing off the tail boom. Luckily, the helicopter landed on its skids and wound up sliding down the runway doing 360's in a brilliant shower of sparks. As it passed the tower the following exchange was heard on frequency:

Tower: "Cobra 23, do you need any assistance?"

Cobra 23: "Don't know, tower, I ain't done crashing yet."

Corollary: If all you can see through the canopy is the direction you came from intermingled with sparks and a commotion from those [poor souls] riding in back, things are not as they should be.

Graduates of Army Pilot's Course No. 4 wait paitently for their turn in the simulator.

"If you are looking for perfect safety, you will do well to sit on a fence and watch the birds; but if you really wish to learn *(about flying)*, you must mount a machine and become acquainted with its tricks by actual trial."
- Wilbur Wright, 1901

South Vietnam (now defunct) pilot.

MYSTERY P-51 PILOT

I cannot vouch for the accuracy of this story, but I can vouch for the pilot of the P-51. I met him many years ago when he had recently retired as a USAF Brigadier General but was often haunting the local airports and military bases during air shows, meets, and pilot roundups. Nicest man you'd ever want to meet; friendly [after all, we were all pilots], professional [ditto], and famous within the Air Force for his service and outside with the public for his other occupation. I am presenting this as a true story, a heart-warming story, and as an example of how we should bring along those airport kids in the world of aviation. We have, after all, had our day; the future of aviation will be in their hands. Let's send them off well-trained, well-equipped, and enthusiastic as all get-out.

This 1967 true story is about an experience by a young 12-year-old boy in Kingston, Ontario, Canada. It is about the vivid memory of a privately rebuilt P-51 from WWII and its famous owner/pilot.

In the morning sun, I could not believe my eyes. There, in our little airport, sat a majestic P-51. They said it had flown in during the night from some U.S. Airport, on its way to an air show. The pilot had been tired, so he just happened to choose Kingston for his stopover. It was to take to the air very soon. I marveled at the size of the plane, dwarfing the Pipers and Canucks tied down by her. It was much larger than in the movies. She glistened in the sun like a bulwark of security from days gone by.

The pilot arrived by cab, paid the driver, and then stepped into the pilot's lounge. He was an older man; his wavy hair was gray and tossed. It looked like it might have been combed, say, around the turn of the century. His flight jacket was checked, creased, and worn - it smelled old and genuine. Old Glory was prominently sewn to its shoulders. He projected a quiet air of proficiency and pride devoid of arrogance. He filed a quick flight plan to Montreal ("Expo-67 Air Show") then walked across the tarmac.

After taking several minutes to perform his walk-around check, the tall, lanky man returned to the flight lounge to ask if anyone would be available to stand by with fire extinguishers while he "flashed the old bird up, just to be safe." Though only 12 at the time I was allowed to stand by with an extinguisher after brief instruction on its use -- "If you see a fire, point, then pull this lever!", he said. (I later became a firefighter, but that's another story.)

The air around the exhaust manifolds shimmered like a mirror from fuel fumes as the huge prop started to rotate. One manifold, then another, and yet another barked - I stepped back with the others. In moments the Packard-built Merlin engine came to life with a thunderous roar. Blue flames knifed from her manifolds with an arrogant snarl. I looked at the others' faces; there was no concern. I lowered the bell of my extinguisher. One of the guys signaled to walk back to the lounge. We did. Several minutes later we could hear the pilot doing his pre-flight run-up. He'd taxied to the end of runway 19, out of sight. All went quiet for several seconds. We ran to the second story deck to see if we could catch a glimpse of the P-51 as she started down the runway. We could not. There we stood; eyes fixed at a spot halfway down the runway. Then a roar ripped across the field, much louder than before. Like a furious hell spawn set loose -- something mighty this way was coming.

"Listen to that thing!" said the controller.

In seconds the Mustang burst into our line of sight. Its tail was already off the runway and it was moving faster than anything I'd ever seen. Two-thirds the way down 19 the Mustang was airborne with her gear going up. The prop tips were supersonic. We clasped our ears as the Mustang climbed hellishly fast into the circuit to be eaten up by the dog-day haze. We stood for a few moments, in stunned silence, trying to digest what we'd just seen. The radio controller rushed by me to the radio. "Kingston tower calling Mustang?" He looked back to us as he waited for an acknowledgment. The radio crackled, "Go ahead, Kingston."

"Roger, Mustang. Kingston tower would like to advise the circuit is clear for a low-level pass." I stood in shock because the controller had just, more or less, asked the pilot to return for an impromptu air show! The controller looked at us. "Well, what?" He asked. "I can't let that guy go without asking. I couldn't forgive myself!" The radio crackled once again, "Kingston, do I have permission for a low-level pass, east to west, across the field?"

"Roger, Mustang, the circuit is clear for an east to west pass." "Roger, Kingston, I'm coming out of 3,000 feet, stand by." We rushed back onto the second-story deck; eyes fixed toward the eastern haze.

The sound was subtle at first, a high-pitched whine, a muffled screech, a distant scream. Moments later the P-51 burst through the haze. Her airframe straining against positive G's and gravity. Her wing tips spilling contrails of condensed air, prop-tips again supersonic. The burnished bird blasted across the eastern margin of the field shredding and tearing the air. At about 500 mph and 150 yards from where we stood, she passed with the old American pilot saluting!! Imagine. A salute! I felt like laughing; like crying; she glistened; she screamed; the building shook; my heart pounded. Then the old pilot pulled her up and rolled, and rolled, and rolled out of sight into the broken clouds and indelibly into my memory.

I've never wanted to be an American more than on that day! It was a time when many nations in the world looked to America as their big brother. A steady and even-handed beacon of security who navigated difficult political water with grace and style; not unlike the old American pilot who'd just flown into my memory. He was proud, not arrogant; humble, not a braggart; old and honest, projecting an aura of America at its best.

That America will return one day! I know she will! Until that time, I'll just send off this story. Call it a loving salute to a Country, and especially to that old American pilot: the late JIMMY STEWART (1908-1997), Actor, real WWII Hero (Commander of a US Army Air Force Bomber Wing stationed in England), and a USAF Reserves Brigadier General, who wove a wonderfully fantastic memory for a young Canadian boy that's lasted a lifetime.

NOT 'RULES'......
MORE LIKE GUIDELINES

Some written in the style of the King James version; some written in plain 'Olde Englisch'. All of them carrying within grains of truth. Heed them all, young Skywalkers; lest on the morrow other swains shalt attempt to console thy grieving widow.

- Inspect thoroughly the quality and quantity of fuel for surely it is the staff of life.

- Check early and often the radiance of the gear warning lights for you will never know the hour of disaster.

- Comply as best possible with the incantations of the tower priests lest chaos and destruction reign within the traffic pattern.

- Imbibe not the fruit of the grape lest thy sandals are firmly planted upon the firmament or verily, thee shallt be firmly planted below the firmament.

- Invoke not the wrath of the FAA lest ye thus shall tread the firmament until the end of days.

- Never fly in a pair of shoes you haven't already walked in.

- Airline pilots are one of the few professionals who guarantee the quality of their work with their lives

- Better higher than lower; better faster than slower.
- The most useless things to a pilot are the altitude above you, the runway behind, the air in your fuel tanks and the airspeed you don't have.

From Bob Stevens:

1. Do not bust your butt.
2. Do not allow anyone else to bust your butt for you.
3. Remember – the pilot is always the first one to the scene of the accident.
4. If in doubt – get out. Or don't go.
5. One peek is worth a thousand cross-checks.
6. Thunderstorms and ice are just like being pregnant – there is no such thing as just a little.
7. Remember – airplanes fly because of Bernoulli, not Marconi [meaning: don't drop the aircraft to fly the microphone]
8. If a crash appears inevitable, hit the softest, cheapest thing you can find as slowly as possible.
9. What you do not say, you do not have to take back at the hearing.
10. A large part of a safe landing is knowing when not to
11. When working with perfect people, be prepared to fly solo.
12. Grieving over past events will not improve the current state of affairs – learning from the will.

13. Never pass up a chance to on-load more fuel or go to the bathroom.

When in doubt – remember rule #1

"There is no reason to fly through a thunderstorm in peacetime."
- Sign over the Ops Desk at Davis-Monthan AFB, Arizona, 1969

"There is no reason to fly through a thunderstorm."
- Sign over the Ops Desk at Udorn RTAFB, Thailand, 1970

NOTES FOR PILOTS -1

These notes were in the same booklet from which the two "Rules of the Air" segments came. Published in 1917 by the "U.S. Army Flying Corps – American Expeditionary Forces", many of these advisements have the ring of truth – if not lawyerly verbosity – of today's rules and regulations. As a student of aviation history [you are one, right?], you will realize these teaching jewels were published a mere 14 years after the Wright Brothers' flight in 1903. Sooo much went on in those years ...

1. **Never go beyond the instructions of the instructor.**

   In 1917 there were no such things as a syllabus or lesson plans; pilots were taught to fly by their instructor who, at the time employed by the US Aero Service [a subdivision of the US Army], pretty much had their own ways of doing things. So following directions was high on the 'you'll do it my way or hit the highway' list. Flight instruction is much more organized now and with scenario-based training being the watchword a student should be able to learn much from the scenarios prepared by the CFI. One of "Drew's Rules of Flying: Learn from the mistakes of others; you will never live long enough to make them all yourself."

2. **The pilot must always inspect the machine before flying.**

   A review of FAR 91.103 Preflight Action - details many of the factors an attention-to-detail oriented pilot in command will satisfy themselves about prior to any flight. Remember, it's not *just out of adherence to the regulations that this is done but also for general safety of and within the flight. No-one but you – assuming you live – is going to be standing in front of the Accident Board stuttering through "State your name, rank and serial number for the Board of Inquiry." Any of you out there recall hearing about "P_7"? [Capital letter 'P' to the seventh power?]*

"Proper Prior Preparation Prevents Piss-Poor Performance."

3. **Always use the safety belt; do not release the belt until after the accident. It will probably save injury, especially if the machine turns over.**

The 1917 rule stated above has been codified in a LOT more detail in FAR 91.107, covering virtually all forms of flying machines and what the pilot, passengers, and even child seating must comply with. If an applicant doesn't brief the examiner about seat/shoulder belt use prior to engine start, it is cause for a failure right then and there when the plane begins to move [91.107(a)(2).

I like this rule, the first sentence assumes there is going to be an accident – sometime, somewhere in a students' life. So always keep the seatbelt fastened, fly the airplane until all the moving parts have stopped moving. Do not unfasten your seatbelt until all movement has stopped [floatplanes are different] and the mags are turned off [key OUT!} and the Master Switch off as well. You will not and cannot fully relax until one of two things occurs: The airplane is safely in the hangar and/or it is tied down securely. THEN you can assume there are no more flight responsibilities to look after – except the paperwork, of course.

4. **If the gasoline gauge cannot be easily read, a piece of cork on the inside will make it more easy to read as it floats on top.**

> This advice is now antiquated in aviation except for Piper J-3 Cubs, Aeronca 7-ACs and the like with a fuselage tank forward of the instrument panel and a floating cork-with-wire fuel indicator [as fuel goes down the floating cork descends into the tank taking a long wire indicator with it – you can 'calibrate' the fuel remaining by the length of wire still visible]. State of the art fuel 'gauge' circa early 1900's.

5. **Unless absolutely alone, a pilot should not attempt to start a motor without assistance.**

> This rule came from when there were no electric starters; pilots started engines by 'swinging the propeller' engaging the magnetos and getting the engine to run. Now, as then, 'hand-propping' an airplane should be done only after some training by experienced personnel AND certain precautions are taken to avoid seeing your aerospace vehicle begin moving briskly about the aerodrome, perhaps to depart terra firma with no pilot aboard, usually resulting in a balled up used-to-be airplane and a very embarrassed used-to-be pilot. See Rule 6 below and "How NOT to Start an Airplane" elsewhere in this book.

6. **If you start your airplane alone, dig a place for the wheels and point the machine into the wind. If possible, tie the tail to something convenient. Blocks may be used in front of the wheels.**

> If you must hand-prop an airplane, MAKE SURE the throttle is at low idle, tie it down AND chock the wheels. Once you get the airplane started, you may adjust the throttle, then gingerly and alertly begin removing the tiedowns and chocks. The last thing

removed is the chock from the side the door you'll use to leap into once the plane is free. Please, please do NOT attempt this without proper and experienced training. I witnessed a Cub come to a roaring start, accelerate forward running over the pilot who barely cleared a propeller rotating at 2,000 rpm and it made its own way halfway down the tarmac finally coming to a halt when a hapless Stinson – through no fault of its own – found itself in the way and then sacrificed its tailfeathers to stop the rampaging Cub.

7. **To get off the ground with the wind, you must have flying speed plus the speed of the wind. This is one of the biggest causes for misjudgment that there is in flying as pilots over-estimate their airspeed because their groundspeed is so great. Bad stalls often result from too little airspeed.**

What is being referred to is a downwind takeoff ["with" the wind}. Over 100 years of collective experience now has shown that downwind takeoffs [and coincidentally, landings] still, to this day, can cause pilots a lot of grief. Takeoffs are not made by timing the takeoff roll ['x-seconds to rotate'] nor are they made by the pilot 'sensing' he's going fast enough along the ground – that's groundspeed; the wings need <u>airspeed</u> to create lift. That's what is referred in the rule as "...have flying speed plus the speed of the wind." To make a takeoff we must fly by the numbers = at a certain <u>indicated airspeed</u> she'll fly. Not by a certain time or by groundspeed sensation. Upshot? We don't make downwind takeoffs. Not nowhere. Not nohow. [Unless you're a bush pilot in Alaska, then all bets - and regulations - are off. Been there, done that, got the t-shirt -ed.].

8. **In getting off the ground with a side wind, be sure and allow the machine to have flying speed before attempting to arise. Then turn slightly into the wind, gain a safe altitude and level out before attempting to turn and go with the wind.**

Can you guess what is being referred to here? Yes-sir – crosswind takeoffs! And the horribly misunderstood 'infamous' downwind turn. As with any crosswind takeoff, always position your flight controls to counteract the winds' effects before beginning the takeoff roll then, as speed increases, slowly bring the controls towards [not at] neutral and you'll know you've made a good crosswind takeoff when the downwind tire lifts off just a second before the upwind tire. Accelerate maintaining directional control with rudders and crosswind drift with ailerons, get to a safe speed and climb away heavenwards! Throughout all turns maintain your airspeed at proper values and you'll not have an issue turning downwind.

It's in the Old Testament somewhere [haven't found it yet] but verily 'tis truth:

"Lose not thy airspeed lest the earth riseth up and smite thee."

9. **In coming in to the field in the direction of the hangars, if the distance is not properly estimated and you find it necessary to put on power and continue the flight, do not**

attempt to climb too steep. Climbing too steep will cause the machine to stall and [crash].

In the early days of flight it was recommended that all planes land 'into the wind'. Sometimes this meant approaching the landing area over the top of a row of hangars [creating the early maneuver of landing over a 50' obstacle]. What they are saying here is "If you must approach the landing field with an approach over the hangars and find you are descending so that you may not clear the hangars, go around! Add power, continue the flight [abort the landing attempt] but do NOT pitch up too fast or dramatically lest the aeroplane thereby stalls [and crashes]. Nowadays we don't have those pesky hangars leaping out into our landing approach flight path, but the basic advice here still is very apropos: If you do not like the landing approach/attempt, add power and go around!* Be careful, however, of the additional power and trim settings which could cause the airplane to dramatically pitch up past the wings' critical angle of attack and result in a low-altitude stall-spin. One doesn't have altitude needed to recover; this gives the opportunity for other pilots to comfort your grieving widow.

> ** Listen to Ken Dravis' song "Go Around"*
> *https://www.youtube.com/watch?v=XQqIc0B-xm4*

10. **If the machine slides in, use more rudder or take off some of the bank, or both.**

What is being referred to here is a slip to a landing; remember, the early aeroplanes did not have flaps or other drag-inducing mechanisms so the only way to manage the rate of descent without a commensurate increase in airspeed was making a slip to a landing. Anyone adept at these maneuvers (we're ALL comfortable with this maneuver, aren't we?) understands that a rudder deflected one way requires the aileron deflection to the other side to achieve the slip [or as stated here, the 'slide']. To then realign the nose of the aeroplane with the wind one reverses the rudder being used and also relieves some - if not all - of the aileron pressure.

Okay, you Naval Aviators, this guy caught ALL the wires between #1 AND #32! Stat THAT!

NOTES FOR PILOTS - 2

Continued from the first section; these rules were developed by the US Army air Service in 1917, just in time for the wind-up for WWI. Most are just as valuable for todays' aviators as they were more than a century ago.

11. If the chine slides out, take off part of your rudder or increase the bank, or both.

The 'Chine' was the angular fuselage top of old biplanes extending from aft of the pilot to where the vertical stabilizer is connected to the fuselage. What is referred to here is a skidding turn, where too much inside rudder is applied to yaw the nose around in direction of the turn. [The chine 'slides out' or out and away from the direction of turn]. To avoid this hazardous maneuver the pilot must decrease the amount of rudder used and/or increase the bank to create a 'coordinated' turn.

12. To get out of a spiral dive, push the elevator forward in all cases.

A 'spiral dive' was the early aviation term for what we now call a spin. Pushing the stick (elevator) forward thus decreases the (exceeded) angle of attack which allows the wings to then begin creating lift. It is presumed that even back then the instinctual tendency of a pilot to pull back on the stick attempting to exit a spin caused many deaths. Knowing much more about the aerodynamics of this maneuver, we know the memory acronym to escape a stall/spin is:

"PARE".

Power = Idle.

Ailerons = neutral.

Rudder = Opposite direction of rotation.

Elevator (stick/yoke) = Forward

13. **Do not trust an altitude instrument. Learn to judge altitude, especially in landings. Barometric conditions may change in a cross-country flight so that even a barometer which is functioning properly may read an incorrect altitude. The altitude of the landing lace may be different from that of the starting place.**

> In aviation's early days there were rudimentary altimeters; however there were no Kollsman windows installed in them. From earlier days than the first fliers the difference of barometric pressures was known and was used to 'predict' weather [high pressure = 'good' weather. Low pressure = 'bad' weather]. Until the technological advancement whereby barometrically adjustable altimeters were invented, aeronauts had to be very careful to not rely entirely on indicated altitudes as flight over some distance very likely would have a change in barometric pressure thereby resulting in an erroneous reading on their altimeters. This is from where the mnemonic "High to low, look out below" comes from: If you fly from a high pressure area to one of low pressure without adjusting the altimeter to the change, you will be lower than indicated on the altimeter. This has in the past killed many unsuspecting pilots and is why the recommendation of

checking one's barometric pressure every 100nm of flight exists for those of us flying below 18,000' (FL 180).

14. **No passengers will be carried without authority from the Officer in Charge of Training. Students will not be allowed to carry passengers except for instruction purposes.**

    Not much to say here; to this very day in the 'Limitations' section of student pilot certificates it reads "Carriage of Passengers Prohibited". [As a DPE I am *gulp* the first passenger for a Private Pilot applicant - see the "Sitzen ist Arbeit?" story elsewhere in this book.]

15. **In case motor is missing pilots will not attempt to leave the ground. If a miss develops in the air a landing will be made immediately.**

    Back then, preflight checks - or 'runups' - were casual at best and mechanical reliability was ... ahhh ... 'iffy'. Despite that learned in training, many pilots knew little of the mechanical intricacies of their aeroplane and thus flight was fraught with unplanned arrivals startling the earth-bound denizens and, at best, shaking up the intrepid aeronaut. Hence the quasi-religious activity of taking part in the "Communion of Touching and Checking the Holy Parts and their Operation" service, being a significant part of a flightcheck and exercising the precepts of general all-around aeronautical health.

16. **It is advisable to carry a good pair of cutting pliers in a position where both passenger and pilot can reach them in case of an accident.**

    This was to allow either pilot and/or passenger to cut their way out of the aeroplane in the event of a crash causing fuselage manglement [I just invented that word - Ed.]. I would *strongly advise every pilot to carry with them a multi-tool <u>on their person</u> (belt) for any 'just in case' event. Plus, they are handy doing minor screw-tightening tasks as well as oil dipstick untightening [because of that body-builder gorilla who 'secured' the dipstick just prior to your flight.]*

17. **No articles should be allowed loose in a machine as the controls may become jammed.**

    There's no commensurate FAR today for this other than the task in the ACS of 'Cockpit Management', i.e. securing one's personal possessions and placing the assets required for the mission at a handy - and safe - location. In the old open-cockpit days, anything loose in the cockpit was liable to be flung earthwards by the wind roiling about the cockpit. [I can recall a flight in a Waco Taperwing biplane (look it up!) flying formation with a friend in a Stearman as lead. Looking over at him, I just caught the blur as his sectional departed the cockpit. When he came on freq to invite me to take lead, I declined saying I was happy flying wing. After several other 'invites' I finally got him to admit losing the chart overboard and then took over lead - and navigational duties. Guess who bought the 'Safety Award' at dinner that night?]

18. **Always fly around the outer edge of a field so as to be able to glide to the field in case of trouble, unless the field is an especially large one.**

    Again, a precaution taken by many early pilots in the event of an all-too frequent engine failure. Landing then at any field [literally, a 'field'] required a look-see to ascertain any hazards lying therein [ditches, cow-paths, soft spots, farmer on a tractor, etc.]. With the advent of side-by-side cockpits with the pilot-in-command sitting on the left side came the 'standard' left-hand traffic pattern so the pilot could easily look down to determine the field suitability.

19. **Always take into consideration the load carried in the machine before a flight is made. Take into consideration the amount of gas, oil, tools, and the weight of the passenger. This weight soon runs up to 350 pounds. The extra weight requires a longer initial run in getting off, a faster landing, a gradual climb and steeper glide. This weight is to be taken into consideration especially if you desire to climb out of a strange field and over obstacles.**

    FAR 91.103 Preflight Action states "Each Pilot-in-Command shall, before beginning a flight, become familiar with all available information concerning that flight." The regulation goes further, mentioning such inconsequential things as "weather reports and forecasts, fuel requirements, alternatives available…, runway lengths at airports of intended use, (and) takeoff and landing data." The regulation from 1917 goes into more detail and reasons for doing what was required because, hey, there was no <u>Pilot's Handbook of Aeronautical Knowledge</u> - or any other detailed reference text - back then. But today's wise [meaning: professionally minded] pilots would benefit greatly by disciplining themselves to perform - and put on paper - all that is mentioned from 1917 to today. In that way the pilot KNOWS what the plane is predicted to be able to do; the pilot isn't guessing, wondering or assuming anything - they KNOW what the airplane can do.

20. **To taxi, apply power gradually and have the machine move slowly. It is a good principle in all cases to apply power gradually, especially on starting a flight.**

    A prudent pilot will yell "Clear prop!" and THEN look around [perimeter check] prior to starting the engine. Remember, the yell-out is a warning; one then must look around to insure no-one is reacting to the warning or trying to get your attention before your crank the engine. THEN we add power to begin movement. I've heard of pilots/applicants say to "taxi at a brisk walk'; if the taxi to the runway is a 'far piece' [southern for a 'long way'] you'll take all day getting to your destination. Rather than a single 'rule' about taxiing, try this: Taxi at a speed whereby if you had to stop with minimal brake effectiveness [weak brakes, mixture to cutoff, throttle to minimum power] you could coast to a stop without hitting anything else. On the ramp in close proximity to hangars, cars, people, and other aircraft - taxi dead slow. Out on the taxiway where the hazards are far away, a little faster taxi speed is okay. All-in-all, just be sensible about taxi speed - adjust it to your surroundings.

Ach, du Lieber, Franz! Za onliest tree in kilometers ... und du hast to shtrike it! Dummkopf!

What's the worst thing that could happen to a pilot? Running out of altitude, airspeed, and ideas all at the same time.

NOTES FOR PILOTS - 3

The third and last section of the Aviation Rules for the US Army air Service circa 1917 as lifted by the author from an old aviation guidebook. Instituted just prior to the nations' involvement in WWI where the US had no serviceable combat airplanes the likes of those in use in Europe, the nation had to develop and turn out airplanes and pilots in prodigious numbers. US developed and built aircraft never saw action in that war but, flying British and French developed and built airplanes, US pilots performed admirably in the short time they were 'Over There'.

21. **Speed as a rule means control. Loss of speed means loss of control.**

    See the Old Testament rule regarding airspeed under Regulation #8 of this part.

22. **Controls should always be worked on the ground prior to a flight to see they function properly.**

    In the "Olden Days" of aviation, airplanes were often referred to as 'bird cages'; there were so many wires going hither and yonder with a multitude of purposes it was said if you released a bird between the wings [these were biplanes, remember?] and it got out, there was a wire missing. Nowadays under FAR 91.103 [Preflight Action] and in many airplanes POH "Check Flight Controls" is mentioned but that's it. A prudent aviator will 'box the controls' [stick/yoke full forward, then completely circumnavigate the entire range of motion forward, left, aft, right and forward again to insure nothing is hanging up in the range of motion and also to make sure nothing inside the cockpit [knee boards, ipads, etc.] is restricting control stick/yoke movement. After all, you don't want that bird escaping, do you?

23. **In case of a landing requiring a glide over hangars or buildings, have sufficient speed as there may be bad air in the vicinity of the buildings.**

    I HATE encountering 'bad' air, I much prefer 'good' air for my aeronautical operations. What they are referring to here is when some object [hangar, row of trees, etc.] interferes with the flow of the air near ground level. I can recall landing a single-seat Skyote [look it up] at a rancher's grass strip where the adjacent corn was as high as an elephants' eye [anyone recall the song that line is from?]. Just as I began the round out at corn tassel height, it seemed like the bottom fell out and I 'arrived' on the field, luckily in a three-point attitude and under directional control. The rancher laughed and then said "Oh, I forgot to warn you about the bad air out there near the corn. Ya gotta carry a few extra knots of airspeed when the corn is high." Thanks for the warning, Ben! Also, mind the effects of winds burbling through and around hangars if your landing runway is downwind of them; you could have an exciting flare and rollout.

24. **Motors have been known to stop during a long glide on account of running the throttle down too long. If the pilot wants to use the throttle for landing, open throttle at intervals during glide. If the machine picks up too much speed, lessen the throttle. It is dangerous to nose down with throttle wide open.**

Most every engine back then was carbureted, and recall they were flying at lower altitudes [msl] where the air humidity was high and thus the engine was liable to suffer the effects of carburetor icing during long, low power glides. We still to this day will apply a burst of power during simulated engine failures and glides to emergency fields to ensure power will be available at the end of the maneuver. If you do this during the drill of simulated power failure and glide and your instructor/examiner asks why, tell them you are merely following a rule from 1917. THAT will get their attention! But leave your spurs at home, okay? Pilots nowadays don't wear spurs while flying.

25. In coming in for a landing on a half turn, get the machine straightened out about one hundred feet above the ground. If continuing the turn when close to the ground, there is always the danger of not getting the low wing up, more so with a dead motor. One will sometimes feel sure that he can straighten out and is somewhat surprised when the low wing hits the ground.

This rule really doesn't apply to today's flying; back then due to the airplane nose being far ahead of the pilot a low altitude circle-to-land approach was standard so the pilot could see where the landing area was because once straightened out and flaring for landing the forward vision was virtually nil. I believe being 'surprised when the low wing hits the ground' is an understatement.

26. In landing, hold the machine off as long as possible. To land at high speed in a strong side wind may wipe off your landing gear.

This rule and the one following emphasize the absolute need to allow the airplanes airspeed to be at the lowest coefficient prior to touching down. This is something many low-time instructors allow their student to do, that is landing while the airplane still has flying speed. Practice holding the airplane off the ground with back pressure on the stick/yoke until one hears the stall warning horn. Once adept at this, then continue holding the airplane off until a stall is accomplished. Ideally you'll be inches above the runway so when the wings give up all lift, it's a miniscule drop to the runway, i.e. a REAL full-stall landing.

27. In coming down with excess speed level out and let the machine skim along close to the ground; do not attempt to force the machine on the ground. If you put the machine on

the ground with more than flying speed the result is bouncing or ricocheting.

See # 26 above: many low experienced pilots tend to rush the plane into being on the ground. This is an invitation for the airplane - which still maintains flying speed - to take the pilot off into a side-to-side excursion/adventure with terra firma not necessarily a part of the landing area(s). If the landing attempt is forced, especially in a tricycle gear airplane, the nose wheel strikes the runway first resulting in a sharp nose-up porpoising. Allowing this to occur sometimes once more, rarely more than twice, results in a nosewheel collapse and much paperwork supplied, and return expected by, the FAA and NTSB [look up: 709 ride].

28. **It is better to land too fast than too slow. Too slow a landing may result in a dangerous stall if the machine is too far above the ground.**

    This rule countermands rules 26 & 27 insofar as many crashes occurred back then by 'ground-shy' pilots allowing airspeeds to deteriorate to dangerously low levels while still too high above the ground. The cure for this, of course, is to maintain proper airspeeds while in a stabilized approach to the runway. Once the runway is made and the landing round out is commencing, power can be reduced to idle, the flare begun, then holding the plane off the ground [flare] until the wings give up their lift and the airplane re-alights upon the planet.

29. **A fire extinguisher will be carried in each machine.**

    Does the reasoning for this rule - back then and today - have to be explained?

30. Smoking in the machine or in the vicinity is prohibited.

Must the reasoning for this rule - back then and today - have to be explained?

Okay, in my day back not only in the last century but also the last millennium, the rule - if I can recall this correctly was "No drinking within 8' of the throttle and no smoking with 50 hours of flying" ... or something to that effect. I hear this regulation has changed some.

"If you're faced with a forced landing, fly the airplane as far into the crash as possible."
- R.A. 'Bob' Hoover, famed airshow pilot

Go to Youtube.com and enter 'Bob Hoover', then watch and be amazed what he could do in a twin on one engine, then in a twin with BOTH shut down! - Ed.

USAAS WWI Pilot wings.

NOW, AT LAST, THE STORY CAN BE TOLD

In the preface of the original Aviator's Bathroom Reader I included the quote from Neal Armstrong [first man on the moon] regarding my book. At the end he says "...the story of me saying 'Good luck' to Mr. Grindowski when I was standing on the moon is a fabrication..."

Well, Neal Armstrong has 'Gone West' as has both Mr. and Mrs. Grindowski, and after having been asked about this numerous times - since I included it in my book - we can now hear 'the rest of the story.'

On 20 July 1969, as commander of the Apollo 11 Lunar Module, Neal Armstrong was the first human to set foot on the moon. His first words after stepping onto the moon have gone down in aviation and space history:

"That's one small step for a man,

One giant leap for mankind."

His step and those words were broadcast around the world, seen and heard by millions. But just prior to re-entering the lunar module, he uttered an enigmatic remark:

"Good luck, Mr. Grindowski."

Many at NASA thought it might be a casual remark to a friend or something to a rival Soviet cosmonaut. Upon checking, however, there was no 'Grindowski' to be found in either Soviet or American space programs. Over the years Armstrong was questioned as to what that comment meant, but Armstrong just smiled and avoided comment.

On 5 July 1995, in Tampa Bay, Florida Armstrong was answering questions when a reporter brought up the 26-year-old question about his comment "Good luck, Mr. Grindowski." This time Armstrong said that since both Grindowskis were now passed away, he could answer the question.

"In 1938, I was a kid in a small mid-western town playing baseball with friends. One of my buddies hit the ball over the neighbor's fence, landing in their yard just under their bedroom window. The neighbors were a Mr. and Mrs. Grindowski. As I got to the ball, I heard Mrs. Grindowski shouting at Mr. Grindowski: "Sex? You want sex? You'll get sex when the kid next door walks on the moon!"

The entire auditorium broke up in laughter.

It is alleged the Armstrong family confirmed the truth of the story. True or not, it's too good not to be passed on.

Can't believe some people still think that the moon landing was faked. – Ed.

"An instrument panel is just something to clutter up the cockpit and distract the pilot's attention from the road, river, or railroad he's following."
- Harold 'Slim' Lewis, US Air Mail Pilot, 1921
Slim was the inventor of IFR flight - I Follow Roads/Rivers/Railways

THE OLD MAN WITH THE BUCKET OF SHRIMP

I shall save commentary until the end of this one; please read it slowly and carefully. This is a wonderful story, and <u>it is true</u>! You will be glad you read it.

It happened every Friday evening, almost without fail, when the sun resembled a giant orange and was starting to dip into the blue ocean. Old Ed came strolling along the beach to his favorite pier. Clutched in his bony hand was a bucket of shrimp. Ed walks out to the end of the pier where it seems he almost has the world to himself. The glow of the sun is a golden bronze now.

Everybody's gone, except for a few joggers on the beach. Standing out on the end of the pier, Ed is alone with his thoughts ... and his bucket of shrimp. Before long, however, he is no longer alone. Up in the sky a thousand white dots come screeching and squawking, winging their way toward that lanky frame standing there on the end of the pier.

Before long, dozens of seagulls have enveloped him, their wings fluttering and flapping wildly. Ed stands there tossing shrimp to the hungry birds. As he does, if you listen closely, you can hear him say with a smile, "Thank you. Thank you." In a few short minutes the bucket is empty. But Ed doesn't leave. He stands there lost in thought, as though transported to another time and place.

When he finally turns around and begins to walk back toward the beach, a few of the birds hop along the pier with him until he gets to the stairs, and then they, too, fly away. And old Ed quietly makes his way down to the end of the beach and on back home.

If you were sitting there on the pier with your fishing line in the water, Ed might seem like 'a funny old duck,' as my dad used to say. Or, to onlookers, he's just another old codger; lost in his own weird world, feeding the seagulls with a bucket full of shrimp. To the onlooker, rituals can look either very strange or very empty. They can seem altogether unimportant - maybe even a lot of nonsense. Old folks often do strange things, at least in the eyes of Boomers, Busters, Millennials and so forth. Most of them would probably write Old Ed off, down there in Florida ... That's too bad. They'd do well to know him better.

His full name: **Edward Vernon *Rickenbacker*** (October 8, 1890 – July 23, 1973). He was a famous flying ace in World War I *[Awarded the Congressional Medal of Honor – ed.]*, and then he was in WWII. On one of his flying missions across the Pacific, he and his seven-member crew went down, ditching in the vast ocean. Miraculously, all the men survived, crawled out of their plane, and climbed into a life raft.

Captain Rickenbacker and his crew floated for days on the rough waters of the Pacific. They fought the sun. They fought sharks. Most of all, they fought hunger and thirst. By the eighth day their rations ran out. No food. No water. They were hundreds of miles from land, and no one knew where they were or even if they were alive. Every day across America millions wondered and prayed that Eddie Rickenbacker might somehow be found alive.

The men adrift needed a miracle. That afternoon they had a simple devotional service and prayed for a miracle. They tried to nap. Eddie leaned back and pulled his military cap over his nose. Time dragged on. All he could hear was the slap of the waves against the raft … suddenly Eddie felt something land on the top of his cap. It was a seagull!

Old Ed would later describe how he sat perfectly still, planning his next move. With a flash of his hand and a squawk from the gull, he managed to grab it and wring its neck. He tore the feathers off, and he and his starving crew made a meal of it - a very slight meal for eight men. Then they used the intestines for bait. With it, they caught fish, which gave them food and more bait; and the cycle continued. With that simple survival technique, they were able to endure the rigors of the sea until they were found and rescued - after 24 days at sea!

'Captain Eddie' lived many years beyond that ordeal, but he never forgot the sacrifice of that first life-saving seagull; and he never stopped saying, 'Thank you.' That's why almost every Friday night he would walk to the end of the pier with a bucket full of shrimp and a heart full of gratitude.

Before WWI he was race car driver. In WWI he first was the driver for General John J. Pershing – CO of all American forces in Europe. He then transferred to the US Army Air Service, becoming a pilot and subsequently America's highest scoring ace with 26 victories. In WWII he was an instructor and military adviser, and he flew missions with the combat pilots. After the war he founded Eastern Airlines (sadly now defunct). Eddie Rickenbacker is a true American hero.

A couple of take-aways here I wish to point out: First, when everything looked bleakest the men in that raft had a service of thanks and of faith. Thankful they survived the mid-ocean ditching and of faith in God they would be rescued from their plight. Both, of course, came to pass. I have no qualms in admitting when I personally went through my time(s) in Hell I prayed a LOT! There's an old saying, "There are no atheists in the trenches." Truer words have never been spoken; and those of you reading this who have been there know that as well.

I encourage everyone to thank God for the blessings received in this life and to have faith that in the end, all will be well. I do not intend this to be proselytizing statements for any one form of faith – or religion – but to acknowledge that, at least in my life, faith in a Creator has been a great source of comfort and of strength through those times of trial and doubt. Anyone who has seen: Skies rivaling the most glorious stained-glass window in the grandest cathedral; heard the song of a smooth-running engine competing with the most harmonious hymn; or have felt the sublime satisfaction after a flight as near perfect as it can get - know that we who fly truly are blessed above all the rest of humanity; those poor groundlings who will never experience that which we experience nor see the sights we see. Let us give thanks for the gift – and blessings – of flight.

Amen.

End of sermon.

Grandfather (old fighter pilot) to teenage grandson (self-absorbed snowflake):

"I wore an oxygen mask while pulling 9 G's, checking six, pumping flares, telling my wingman to "BREAK LEFT", selecting auto-guns, locking onto a bandit, selecting AIM-9 missiles, keeping visual while gaining a tally, getting a 1500 MHz tone on top of 5 other frequencies, watching my altitude, planning an egress, shooting the bandit, telling wingman to "BUG OUT SOUTH", reforming into a tactical formation, pushing it up, taking it down, short range radar, and resetting the CAP ... and all you gotta do is remember to get a gallon of milk!"

'PEANUTS' PHILOSOPHY

The following is philosophy from Charles M. Schultz [1922 – 2000], the creator of the "Peanuts" comic strip. You don't have to actually answer the questions. Just read straight through and you'll get the point. We pilots exist in a solitary world, perhaps a co-pilot/first officer at our elbow but still essentially alone, responsibility and authority heaped on our shoulders with the welfare of all aboard literally in our hands. Treasure your family and friends, tell those who mean something to you how special to you they are. You may not have the chance later to do so after they - or you - are gone.

1. Name the five wealthiest people in the world.
2. Name the last five Heisman trophy winners.
3. Name the last five winners of the Miss America.
4. Name ten people who have won the Nobel or Pulitzer Prize.
5. Name the last half dozen Academy Award winners for best actor and actress.
6. Name the last decade's worth of World Series winners.

How did you do?
The point is none of us remember the headliners of yesterday. These are no second-rate achievers. They are the best in their fields. But the applause dies. Awards tarnish. Achievements are forgotten. Accolades and certificates are buried with their owners.
["All glory is fleeting." – General George S. Patton]

Here's another quiz. See how you do on this one:
1. List a few teachers, flight instructors or drill instructors who showed you the righteous way.
2. Name three friends who have helped you through a difficult time.
3. Name five people who have taught you something worthwhile.
4. Think of a few people who have made you feel appreciated and special.
5. Think of five people you enjoy spending time with.

Easier?

The lesson: The people who make a difference in your life are not the ones with the most credentials, the most money, or the most awards. They are the ones who <u>cared about you.</u>

[Pass this on to those people who have made a difference in your life. "Don't worry about the world coming to an end today. It's already tomorrow in Australia." – Ed.]

© United Features Syndicate
Used without permission and imploring forgiveness for the cause of Aviation Safety.

PILOT APTITUDE TEST

In flight school this test was handed out with the admonishment: "Not all y'all are gonna pass this hyar exam; those whut do er gonna have a long career in the service uv yer country. Youse udder guys is gonna go to Viet Nam. Good luck! Y'all gots 10 minutes."

Let's see how well you can do ... for you old guys, even after all those years, you should get ONE right!

How fast can you determine the words and fill in the blanks?

1. _ _ NDOM

2. F _ _ K

3. P _ N _ S

4. PU _ _ Y

5. S _ X

6. BOO _ S

Answers:

1. RANDOM

2. FORK

3. PANTS

4. PUTTY

5. SIX

6. BOOKS

You got all 6 wrong, didn't you? I'll bet you never rose above 0-2/W-2/first officer/co-pilot, did you? Well, just proves you don't have Alzheimer's, but you're still a pervert.

POLITICALLY CORRECT COCKPIT COMMUNICATION

This was meant for you old hands [any of you left out there?] who may need some ... ahhh ... guidance in the fine and delicate art of in-cockpit communication. Since the new crop of FO's may have come from an environment where if their feelings got hurt they would retreat to a 'safe space', we must afford them the opportunity to take out their grief and frustration on a Play-dough doll and then return – albeit with a few tears down their rosy cheeks and a some sniffles which may need a hanky to remove – to the cockpit with their feelings assuaged and self-esteem intact. After all – as Captains who care about the well-being of our crew, it's the least we can do.

To: All Flight Crew Personnel

It has been brought to the Chief Pilot's attention that some individuals throughout the company have been using foul and inappropriate language during the course of normal conversation in the Cockpit.

> Due to complaints received from some first officers who may be easily offended, this type of language will no longer be tolerated. We do realize, however, the critical importance of being able to accurately express yourself when communicating within the cockpit.
>
> Therefore, a list of" TRY SAYING"; new phrases has been provided in the Operations Manual so that proper exchange of ideas and information can continue in an effective manner without risk of offending our more sensitive employees and to guarantee an exchange of information and ideas which will ensure safe and respectful flight operations.
>
> *I. M. Wright*
>
> Chief Pilot

TRY SAYING: I'm certain this isn't feasible.

INSTEAD OF: No f**king way.

TRY SAYING: Really?

INSTEAD OF: You've gotta be shitting me!

TRY SAYING: Perhaps you should check with Flight Ops.

INSTEAD OF: Tell someone who gives a shit.

TRY SAYING: I wasn't consulted on that issue:

INSTEAD OF: It's not my f**king problem.

TRY SAYING: That's interesting:
INSTEAD OF: What the f**k do you know?

TRY SAYING: I'm not sure this can be implemented.
INSTEAD OF: That shit won't work.

TRY SAYING: I'll try to schedule that.
INSTEAD OF: Why the hell didn't you tell me sooner?

TRY SAYING: He's not familiar with the procedures.
INSTEAD OF: He's got his head up his ass.

TRY SAYING: Allow me to enlighten you about this matter.
INSTEAD OF: Keep your eyes open and your goddam mouth shut.

TRY SAYING: You need to speed up your task management.
INSTEAD OF: You sure are a worthless P.O.S., aren't you?

TRY SAYING: I don't think you understand.
INSTEAD OF: Shove it up your ass.

TRY SAYING: I love a challenge.
INSTEAD OF: Let's just do it my way; okay with you?

TRY SAYING: That suggestion warrants serious consideration.
INSTEAD OF: How in the world did you get through flight school?

TRY SAYING: You are somewhat insensitive.
INSTEAD OF: You're a Shit Head.

TRY SAYING: She's an aggressive flight attendant.
INSTEAD OF: Are you sleeping with that Bitch?

TRY SAYING: I think you could use more training.
INSTEAD OF: You don't know what the f**k you're doing, do you?

POSITIVE ATTITUDE

I use a Marine pilot because that's how this story came to me – in the retelling you may use any service that suits the need, environment and/or company. ALL pilots/aviators KNOW a positive attitude is a prerequisite for flight, along with a good plan, a better back-up plan, knowing where the 'back door' is, how to get there, and how/when to touch all the 'lucky parts' of the aircraft.

After his warplane was hit and he was forced to eject, the Marine Corps fighter pilot finally regained consciousness. He was in a hospital, in a lot of pain. He found himself in the ICU with tubes/IV drips in both arms, a breathing mask, wires monitoring every function and a nurse hovering over him, looking worried. It was obvious he was in a life-threatening situation.

The nurse gave him a serious look, straight into his eyes. Knowing he was not only a fighter pilot, but a Marine, she spoke to him softly and slowly, enunciating each word: "You … may … not … feel … anything … from … the … waist … down."

Somehow, he managed to mumble a reply, "Can I feel your tits, then?"

And that, my friends, is an example of a positive attitude.

Segué to the next day – same Marine, same hospital, same nurse …

Wearing the oxygen mask, the Marine fighter pilot asks his nurse: "Are my testicles black?"

The nurse gently takes out his 'package', inspects them gently and thoroughly, returns them to proper placement and says, "They look fine to me."

Taking off the O^2 mask, he asks again in a slow and deliberate method: "That ... was ... nice ... thank ... you ... but ... I ... asked ... 'Are ... my ... test ... results ... back?'"

Because he tried hiding a bomb in his shoe, Richard Reid forced us to remove our shoes in the TSA line at airport security. Thank goodness he didn't hide the bomb in his underwear.

QUESTIONS FROM STUDENT PILOTS
OR CONFUSION IS THE FIRST STEP TOWARDS KNOWLEDGE

As an instructor pilot/ flight instructor for more years than I care to recount, I have had many sharp Grade A students whose questions caused me to scramble in finding the answer(s) to their very thoughtful inquiries. Trying to stay half a step ahead of these tyros was a great challenge ... and a great joy; for I took credit [unashamedly and for good reason, natch!] in the fact that their budding brains were ranging far and wide throughout the subject matter(s) I had presented. These "Young Skywalkers" went on to command the hottest ships and fleet airliners "... holding all those lives in the palm of (their) hand."

[See: https://www.youtube.com/watch?v=8XC3Hc-rAkk]

THEN ... *there were the others, those optimistic hopefuls whose imaginations, colored by too many Hollywood 'aviation epics', allowed their ahhh ... intellect - loosely described - to wander far off the tarmac of reality and bend, if not break the "bonny laws o' physics' {engineer Scott, the original Star trek TV series] and aerodynamics. Collected here are some of those questions I received during the schooling of these 'intrepid* *aeronauts' who intellectually are still exploring where "... no man has gone before."*

From a young wrench [mechanic]: Every time I drop a tool, I tell myself at least I'm not working on a floatplane.

Same mechanic: If I don't have a torque wrench can I just push hard enough until my wrist snaps?

Asked of a class of mechanic hopefuls: Which is harder to find, heavier, or more expensive? A bucket of propwash or a ball of flight line? *I was amazed they took that question seriously!*

Asked from the rear of the class: Can you go over the Corleone Force and the Borealis Effect again?

If most traffic patterns are to the left, why doesn't the right wing have more bugs on it?

In Australia:

- Do pilots sit on the right side of the airplane?

- Do they land on the other side of the runway?

- Do helicopter rotors turn the other way?

You are flying a 747 coming from South America with a load of parrots. If they all start flying around the cargo hold, does the airplane weigh less?

So, if you're inverted on the localizer, is the needle reverse sensing?

I was so intrigued by THIS question I sallied forth in a Super Decathlon 8KCAB to ascertain the answer, which is: No, the needle is NOT reverse sensing, it will still indicate whether you are left or right of the localizer. That being said ... the pilot IS.

My favorite question to ask in ground school comes immediately after discussing Bernoulli's Principle and how a wing creates lift. I ask the class "In the spring and fall you see the geese flying overhead and they always fly in a 'V'. One side of the 'V' is always longer than the other. Why is that?" Then I disappear for their break.

When the class reconvenes there are a multitude of explanations: the strongest goose creates a 'bow wave' for the weaker geese to ride; the wingtip vortices also create a 'wave-like force' the geese can ride like a surfer rides a wave; the longer side of the 'V' is the downwind side, and so on. When asked for the reason, it simply is:

Geese don't know Bernoulli from Shinola, there's just more birds on that side.

Corollary: "Any landing you can walk away from is a good one" is NOT an official FAA definition.

REAL SUPERHEROES

I turned up in Colorado right at the end of the Rocky Mountain Airways days. The planes, pilots, and kind of flying they did was legendary in the state known for serene mountain views from above combined with turbulence rivaling cyclonic discombobulation coupled with zero-zero inflight visibility due to snow ... oftentimes all occurring during the same flight!

It's interesting how the world is fascinated by Hollywood 'superhero' films. The mega-million-dollar box office proceeds serve to illustrate the insane level of interest in 'entertainment' of a spellbound populace. These 'superheroes' are not real, they are actors just playing like superheroes and do so with the magic of digital cinema, costumes, green screen, harnesses, and ropes to give the illusion of super strength and super speed. However, superheroes have walked among us. I know because I spent the better part of 15-years with them.

The superheroes I knew looked like ordinary people - and they were - except for a few traits that raised them above common people. These superheroes served others, but it was the effort and determination that drove them that made them superheroes. It is much easier to have the illusion of a being superhero today, with modern technology and its instant access to information. The superheroes of past lived in the modern world, but there were no cell phone or computers. In fact, there were no cordless phones as the handset was wired to the base and the base was plugged into the wall or post. Public phones were pay phones and required pocket change to use them. There were no handheld computers, in fact there were no personal or desktop computers. There was no Facebook, internet, twitter, Instagram, because there was no internet. Fax was the biggest technological advancement and only the large companies had such a marvel.

Aviation was on the leading edge of technology, but change was slow and steady as over a 40-year period not many big jumps in aviation had been made. The superheroes of the past could fly, they had wings and they even had telepathy. The superheroes I knew were Rocky Mountain Airways pilots. Yes, they had wings on their chest, and they could fly. Boy, could they fly! Modern day pilots deserve a great deal of respect, but to put things in perspective, todays fully automated, glass-cockpit aircraft can fly themselves and the assistance they get from ground-based instruments and communications are light-years ahead of aircraft like the De Havilland Twin Otter and Dash-7, which had little more than needle-ball- and airspeed instruments, and the pilots had very limited ground based assistance.

The story begins in 1965 when the company was founded by Gordon Autry as Vail Airways. Gordon piloted the 6-passenger Aero Commander. While the early days were marked with boot strap ingenuity and simple promotional gimmicks, the airline began to take shape. Professional timetables were circulated showing the all-encompassing reason for the airline – skiing. By the end of the first year a total of 240 passengers had been carried. During those initial years the operation was completely shut down during the summer months. There simply wasn't enough traffic. The operation at the Eagle Airport (EGE) was VFR only which simply meant flights could only be made in clear skies. So that a better flight completion could be possible, Mr. Autry himself installed an NDB in 1967 giving the ability to make instrument approaches to the airport.

In 1968, Mr. Autry applied for and was awarded a route to Aspen (ASE). At this time the name Vail Airways was changed to Rocky Mountain Airways. RMA carried over a million people to the ski areas in its fleet of unpressurized, 19- passenger de Havilland Twin Otters. Passengers often imitated the two-man crew by removing the oxygen mask and sucking on the tube. It was not unusual for the passengers to fill up their sick sacks as the aircraft bounced around and ice was slung off the props onto the side of the fuselage. Non-precision approaches allowed the airline all-weather capability, but better approaches were desired, and in 1972 RMA entered into a joint study program with Singer Kearfott to evaluate and provide the necessary documentation for a microwave landing system (MLS), a full-precision approach called "TALAR" A system that had been developed for military use in Southeast Asia to permit precision landing approaches in terrain and weather conditions that would distort conventional radio beam Instrument Landing Systems (ILS).

Company-owned MLS were installed in Steamboat Springs (SBS) and ASE in 1973. In addition to TALAR, RMA installed electronic aids at SBS and ASE including strobes, obstruction lights, Visual Approach (VASI) lights and runway lights. RMA established Supplementary Aviation Weather Reporting Stations (SAWRS) for its own use in SBS and WHR, which were approved by the National Weather Service. RMA pilots flew the steepest high angle precision approaches in the United States. Aspen and Steamboat were 6° and the Avon STOLport was flown at 7° which caused the passengers to literally slide forward in their seats and hang on their seatbelts!

Telepathically, they must have had the ability to read minds, because if you wanted a message to be spread quickly, you just told a pilot that it was confidential information and in less than 20 minutes the entire airline knew and generally other airlines also knew! Although archaic by the standards of today, they did have air-to-ground radios, but the frequencies were monitored by FAA and the company. But somehow, they spread the word! The reason the RMA pilots were superheroes was because they had a superhero father, like Thor's father Odin, only their father Gordon Autry was shorter. Gordon stood 5'7" tall, but he acted like he was 7' tall and most everyone thought he was!

But it was the environment that Gordon created that encouraged and allowed people be superheroes – the freedom to fail! The magic of the RMA days was the lack of government interference and a combined loyalty and drive to succeed! The airline grew out of the cash box, which meant it was not beholding to influences that could direct it by personal agendas. And the airline had a sense of 'family' where everyone depended on everyone else and the underlying feeling of responsibility was that cancelled flights, for whatever reason would bring the company closer to a shut down. The lack of government interference was by design. RMA was self-sufficient as it funded and built its own infrastructure. Gordon had a key philosophy: if you take government money, the government will tell you how to run your business. And that applied to not only the federal government, but local governments as well.

By way of example RMA paid for and constructed passenger terminals, non-precision and full precession landing aids including runway and obstruction lights, VASI and REIL. RMA provided its own shuttle service between the Eagle Airport and Vail. The best example was the private funding and construction of the Avon STOLport, an entire airport with runway, ramp terminal, full precision TALAR approach and all the secondary aids, also, the construction of a water and wastewater system to serve the terminal. Rocky Mountain Airways pilots flew for Vail Airways and RMA between 1965 and 1986, when the airline was sold to Texas Air and began operating as Continental Express. RMA flights departing Denver (DEN) carried enough fuel for a round-trip plus a 30-minute reserve. Twin Otter and Dash 7 Captains were known for their aviation skills and perseverance. They needed weather minimum to depart DEN and then they needed landing minimums at their destination to be legal to start the approach.

Flights to the ski destinations were dispatched with enough fuel to make a roundtrip plus 45-minuters of reserve fuel. If a flight started the approach and the station told them the weather had gone below minimums, it was at the Captain's discretion as to continue the approach or execute a missed approach. RMA captains would generally continue the approach and often execute a landing as mountain weather fluctuated and would frequently go above minimums! If the weather was below minimums when the flight was ready to start its approach, the aircraft would hold if it could, to see it the weather improved enough to begin the approach.

When RMA began flying as Continental Express the pilots no longer acted like superheroes as the airline was now part of a larger organization that had deep pockets and had a different standard of dispatching, completing flights and procedures in-route or making a missed approach! The new environment was just different from the old RMA! The RMA standards were incredibly high, and it was a real sense of accomplishment to become a Rocky Mountain Airways Captain. Those pilots of yesteryear were Real Superheroes - their like may never be seen again.

"Pilots track their lives by the number of hours in the air, as if any other kind of time isn't worth noting."
- Michael Parfit, 2000

REGARDING HELICOPTER PILOTS

Much has been written regarding helicopter ... ahhh ... 'flight' [and that term is very loosely used here], most of which goes along the lines of:

"Helicopter defined: A bunch of spare parts flying in close formation."

"Anything that screws its way into the sky is there according to unnatural principals."

"Helicopters don't fly, they just beat the air into submission – sometimes the air wins."

As a 'final' word on the matter, have you ever wondered why there are no "Antique Helicopter Fly-ins"? There's a reason for this and I'll wager even a Student Pilot/2nd Lieutenant/W1 could figure out why.

You never want to sneak up behind an old high-time helicopter pilot and clap your hands. He will instantly dive for cover and most likely whimper ... then get up and smack the crap out of you.

There are no old helicopters lying around airports like you see old airplanes. There is a reason for this. Come to think of it, there are not many old high-time helicopter pilots hanging around airports either, so the first issue is moot.

Graduates of Army Pilot's Course No. 4 wait paitently for their turn in the simulator.

You can always tell a helicopter pilot in anything moving: a train, an airplane, a car or a boat. They never smile, they are always listening to the machine and they always hear something they think is not right. Helicopter pilots fly in a mode of intensity; actually more like "spring loaded" while waiting for pieces of their ship to fall off.

Flying a helicopter at any altitude over 500 feet is considered reckless and should be avoided. Flying a helicopter at any altitude or condition that precludes a landing in less than 20 seconds is considered outright foolhardy.

Remember in a helicopter you have about one second to lower the collective blade pitch in an engine failure before the craft becomes unrecoverable. Once you've failed this maneuver the machine flies about as well as a 2-ton meat locker. Even a perfectly executed autorotation only gives you a glide ratio slightly better than that of a brick.

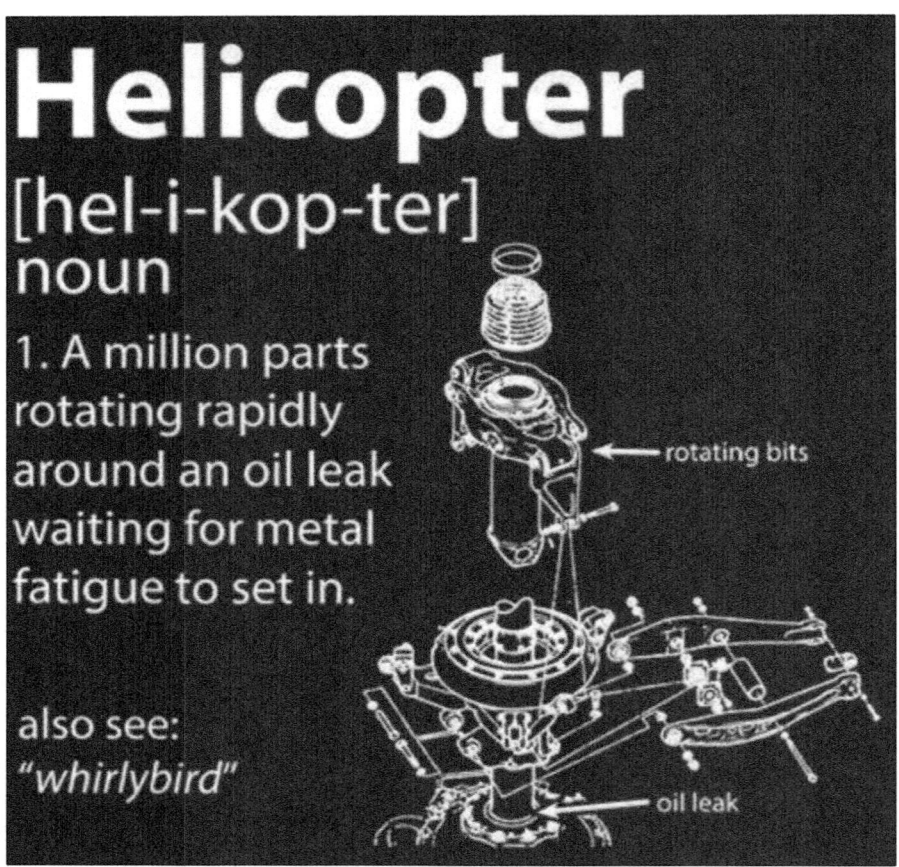

When your wings are leading, lagging, flapping, precessing and moving faster than your fuselage there's something unnatural going on. Is this the way men were meant to fly?

While hovering, if you start to sink a bit, you pull up on the collective while twisting the throttle, push with your left foot (compensate for torque) and move the stick left (more translating tendency) to hold your spot. If you now need to stop rising, you do the opposite in that order. Sometimes in wind you do these many times each second. Great fun is letting a fighter pilot go for a ride and trying this.

For Helicopters: You never want to feel a sinking feeling in your gut (low "g" pushover) while flying a two bladed under slung teetering rotor system. You are about to do a snap-roll to the right and crash. For that matter, any remotely aerobatic maneuver should be avoided in a Huey. *(That's a fact, Jack! -Ed.)*

Don't push your luck. It will run out soon enough anyway. If everything is working fine on your helicopter, consider yourself temporarily lucky because something is about to break.

There are two types of helicopter pilots: Those that have crashed, and those that are going to.

Harry Reasoner once wrote the following about helicopter pilots:

"The thing is, helicopters are different from planes. An airplane by its nature wants to fly, and if not interfered with too strongly by unusual events or by an incompetent pilot, it will fly. A helicopter does not want to fly. It is maintained in the air by a variety of forces and controls working in opposition to each other, and if there is any disturbance in this delicate balance the helicopter stops flying; immediately and disastrously. There is no such thing as a gliding helicopter. This is why being a helicopter pilot is so different from being an airplane pilot, and why in generality, airplane pilots are open, clear-eyed, buoyant extroverts and helicopter pilots are brooding introspective anticipators of trouble. They know if something bad has not happened it is about to."

Having said all this, I must admit that flying in a helicopter is one of the most satisfying and exhilarating experiences I have ever enjoyed: skimming over the tops of trees at 100 knots is something we should all be able to do at least once.

Many years later I know that it was sometimes anything but fun, but now it IS something to brag about for those of us who survived the experience.

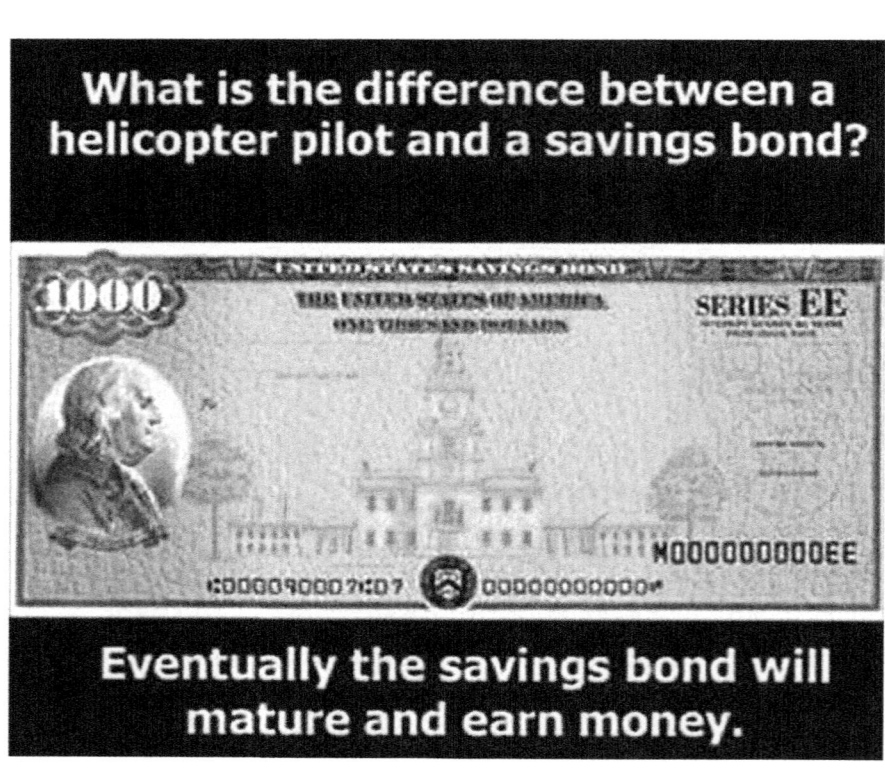

I have had a LOT of fun at the expense of helicopter pilots in this, and the first volume of, the Aviator's Bathroom Reader. Mostly because even this many years later, these guys are a bunch of crazy Mofo's; and when one hears the stories of adventures long gone by, all of them occurring from ground level to <u>maybe</u> tree-top altitudes, one cannot help but wonder "Maybe, just maybe, these guys have had more than one screw loose for a long, long time." But when you are standing, frightened and scared to death, in the middle of 'Indian territory' and hear that distinctive sound of rotor blades at max rpm coming your way, all you can think of is "Thank you Lord, for the guys in these 'flying targets' coming to get me." It's just one of the reasons why, after the rescue, those guys didn't have to buy a drink all night.

The following was written by Joseph Galloway, a Vietnam War correspondent who, in a moment of insanity, got on board a Huey and rode into the Battle of Ia Drang; his experiences later published in book form as <u>We Were Soldiers Once ... and Young</u>. This was later made into a movie starring Mel Gibson and Sam Elliot. It is as valid today as it was then. Thanks, fellows, for willingly flying into the Valley of Death; and thanks, Lord, for allowing them to fly out the other side.

GOD'S OWN LUNATICS

By: Joe Galloway

13 November 1941 - 18 August 2021

"I don't know if there's anybody here today that didn't thrill to the sound of those blades. That familiar 'wop-wop-wop' is the soundtrack of our war. The lullaby of our younger days. To someone who spent his time in 'Nam and the grunts, I've got to tell you that noise was always great comfort. It meant someone was coming to help. Someone was coming to get our wounded, someone was coming to bring us water and ammo, someone was coming to take our dead brothers home, and eventually someone was coming to give us a ride out of hell. Even today when I hear it I stop, catch my breath, and go back to those days. I love you guys as only an infantryman can; no matter how bad things were, if we called, you came. Down through the rivers of green tracers and other visible signs of a real bad day off to a real bad start. To us, you seemed to be beyond brave and fearless, that you would come to us in the middle of battle in those flimsy, thin-skinned crates, and in the storm of fire you would sit up there behind that thin plexiglass seeming so patient and so calm and so vulnerable waiting for the off-loading and on-loading; we thought you were god's lunatics - and we loved you ... still do. We're the fortunate ones; we survived when so many better men gave up their precious lives for us. We owe them a sacred debt - to live each day to its fullest. What they're saying, if you listen hard enough, is this: "We're at peace, and so should you be. And so should you be."

- Dedicated to the 4,095 helicopter pilots, crew members, and observers lost in the Vietnam War.

https://www.youtube.com/watch?v=CqYOAqxlL_Y

REMEMBER 'DEAD BUG'?

Those with more decades behind than ahead can relate to this; what does one remember of those days? The boredom, the moments of abject fear, the hard work, the memorable flight(s) where, if we relax, sit back, and close our eyes we can still feel the flight controls, smell the smells and feel the vibrations. What do you remember?

As we get older and we experience the loss of old friends, we begin to realize that maybe we bullet-proof pilots won't live forever. We aren't so bullet-proof anymore. We ponder ... if I we're gone tomorrow; "Did I say what I wanted to my Brothers?" The answer is "No!" Hence, the following random thoughts:

When people ask me if I miss flying, I always say something like, "Yes, I miss the flying because when you are flying, you are totally focused on the task at hand. It's like nothing else you will ever do (almost). " But then I always say, "However, I miss the squadron and the guys even more than I miss the flying."

Why, you might ask? They were a bunch of aggressive, wiseass, cocky, insulting, sarcastic bastards in smelly flight suits who thought a funny thing to do was to fart and see if they could clear a room. They drank too much, they chased women, they flew when they shouldn't, they laughed too loud and thought they owned the sky, the bar, and generally thought they could do everything better than the next guy. Nothing was funnier than trying to screw with a buddy and see how pissed off they would get. They flew planes that leaked, smoked, broke, couldn't turn, burned fuel too fast, never had working autopilots or radars, and with systems that were archaic next to today's new generation aircraft.

But a little closer look might show that every guy in the room was sneaky smart and damn competent and brutally handsome in their own way! They hated to lose or fail to accomplish the mission and that seldom happened. They were the laziest guys on the planet until challenged and then they would do anything to win. They would fly with wing tips overlapped at night through the worst weather with only a little 'Form' light to hold on to, knowing their flight lead would get them on the ground safely. They would fight in the air knowing the greatest risk and fear was that another fighter would arrive at the same six o' clock the same time they did. They would fly in harm's way and act nonchalant as if to challenge the Grim Reaper.

When we flew to another base, we proclaimed that we were the best squadron on the base as soon as we landed. Often, we were not invited back. When we went into an O' Club, we owned the bar. We were lucky to be the "Best of the Best" in the military. We knew it and so did others. We found jobs, lost jobs, got married, got divorced, moved, went broke, got rich, broke some things, and knew the only thing you could count on -- really count on -- was if you needed help, a fellow pilot would have your back.

I miss the call signs, nicknames, and the stories behind them. I miss getting lit up in an O' Club full of my buddies and watching the incredible, unbelievable things that were happening. I miss the crew chiefs saluting as you taxied out of the flight line. I miss lighting the afterburners, if you had them, especially at night. I miss going straight up and straight down. I miss the cross countries. I miss the dice games at the bar for drinks. I miss listening to BS stories while drinking and laughing until my eyes watered.

I miss flying upside down in the Grand Canyon and hearing about flying so low that boats were blown over. I miss coming into the break hot and looking over and seeing three wingmen tucked in tight ready to make the troops on the ground proud. I miss belches that could be heard in neighboring states. I miss putting on ad hoc Air Shows that might be over someone's home or farm in faraway towns.

Finally, I miss hearing "DEAD BUG!" called out at the bar and seeing and hearing a room full of men hit the deck with drinks spilling and chairs being knocked over as they rolled in the beer and kicked their legs in the air—followed closely by a Not Politically Correct Tap Dancing and Singing spectacle that couldn't help but make you grin and order another round.

I am a lucky guy and have lived a great life! One thing I know is that I was part of a special, really talented bunch of guys doing something dangerous and doing it better than most. Flying the most beautiful, ugly, noisy, solid aircraft ever built. Supported by ground troops committed to making sure we came home! Being prepared to fly and fight and die for America.

Having a clear mission. Having fun.

We box out bad memories from various operations most of the time but never the hallowed memories of our fallen comrades. We are often amazed at how good war stories never let truth interfere and how they get better with age. We are lucky bastards to be able to walk into a Squadron or a bar and have men we respected, and love shout our names, our call signs, and know that this is truly where we belong.

We are Pilots.

We are Few.

We are Proud.

I am privileged and proud to call you Brothers

Push it Up & Check SIX!

"Yea though I fly through the valley of the shadow of death, I fear no evil - for I fly the biggest, baddest, meanest, fastest MoFo in the whole damn valley.
- USAF mantra, Southeast Asia War Games [Vietnam]

REMEMBER THE GOOD THINGS ABOUT BEING A 'FREIGHT DOG'?

Neither do I. Yes, it's a flying job. Yes, you're being paid [sort of]. Yes, you're usually the captain of a one-man crew. So … ? The following is a 'Doggers' view back on their life and experiences sorta like others found elsewhere in this book.

- Your airplane was getting old … when you were born.

- You haven't done a daylight landing in over a year.

- ATC advises there's smoother air at a different altitude … and you don't give a shit.

- You see the FBO begin to roll out a red carpet … then they quickly roll it back up again when they realize it's you.

- You call the hotel van to pick you up and they don't understand where you are on the airport.

- Center asks you to "Keep those chickens quiet!" so they can hear your transmissions.

- Your airplane has over 75,000 cycles.

- Your airplane's nickname is "Old oil can."

- The lady at the FBO locks up the popcorn machine after hearing you say you're going to "make a meal of it."
- Your airplane has at least eight faded company logos on it [all defunct].
- You wear the same shirt for a week ... and no-one complains.
- Center mispronounces your callsign more than three times ... during the same flight.
- Your Director of Operations mysteriously changes the plane's max take-off weight just before Christmas.
- Every FBO requires you park out of sight around back.
- You walk barefoot through the terminal ... because you just woke up.
- Your airplane doesn't leak oil ... it is just 'marking its territory.'
- The entirety of your personal possessions can fit in a suitcase and flight bag.
- All the other pilots wait for you to be the first to 'test the squall line'.
- All the other airplanes wait to see if you get in.
- You request the 'Visual' when it's 300' OVC and ½ mile viz.
- You make no attempt to deviate around weather.
- You never check weather ... 'cause you're going anyway.
- You have an emotional reunion with your newly assigned Beech 99 because 25 years ago you used to fuel it when it had 'only' 18,000 cycles and the windows weren't painted over.

- You've slept in the FBO 'lounge' more than in the house you grew up in.

- Upper management thinks the derelict fuel truck you sleep in is a 'crew domicile'.

- You carry a 'personal' step ladder in the airplane.

- You've changed tires, starter-generators and ADIs but you're neither an A&P nor "Twidget" [avionics tech].

- You have a 'secret' Mexican family in Del Rio, Texas.

- The tip tanks serve as an alarm clock when they run dry.

- You become VERY proficient at night aileron rolls to stay awake.

- Center's first call to you is: "Hey Mailbag 216 wake up! I know you're sleeping up there!"

- On a clear night you consider it normal to make a low pass [or two] to 'clear the ground fog' and deer off the runway.

- Your hero is a crusty old captain who has both dead-sticked a DC-3 at night to a safe landing AND declared an emergency when the co-pilot tried to pee out of an old antennae hole and was nearly castrated.

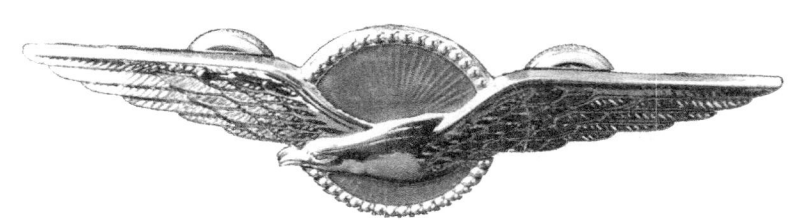

Netherlands - WWII Colony pilot wings.

REPLY LETTER FROM NASA

Inventiveness and creativity in America is NOT DEAD – it's merely being redirected in ... ahhh ... more novel ways and directions. I would love to see the original letter to NASA from this budding 'space-man' [or would a better description be 'spaced-out man?"] but by now I'm sure it is firmly and deeply buried in NASA's "Do I Really Have to Answer This?" file. I include a picture of NASA's reply letter and a more readable transcript below; I have to wonder what else Mr. Jones has come up with recently? I've found that having ideas is the easy part – the real challenge comes when attempting to make the idea a reality. Remember, the parachute came about because someone tied a bedsheet to himself, then jumped off a barn roof.

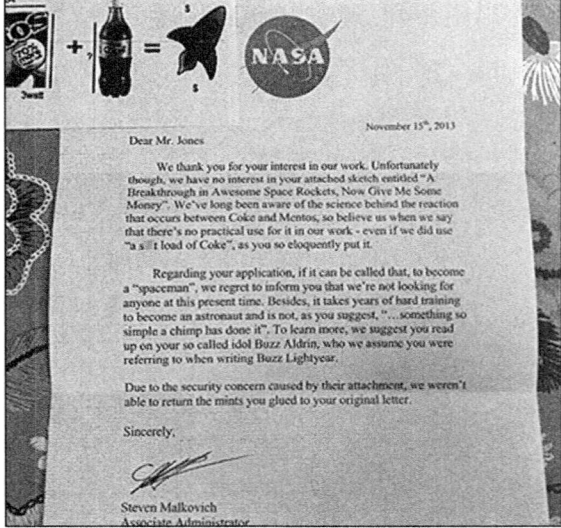

NASA

November 15th, 2013

Dear Mr. Jones

We thank you for your interest in our work. Unfortunately though, we have no interest in your attached sketch entitled "A Breakthrough in Awesome Space Rockets, Now Give Me Some Money." We've long been aware of the science behind the reaction that occurs between Coca-Cola and Mentos, so believe us when we say there is no practical use for it in our work – even if we did use a "shitload of coke", as you so eloquently put it.

Regarding your application, if it can be called that, to become a "spaceman", we regret to inform you we are not looking for anyone at this present time. Besides it takes years of hard training to become an astronaut and is not, as you suggest "… something so simple a chimp has done it."

To learn more, we suggest you read up on your so-called idol Buzz Aldrin, who we assume you were referring to when writing 'Buzz Lightyear'.

Due to the security concern by their attachment, we weren't able to return the mints glued to your original letter.

Sincerely,

Steven Malkovich
Associate Administrator

Several thoughts come immediately to mind:

1. Just how many Mentos would it take to launch a rocket [of ANY size]?

2. Just how much is a "shitload" of Coke?

3. Once begun, how would you control the reaction [think: solid-fuel rocket that's either burning or not]?

4. Can you imagine the reaction of the NASA HAZMAT [Hazardous Materials] team to the unidentified white pill-like objects glued to the original letter?

5. How long and by what means/tests did they finally determine those objects were Mentos?

6. Were those Mentos destroyed or impounded into NASA's archives?

"I know, but this guy doing the flying has no airline experience at all. He's a menace to himself and everything in the air ... yes, birds, too!"
- Air Traffic Controller, 1980 movie *Airplane*

Austria-Hungary, Emperor Franz-Josef 1913 – 1916.

RULES OF THE AIR:
HOW TO FLY YOUR MACHINE - I

I ran across a little pamphlet dated June 1917, published by the U.S. Army Flying Corps, American Expeditionary Forces - which means these rules were part of pilot training over 100 years ago. While some are arcane and now no longer valid, many are the predecessors to the rules, regulations and procedures we now follow over a century later. So when you don your leather flying coat, helmet, goggles and scarf, take a moment to recall these rules – for indeed they are 'rules' and not merely guidelines.

The 1917 regulations are in boldface.

1. **Before starting, see that the section of the field you are going to use in making your get-away is clear and no machines are landing or gliding into this section of the field. Locate position of all machines in the air.**

    A good practice at non-towered airports is, after the pre-takeoff checks have been accomplished, to perform a taxiing 360° turn to check the traffic pattern for other planes. Not everyone uses their radio, y'know.

2. **If other machines precede you in starting, allow them to gain a distance of at least half a mile before following. Do not follow in trail; propeller wash will thus be avoided.**

    Give the plane taking off ahead of you a little room to get airborne; you won't be right on their tail if they have a problem ... AND ... little airplanes create wake turbulence and wingtip vortices just like the big guys do. Be alert!

3. **Machines with dead motors have the right of way over all others.**

FAR 91.113(c) In distress. An aircraft in distress has the right-of-way over all other traffic.

AIM 6-1-2(a) states "Pilots (should) not hesitate to declare an emergency when they are faced with distress situations…" and (b) "Pilots who become apprehensive for their safety should <u>request immediate assistance</u>."

Never, ever be reluctant to declare an emergency if you are in any way 'apprehensive' about the outcome of your flight. The sooner you call for help the more time you have to obtain aid & assistance – done quickly enough could save lives whereas waiting longer may not have a happy ending to the event. And don't worry about 'breaking the rules'; FAR 91.3 (b) states: "In an in-flight emergency requiring immediate action, the pilot in command may deviate from any rule of this part to the extent required to meet that emergency." I have had to do just that several times and there was never a negative ramification afterwards.

4. **Machines gliding into a field have the right-of-way over those about to leave. Machines landing have greater speed than those leaving so be careful not to misjudge your start and be overtaken by another machine that is powerless to keep from having an accident as the result of your misjudgment.**

FAR 91.113(g) Landing aircraft, while on final approach to land or while landing, have the right-of-way over all other aircraft in flight or operating on the surface.

5. **Before beginning a glide, see that no machines are under you. Those flying beneath you have the right-of-way.**

FAR 91.113(g) Landing. When two or more aircraft are approaching an airport for the purposes of landing, the aircraft at the lower altitude has the right-of-way, but shall not take advantage of this rule to cut in front of another aircraft…

If you fly a low-wing aircraft, be alert to another aircraft below you if you are descending. If you fly high-wing aircraft, be alert to another aircraft above descending on top of you.

6. **In flight, before making a turn, see that no machines are dangerously near on your flanks.**

   LOOK FIRST in the direction you wish to turn, MAKE SURE the sky is clear, and THEN begin the turn.

7. **Machines approaching head-on pass to the right at an interval of at least 150 yards.**

   FAR 91.113(e) Approaching head-on. When approaching each other head-on, or nearly so, each pilot of each aircraft shall alter course to the right.

8. **In passing a machine going the same direction, have an interval of at least 200 yards.**

   FAR 91.113(f) Overtaking. Each aircraft that is being overtaken has the right-of-way and each pilot of an overtaking aircraft shall alter course to the right to pass well clear.

9. **In passing over or under another machine, the interval must be at least 150 yards.**

While there is no specific FAR guidance regarding flying over and/or under another airplane [outside of formation flight], there are some generalized regulations:

FAR 91.111(a) No person may operate an aircraft so close to another aircraft as to create a collision hazard.

FAR 91.113(b) General. When a rule of this section gives another aircraft the right-of-way, the pilot shall give way to that aircraft and may not pass over, under or ahead of it unless well clear.

10. **Hangars must be cleared by at least 50 feet in all flying.**

    FAR 91.119(c) Over other than congested areas. ...the aircraft may not be operated closer than 500' to any person, vessel, vehicle or structure [hangar].

"Mix ignorance with arrogance at low altitude and the results are almost guaranteed to be spectacular."

RULES OF THE AIR:
HOW TO FLY YOUR MACHINE - II

In the first part of this two-parter we reviewed some rules of flying from 1917 and then referred to some of the modern-day regulations which cover the same topic(s). This illustrates to those of us flying today the rules and regulations by which we must abide today have a deep background in aviation's history and, while not elucidated with today's lawyerly verbosity, still are as relevant today as they were 100 years ago.

The 1917 regulations are printed in boldface.

USAAC WWII Flight Nurse Wings.

11. **After gliding in preparation to making a landing, if the section of the field you are going to use is not clear, continue flight.**

   Whenever landing considerations are not satisfactory, a go-around [rejected landing] is warranted. Airplane Flying Handbook, pg. 8-12]

   "You Can Always Go Around" by Ken Dravis [Thanks, Ken!] https://www.youtube.com/watch?v=lr5d3sGxSXQ

12. **While in flight, keep a constant lookout for machines in all directions.**

   "Always keep your head on a swivel." "Beware the Hun in the sun." "Never fly straight-and-level for more than 5 seconds." These are all old sayings which came out of the combat experiences from WWI through today. While thankfully no-one is hunting us in the skies these days, these truisms still maintain their validity. The most dangerous airplane out there is the one you don't see.

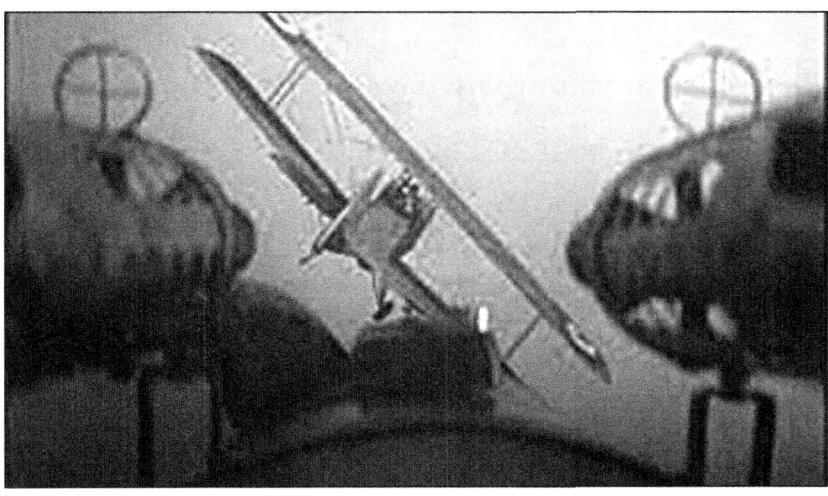

13. **After landing, never turn short; remain in position where the machine rests until you have determined that a sufficiently clear field exists in all directions for taxiing or continuing the flight as the case may be.**

    One needs to land their ship and then, without excessive delay, exit the runway safely and under control. Keep in mind, there is no rush to clear the runway – until you are off, it belongs to you. If someone else has followed too closely, well – they need the go-around practice. Clear the runway by going past the Hold Short markings and then stop. NOW is the time to perform your after-landing flows and checks, not while you are still in motion.

14. **Never fly in heavy fog. However, if caught in a fog, always make your landing on the training field from the left in order to avoid possible accident if landing is made from the right.**

    I'm not 100% sure, but I am thinking this is where the standard left-hand traffic patterns came from.

15. **If the flight is begun and conditions arise thereafter that are hazardous, land as soon as possible.**

    If you ever are in doubt about your safety, either get to the very closest airport available OR make a precautionary landing. This is when the pilot lands on a self-chosen piece of ground, under control, with power available, all of their own choosing. It's better than a forced landing where one must land on whatever ground is below you, no choice in the matter, perhaps without power and you have but one try at it. [Helicopter pilots know this, which is why they never fly more than a few hundred feet agl.]

16. **At all times keep the machine in such a position with reference to suitable ground that a landing may be affected at any time.**

   As you fly and scan the sky for traffic, when your eyes go below the horizon, check out the terrain below for a 'suitable' emergency landing field. You will never know when you will need one and a suitable field just past is better than an unknown one ahead.

17. **Returning to hangars after flight, taxi at a slow rate of speed and stop the machine before reaching the dead line.**

   What is a 'safe' taxi speed? I've heard it said a 'brisk walk.' Heck, even a brisk walk will result in a 10-minute taxi if you must go far. I recommend taxiing at a speed that, if you must come to a stop with minimal use of brakes, you can pull power & mixture and coast to a stop without hitting anything. In the

tie-down area you taxi dead slow; out on the clear taxiway you might go a little faster. Use good judgement here!

18. Never continue flying when a machine feels uncomfortable to you or you feel that something is wrong.

Pretty much self-explanatory.

19. Do not turn the machine sharply in taxiing. The tail skid damages the fuselage many times. Hold elevator forward in taxiing, it loosens the weight on the tail.

Well, we don't have tail skids anymore, but tight turns should be accomplished with care, so a wingtip doesn't encounter some other solid item thus causing embarrassment and financial woe to said unwary pilot.

"Our two greatest problems are gravity and paperwork. We can lick gravity, but sometimes the paperwork is overwhelming.
- Dr. Werner von Braun
-Corollary: When the weight of the paperwork equals the weight of the airplane, you're almost ready to fly.
- Donald Douglas

SANTA'S RAMP CHECK

No, this is NOT "Santa's FAA Flight Check; that well-known and well-loved rendition of an FAA line check for Santa where he's "going to lose one on takeoff." It's ANOTHER FAA/Santa saga encompassing the second and first greatest lies in aviation [2nd: "I'm from the FAA and I'm here to help you." 1st: "I'm so glad to see you here."]. Those of ~~you~~ us who have endured a ramp-side 'discussion' of our - and the airplane's - fitness to fly might relate to a few of these. Those of you who have not - prepare thyself.

Many thanks to the Pilot of America forum:

I don't CARE if you live at the North Pole, you still need a compass deviation card.

"Where's the STC for these bells?"

Whoa, cowboy. FAA doesn't have the jurisdiction here. Because the North Pole isn't a land mass, and the nearest populated place is Nunavut, Canada has rightful jurisdiction over the sleigh and its operator.

While Canada must deal with airworthiness certification (I'm sure it's experimental) and pilot qualification (unless it's an N-numbered sleigh), the FAA does have jurisdiction for operations in USA airspace.

An eight-engine experimental? OMG *[Nine, counting 'Reindeer Lead"]*!

So, who's leaving Santa a CPAP instead of milk and cookies this year?

Santa has a BMI WAY over 40.

If the airman visiting his AME explains that he is afraid of Santa, which box does he check on the MedXpress form that he's Claustrophobic?

The type certificate says, "Powered by EIGHT tiny reindeer." If you want to fly this back to the North Pole, we're going to need to see all eight.

TFR? What TFR?

I don't see a transponder in here. No presents for anyone inside the Washington ADIZ.

While 14,657,876,154 landings in one night are impressive, they don't meet the requirements for currency.

Flashing red light must be visible from all directions. One light on the nose is unacceptable.

"If the pilot of this thing is who I think it is, he's definitely operating over gross."

"I know you have a long way to go, but if we hear you've exceeded 250kts under 10,000 you're going to have some explaining to do."

"The GPS database appears out of date; just how did you expect to file /G and be legal?"

The TCDS do not allow operations on skis

Do you have an STC for that 9th reindeer?

Rooftops are not designated runways.

"Have you complied with 91.103 for all 14,657,876,154 locations you will be landing? I assume this can be verified with a briefer's recording?" Assuming it took 30 seconds per landing point, a briefing would take a total of 2,035 hours and 43 minutes.

You didn't file your passenger manifest electronically at least an hour before departing for the U.S. Airspace!"

"Have you had any eggnog within the past 8 hours?

SAY YOUR LAST KNOWN POSITION?

I suspect the answer was "When we were number one for takeoff." If ever there was a good example of a bad example of inept flight management, this is it. I have taught this one of many 'Drew's Rules of Flying' for years:

IN GOD WE TRUST ... EVERYTHING ELSE WE CHECK - AND DOUBLE-CHECK!"

I don't care how many times you've flown your own plane; gremlins have been known to mess with airplanes 'safe and secure' in their own hangars. If the PIC doesn't perform thorough preflight inspections AND abide by the published checklist(s) bad things can, and often do, happen. Where were the pilot's minds when this event began to unfold? Why did it take so long to discover the issue? Who was responsible for quality control and the accurate input - and checking on - the data entered into the FMS? Inquiring minds [like the airline safety review board and perhaps the British version of the FAA] want to know.

London (CNN) — Passengers on a British Airways flight from London's City Airport to Dusseldorf in Germany were met with a surprise Monday morning when their plane touched down Edinburgh, the capital of Scotland. The travel error happened because of an incorrectly filed flight plan, leading both the pilot and cabin crew to believe the flight was bound for Edinburgh. The flight was operated by German leasing company WDL Aviation on behalf of the British Airways subsidiary airline BA CityFlyer. The incorrect flight plan was filed at WDL Aviation's offices in Germany.

After landing in Edinburgh, the plane took off a second time for Dusseldorf. Piotr Pomienski, a student at Imperial College London, told CNN his girlfriend Zsófia Szabó was on the plane that landed in Edinburgh by mistake. "I saw on Flightradar that the flight was flying north instead of south, but I assumed it was a system error of some sort. That is until she wrote to me that they're in Edinburgh." Szabó told CNN she realized something wasn't right when she saw mountains outside the plane, instead of the "usual German industrial landscape."

"When we started descending and I saw some taller hills/mountains, I did think that this isn't how Eastern Netherlands/Western Germany should look like but I assumed we took some small detour," she said. "Then my colleague sitting across the aisle from me told me to check Google Maps -- and it showed us being around Carlisle." "The information then spread around quite quickly. Everyone started asking everyone else where they were going -- everyone was for Dusseldorf."

"When we landed there was a bit of a hilarious moment when the flight attendant asked for a show of hands for the people going to Dusseldorf, which turned out to be everyone," she said. The captain subsequently apologized to the passengers, telling them the plane would refuel before heading to Germany.

"Most of us found this situation quite funny," Szabó said. "People were on phone calls trying to convince everyone that they've arrived in the wrong city." Another passenger on the flight, Son Tran, told CNN: "Most passengers sleep or work through this flight so no one really noticed we were not flying over the Channel. We only realized we are in Scotland once we descended on approach and asked the crew."

In a statement, a spokesperson for British Airways said the airline was working with WDL Aviation "to establish why the incorrect flight plan was filed." "We have apologized to customers for this interruption to their journey and will be contacting them all individually," the spokesperson said.

WDL Aviation said in a statement: "We are working closely with the authorities to investigate how the obviously unfortunate mix-up of flight schedules could occur. At no time has the safety of passengers been compromised. We flew the passengers on the flight with number BAXXXX (# redacted) to Dusseldorf after the involuntary stopover in Edinburgh."

"Both optimists and pessimists have contributed to aviation; the optimist invented the airplane, the pessimist the parachute."
- George Bernard Shaw

SECRET TO A LONG MARRIAGE

As I was dating the woman who later became my wife, we spoke of our future life together and, as this was the second go-around for both of us, some of the 'ground-rules' under which we would operate. It was all pretty simple, really, we both knew of and accepted the demands made on us by our respective employments and were good with that. Since I was traveling some, she solidified in her mind I was not someone with a 'roving eye', which I was not [If there's anything I have learned about being in a relationship, it is if I <u>ever</u> thought being involved with one woman wasn't enough, I know being involved with two is '<u>way</u> too many]. Plus she told me if she ever discovered that I was cheating on her I would unexpectedly die in my sleep, simple as that. Since I sleep with both eyes closed, I figured "Well, that's words to the wise."

The old Airline Captain was asked how he and his wife had managed to be married for 45 years and never had an argument.

He said that soon after they were married, they went on vacation at an Arizona horse ranch. While they were out riding one morning, the horse his wife was riding threw her off.

She picked herself up, caught the horse and as she patted him she said, "That's once."

A little later the horse threw her again. She picked herself up, caught the horse and as she patted him, she said, "That's twice."

A little later the horse threw her again. She picked herself up, caught the horse and as she patted him, she said, "That's three times." She pulled out her gun and shot the horse. I grabbed her by the shoulders, shook her and said, "What the hell are you thinking? You idiot, you just shot that horse."

She looked at me and said, "That's once."

SERVICE RULES OF ENGAGEMENT [ROE'S]

A lot of fun with inter-service rivalries, none without a slight semblance of truth and a larger semblance of BS. The first submission, Marine Corps rules, closely approximates the "Rules for a Gunfight" and thus should be memorized by anyone carrying a concealed weapon. You never know when a bad guy will appear – they always have the advantage of knowing when they are going to strike. We have to react to their appearance and by definition reaction is always slower than action. The rest of this is submitted for humor factor only – all the men and women in the service of our country require and <u>deserve</u> our honor and respect for performing a mostly thankless and occasionally very dangerous job.

Marine Corps Rules:

1. Be courteous to everyone, friendly to no one.
2. Decide to be aggressive enough, quickly enough.
3. Have a plan.
4. Have a back-up plan, because the first one probably won't work.
5. Be polite. Be professional. But have a plan to kill everyone you meet.
6. Do not attend a gunfight with a handgun whose caliber

does not start with a '4.'
7. Anything worth shooting is worth shooting twice. Ammo is cheap. Life is expensive.
8. Move away from your attacker. Distance is your friend. *(Lateral and diagonal preferred.)*
9. Use cover or concealment as much as possible.
10. Flank your adversary. When possible, protect yours.
11. Always cheat; always win. The only unfair fight is the one you lose.
12. In ten years, nobody will remember the details of caliber stance, or tactics. They will only remember who lived.
13. If you are not shooting, you should be communicating your intention to shoot ... or be reloading.

Navy SEAL Rules:

1. Look very cool in sunglasses.
2. Kill every living thing in sight.
3. Adjust Speedo.
4. Check hair in mirror.

US Army Rangers' Rules:

1. Walk in 50 miles wearing 75-pound rucksack while starving.
2. Locate individuals requiring killing.
3. Request permission via radio from 'Higher' to perform killing.
4. Curse bitterly when mission is aborted.
5. Walk out 50 miles wearing a 75-pound rucksack while starving.

US Army Rules:

1. Curse bitterly when receiving operational order.
2. Make sure there is extra ammo and extra coffee.
3. Curse bitterly.
4. Curse bitterly.
5. Do not listen to 2nd LTs; it can get you killed.
6. Curse bitterly.

Note: Reportedly the US Army is returning to the 'Pinks and Greens' uniforms of WWII fame.

US Air Force Rules:

1. Have a cocktail.
2. Adjust temperature on air-conditioner.
3. See what's on HBO.
4. Ask 'What's a gunfight?'
5. Request more funding from Congress with a 'killer' Power Point presentation.
6. Wine and dine "key' Congressmen, invite DOD and defense industry executives.
7. Receive funding, set up new command and assemble assets.
8. Declare the assets 'strategic' and never deploy them operationally.
9. Hurry to make 13:45 tee-time.

10. Make sure the base is as far as possible from the conflict, but close enough to have tax exemption.
11. Always have ICE CREAM

US Navy Rules:

1. Go to Sea.
2. Drink Coffee
3. Insert SEALS
4. Deploy Marines,
5. Launch Aircraft and Missiles 350 miles away from fighting
6. Drink more Coffee

"SHIT-HOLE" DEPLOYMENTS

Notwithstanding the leftist furor over President Trump's use of this term to describe areas of this planet which barely have Stone Age technology, our brave men and women in uniform keep being sent there [my nephew twice!] to combat the evil and cancer emanating therefrom. Some signs you're being deployed to a 'shithole' are listed below, passed on by a Chief Master Sergeant who finally had enough. Other signs of 'shithole deployment' are inhabitants who revere four-legged critters not only as holy beings but also as acceptable sexual partners, treat women as ranking well below said critters on the respect ladder and desire the world 'return' to the mores and habits of 1300 years ago [except, of course, for the acquisition and use of Rocket-propelled grenades and AK-47's].

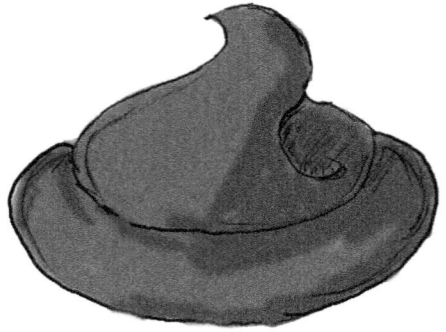

You might be deploying to a "Shit Hole" if...

1. If your CSM/boss tells you to update your Gamma Globulin, Yellow Fever, Malaria, Dysentery, Tetanus and other fun immunizations - You might be deploying to a Shit Hole.

2. If the Mobilization NCO tells you not to waste your time bringing a radio, or any other electronics, as there is no electricity and there are no signals - You might be deploying to a Shit Hole.

3. If the Travel Pay folks give you a travel advance and the Per Diem rate is only $8.00/day, for everything - You might be deploying to a Shit Hole.

4. If the "Area Cultural" briefing is only 30 minutes long, but the briefing on communicable diseases is 3 hours long - You might be deploying to a Shit Hole.

5. If the "Area Cultural" briefing includes facts that some leaders in the host country keep young boys as sexual slaves - You might be deploying to a Shit Hole.

6. If the "Area Cultural" briefing includes facts that male members of that society have multiple wives, but also engage in sexual activity with barnyard animals - You might be deploying to a Shit Hole.

7. If the "Medical Briefing" includes recommendations not to walk barefoot, drink the local water, or eat ANY food from the local economy - You might be deploying to a Shit Hole.

8. If the "Medical Briefing" includes information that the roadside ditches not only serve as flood control, but also as a common latrine - You might be deploying to a Shit Hole.

9. If the Daily Report for your new assignment includes an area for "Number of Personnel Med-Evaced" from theater for unknown diseases - You might be deploying to a Shit Hole.

10. If the monetary exchange rate is greater than 50 to 1 for local currency to US Dollars - You might be deploying to a Shit Hole.

"In spite of the opinions of certain narrow-minded people who would shut up the human race upon this globe, we shall one day travel to the moon, the planets and the stars with the same facility, rapidity, and certainty as we now make the ocean voyage from Liverpool to New York."
- Jules Verne   Early 'Science Fiction' author, 1865
[Many of his 'wildest ideas' are now reality. - Ed.]

Communist Bulgaria 1946 – 1990.

SHOT DOWN BY A W-2

The setting was the O'Club at Kadena AB ... circa late 60's or early 70's. The participants were an SR-71 crew, a Captain and Co-pilot from Continental, and two young schoolteachers for the US Government schools in Okinawa (actually, the last two should be called 'targets of opportunity').

Ain't no way to say it nicely; but 'Round Eyes' were a hot commodity in those days, especially unmarried ones. Our two young ladies were enjoying the unabashed and total focus of the four gentlemen sitting at the two tables on either side of them. 'Fight on'!

Since it was a 'Dirty Shirt' bar, our two young studs were in flight suits, hepped up a little from their latest 'overflight' mission; fearless and bullet proof - they surveyed the opposition and knew they were already in the saddle or soon would be No real threat on the scope.

The Captain, while still handsome, was a bit long in tooth, a former Spad driver he was; his co-pilot was of the jet age, having flown 'Scooters' on little boats, until opting for the 'Good Life' that the airlines promised. Our two young damsels were almost immediately overwhelmed by the two young 'flat bellies' in their form fit flight suits covered with patches. They represented all that was good about virile, young, American manhood. They were in awe.

Even though the good Captain had bought their drinks, it was obvious our two SR types had the upper hand. One of the young ladies, looking at a patch on the shoulder of one of the two studs, asked what it meant. The patch was red (compliments green, Air Force guys know about such things). In the middle was the word 'Habu' and just above it was a sinister looking snake. Above it was written "Lockheed Super Bird SR-71". Just below that was "MACH 3 +" and just below that was written "80,000 +".

'Studley Do-right'; knew it was time for the kill; he told the young ladies that 'Habu' was the nickname of the airplane he flew; since they were new on the island, they weren't familiar with the notorious venomous snake that lived in the jungles surrounding them. At this point the prettier of the two sweet young things asked, 'What does match three mean'? Our steely eyed young buck knew it was all over but the shouting, loud enough for most of the club to hear. He firmly, but politely corrected her mispronunciation and explained that Mach was a technical word that stood for the speed of sound... 'Mach 3+ means I've flown over 3 times the speed of sound' and in a moment of sheer brilliance, he looks at the two airline types and says to the Captain, 'Hey old man, you ever been above Mach 3'? In a humble mumble... the good Captain acknowledged he had not.

Studley knew her next question, and before she could even ask, he went on to explain that the 80,000+ stood for flying above 80,000 feet. And then Studley went too far; in a final move intended to seal the deal, Studley, erect and steely eyed, looked at our humble Captain and said what he should not have said; 'Ever been above 80,000 old man'?

Our humble Captain looked at Studley; then ignoring his protagonist, he cracked a half smile, stared at the two young sweet things, looking for signs of understanding for what he was about to say. He then very calmly and eloquently said, "Only on my W-2 form, Hotshot, only on my W-2!"

Studley had no idea he'd just been smoked! He had no idea; that the other gender, no matter what degree of blondness, or air filling of head, wouldn't know Mach from match but they all knew what a W-2 was; it was a 'woman thing'; it was innate. It was in their bones; and shortly it was over. Our good Captain then said, 'Why don't you ladies join us for dinner'? An agreement was quick in coming and as they left for parts unknown, Studley sat there stunned, having no idea what went wrong.

As Corkey was fond of saying, 'The genies of fate had just urinated on the best intentions of a young man'. A simple government form, had just trumped the fastest and highest flyer in the world. Ain't life a bitch?

"To most people, the sky is the limit. To those who love aviation, the sky is home."
- Jerry Crawford

"The sky is not the limit, the ground is."
-Captainette Christine Wolff

Prussia Balloon Pilot.

SIX TYPES OF MAJORS ONE MEETS IN THE MILITARY

Okay, those who have been there will recognize those detailed here only because they've been there and know about those who are assigned here, or there, or where-ever. In the civilian world these people can also be found out easily pretty much by the sole fact they have to wear a tie to work every day.

An O-4 is a strange military bird. Majors are no longer "one of the boys." They're middle management. They're the adult supervision. Making major is like going from single-A baseball to AAA. It's kind of a big deal, but you're still not in the major leagues just yet. Making captain requires a pulse; making major requires a functional cerebellum. It's the stage when officers either stall out and crash, career-wise, or set themselves up for reaching the next level. Because of this, it doesn't necessarily make once normal individuals into lobotomized morons, but it often reveals the moron inside. Promotion to major breaks up the once mighty pack of company-grade officer peers into several distinct breeds, each with unique characteristics. Here's Task & Purpose's illustrated guide to the six types of majors you find across the military.

The Superstar

As much as everyone hates majors, we must admit that some of them actually know some things. The Superstar knows *everything*. What's worse, he *knows* he knows everything. He's the one guy who did Top Gun or WTI or Ranger School or flew the space shuttle, and everyone knows he deserved it. Everyone hates that SOB anyway, but they also feel guilty for hating him, because they realize he actually deserves his good fortune. It'd almost be better if he sucked. That way everyone could hate him without feeling guilty about it.

The Superstar's path is not necessarily for everyone. Most people aren't willing to take multiple deployments, do all the right schools, go to the Pentagon, and then shuffle back to the operating forces again. But as with the Stations of the Cross, the Superstar knows he must pass through all that suffering for the greater good. After suffering through the staff jobs, one day he will ascend to heaven with an office in the E-ring, probably while Handel's "Hallelujah Chorus" sounds in the background. Yeah, screw that guy.

The Company Man

The Company Man believes that if he does everything right; he still might make it to the top. He does all the field-grade duties, from filling any white space in a schedule with "hip-pocket" PME to speaking...his....punctuation, period (speaking one's punctuation aloud being an early side effect of frontal lobotomies). However, *comma*, he's not a natural like the Superstar (period). The Superstar can be hard on people because everyone knows he's awesome. The Company Man is hard on his people, especially about rules and procedures, but his people often can't stand it because his chief talent is knowing the rules.

The Company Man is a Xerox of the Superstar. At first glance it looks like he has his act together — and he does, on paper, at least. But it's a flat copy of the original. Something is just slightly off. It's the uncanny valley of military excellence. He will most likely succeed, though; for if nothing else, the military loves people who follow rules. While many of his contemporaries' crash and burn with their sundry improprieties, the Company Man walks the righteous path.

The Burnout

The burnout isn't truly a case of DGAF because he actually does give a f**k, but he wants other people to give that f**k for him. He has brought the mission order to a whole new level: "I don't give a f**k what you do. I just don't want the colonel yelling at me. If he yells at me, I yell at you, understand? Now get started, it's almost 1400 and for some reason I'm still here."

The burnout's energy level makes Jabba the Hut look like Richard Simmons. That's because he's tired. He's deployed so much that his kids think they have an uncle named Jody. He knows he can't keep going like this. He's got to turn himself around and become a Company Man or something, or else he'll become The Passed Over For Promotion.

The Passed-Over for Promotion

The Passed-Over may be the way he is for any number of reasons. Maybe he's a former Superstar who crashed and burned. Maybe he was a Burnout who never recovered. Maybe he was a talented officer who didn't know how to play the game. Or maybe he just sucked all along.

Nevertheless, assuming he's reached sanctuary and has his retirement locked up, he's reached a nirvana few officers ever truly reach actually, truly running out of shits to give. The military may be screwing him, but he's taking advantage of his dire straits so he can lay back and enjoy it. They won't send him back to a line unit. If he plays his cards right, he can get that choice gig working for the base or something and joining the ranks of the "in by 09-ish, PT at 1100, out by…eh…1500-ish, give or take an hour."

Sure, his pride took a hit in the shorts when he read the promotion list and didn't find his name on it. But since then, the liberation from giving a shit has been, well, liberating. The first time it happened, it kind of sucked to have his former subordinates calling him by first name, but now he's realized that being the military's version of Van Wilder suits him. The senior NCOs, the lieutenants, the captains, and even his commanding officer ask for his opinion all the time now. Not giving a shit is his superpower. He sometimes wonders whether, if he had stopped giving a shit much earlier, things might have been better.

The Mustang, aka Methuselah

The Mustang has more Good Cookies (Good Conduct Medals) than a box of Chips Ahoy, and he's an officer. He has campaign medals no one even recognizes. Where the hell is Kosovo, or for that matter "Southwest Asia," anyway? The junior enlisted troops love the Mustang. They think it's cool as hell that someone went from enlisted to officer. The senior enlisted troops are not nearly as enamored, because the Mustang doesn't fall for their bullshit. "It doesn't take all day to do that, gunny. If you need time off, how about you just freakin' say it?"

The Mustang is not, objectively speaking, that much older than his contemporaries. But whatever happened during those seven or eight extra years of enlisted service, it sure looks like it got to him. As they say, "It's not the years, it's the mileage." Apparently, the Mustang hasn't just been around the block, he's been around the planet. Twice.

The Weirdo

The Weirdo was just a little bit off when she was a captain. Sure, she liked video games more than most, and for some reason she attended renaissance fairs in full costume, but she wasn't that bad. She was a strange deployment roommate, but other than the whole ordering-drinks-with-umbrellas thing, she was an okay person.

No one was surprised when she earned a prestigious fellowship to study an obscure field that none of her former colleagues could name, much less understand. She disappeared for five years and came back... well, not *that* different from before, but different enough.

Before she went away for her fellowship, advanced degree, or sabbatical, her weirdness was okay, because she was as tactically proficient as her peers. Now, though, even the lieutenants know more about the weapon systems and her unit operations. And one of those lieutenants also wants to stab the Weirdo in the eye because she kicked back the training schedule twice for corrections because it didn't use "Lean 6-Sigma" principles and show awareness of the "theory of constraints," whatever the hell those are.

Spock: "Captain, during our visit to Planet 'Terra Incognita' a few parsecs ago, I came across a curious ancient artifact which, surprisingly, is quite useful. I have determined it can, with proper data inputs, perform calculations within the time - space continuum of dilithium consumption, distance over time calculations appropriate even to parameters of the Enterprises capabilities, speed estimations up to Warp 7 and even these can be adjusted for the solar winds extant in this quadrant of the galaxy. The race of humanoids on that planet must have been quite adept and skilled at three-dimensional travel, which is quite illogical, considering everything else we've learned about their rudimentary civilization."

Kirk: "No shit?"

SOUTHERNERS ARE SO POLITE

I have family in the Deep South of the USA, locally known as "L.A." = Lower Alabama. As a matter of fact, the hometown airport is just a few miles – or for you Army helicopter pilots, a half-days flight – west of Fort Rucker. The airport café at Andalusia, Alabama - South Alabama Regional Airport [79J] - holds the distinction for the best airport ribs for miles around [every Friday, BTW ... and fried catfish on Thursdays] and good fuel prices if you're going to/from Sun-and-Fun down Florida way every Spring. We like to meet for breakfast [0730], watch the crew bus from 'Mother Rucker' pull up, all the helicopters fly in to refuel hot and then watch ... from a distance, mind you ... the antics of those trying to learn the flight characteristics of helicopters [Clue: Helicopters don't fly, they just beat the air into submission – sometimes the air wins.]

But no matter what, Southern genteel civility abounds as evidenced by this tower transmission from Atlanta [KATL] tower:

Atlanta Tower: "Saudi Air 511 -- You are cleared to land on runway 9R."

Saudi Air: "Thank you, Atlanta. Acknowledge cleared to land on runway 9 Right. Allah be praised."

Atlanta Tower: "Iran Air 711 - You are cleared to land on runway 27L."

Iran Air: "Cleared to land on runway 27 Left - Allah is Great."

Pause....

Saudi Air: "ATLANTA TOWER - ATLANTA TOWER!"

Atlanta Tower: "Go ahead Saudi Air 511"

Saudi Air: "YOU HAVE CLEARED BOTH OUR AIRCRAFTS FOR THE SAME RUNWAY GOING IN OPPOSITE DIRECTIONS. WE ARE ON A COLLISION COURSE . . . . . INSTRUCTIONS, PLEASE!"

Atlanta Tower: "Well, bless your lil' ol' hearts, and praise Jesus. Y'all come ahead and tell Allah 'hey' for us now, y'heah?"

"It is not necessarily impossible for human beings to fly, but it so happens that God did not give them the knowledge of how to do it. It follows, therefore, that anyone who claims that he can fly must have sought the aid of the devil. To attempt to fly therefore is sinful.
 - Roger Bacon, 13th century Franciscan friar

THANKSGIVING ON THE 'HIGH LINE'

I got to Colorado too late to be a part of Frontier Airlines – the "Old Frontier" as it is lovingly referred to by those whose careers took them around the Rocky Mountain west in Convair 580's, DC-3's, and other relics from the days when an ADF was the most sophisticated navigational equipment on board [Do you remember, let alone recall how to use them?] and in between approaches you could listen to the local farm and ranch reports, weather rumors, news, gossip and, of course, BOTH kinds of music [country AND western – natch!]

A little over fifty years ago Frontier Airlines (the original Frontier Airlines) ran an air service for some small towns in Montana and the Dakotas they called it the "High Line". The "High Line" was based in Great Falls, Montana. Every morning two airplanes took off from Great Falls and flew east. One made stops in Havre, Glasgow, Wolf Point, Williston, and Minot. The second airplane flew a more southern route from Great Falls to Lewistown, Billings, Miles City, Glendive, Sidney, and Williston. When the airplanes reached the eastern terminus they turned around and retraced their route back to Great Falls. It was full days flying by the time the planes were back in Great Falls. Frontier flew it for years with their dependable old DC-3s.

This was the days of the CAB (Civil Aeronautics Board) who dictated where and how often an airline would fly serving large and small communities across the nation. As the loads dwindled and the DC-3 got more expensive to maintain and operate Frontier decided to replace them with a couple of De Havilland's new DHC-6 Twin Otters. Down in Southern California a small operator Golden West Airlines was just getting started. They were a recent amalgamation of four airlines Aero Commuter, Golden West Airlines, Cable Commuter, and Skymark Airlines operating under the name Golden West Airlines. Golden West was the biggest Twin Otter operator in the country at that time and not all the aircraft were needed to operate the Golden West schedules. In the fall of 1970 they contracted with Frontier Airlines to operate the "High Line" until Frontier could get their new aircraft on line and their crews trained.

So Thanksgiving Day 1970 found my copilot and myself flying east in the morning headed eventually for Minot with several intervening stops. There was a great guy in Glasgow that managed the airport, operated a small fixed base, and was contracted by Frontier to handle the P-M-X. P-M-X being passengers, mail, and express (cargo). The fellow's name was Vick; I don't know that I ever knew his last name. He had eked out a living in aviation up in that part of the country for many years. I'm talking biplanes on skis and radial engine Stinson's. I liked Vick and his family all of whom helped him operate the airport. I remember his son was there and he the son had a new baby. I always tried to manage my fuel so I could buy fuel from Vick.

As we departed Glasgow on the east bound leg Thanksgiving morning, I jokingly said to Vick something like "we'll see you for dinner" and didn't give it another thought. In Minot at the end of the east bound run a passenger that owned a hotel insisted that we ride into town and have lunch at the hotel, which it turned out he bought.

West bound again the weather deteriorated and the wind was on the nose of the airplane about 40 knots. The Otter cruised about 150 knots true air speed, so we were only making around 110 knots over the ground. By the time we made approaches at Williston and Wolf Point we were running late. By the time we pulled into Glasgow we were well behind schedule. It was dark and snowing pretty good. The ramp was sloppy with slush that was trying to freeze. We got the paperwork finished and quickly loaded the passengers and got the plane closed. I was looking out into the dark in front of the airplane for Vick to give me the hand signal that it was clear to start the engines. When there was a knock on the cockpit door, the twin Otter had an exterior door on either side of the cockpit for the crew to use to climb in and out of the airplane. When I looked out I could see Vick standing just below the door with what appeared to be a package in his hands.

I opened the door and Vick handed up a brown paper grocery bag and said something about Thanksgiving dinner. We, me and the copilot said thanks and set it on the floor between us. We got the engines started and took off for Great Falls by way of Havre. We climbed up high enough to be sure the ice wasn't sticking to the airplane and took the bag off the floor to get the sandwiches or whatever was in the bag Vick gave us.

I think of that Thanksgiving every year at this time and of Vick and his family his kids and grandkids. You see in that brown paper bag was two complete Thanksgiving turkey dinners. Not just a couple of slices of turkey but two complete dinners right down to china plates and silverware, dressing, cranberry sauce, mashed potatoes with gravy, two slices of pumpkin pie, two cokes, and two drumsticks. We both sat there just a bit this side of nirvana munching on those two dinners in the quiet solitude of the De Havilland's cockpit having Thanksgiving dinner on the High Line.

Hope you all had a great Thanksgiving!

Fred Austin
Golden Age Aeroplanes

I sent this to a good friend who's first assignment when he joined "The Old Frontier" – after flying Twin Otters at Rocky Mountain Airways [also now defunct] – was The High Line out of Great Falls, Montana ["We called it 'Alcohol Falls'"]. He said since he was a new captain, he would be a 'by-the-book' kind of guy, so one day a few miles out of Great Falls he asked his copilot to call for a 'runway condition report'. There was a few moments of silence on the other end of the frequency, then a succinct and telling reply: "Well, the runway was asphalt the last time we saw it, but that was back in September. It's been covered with ice and snow since then [it was February] so you're on your own."

"There I was out of altitude, airspeed, and ideas all at once and in fog so thick I couldn't see the instruments. The only way I knew I was inverted was my air medals were in my eyes. But I knew I was in real trouble when the tower called and told me to climb to field elevation."

Manchukuo Pilot - 1932 - 1945 as Japanese 'Protectorate'.

THE FIVE TYPES OF AIRLINE PILOTS

So, which type did you fly with today? On the other hand, which one are YOU? The following was sent to me by a flight attendant who, having put in over 16 years in the rear cabin, has unique and telling views on who/what walks/struts/slithers onto the flight deck of the airliner she happen to be working that day. Do keep in mind this was written with more humor in mind than an actual condemnation of pilot types, for once the cockpit door closes and the engines are started, there is nothing but professionalism coursing throughout the 'front office'. She has reminded me, however, of the difference between a jet engine and a pilot; that being the engine stops whining once the flight is over.

The Military "Type A" Personality

This flight deck officer stands at full brace even when 'at ease,' always maintains a stern countenance and is only 'comfortable' when in command and issuing orders. If not a captain, he/she will upgrade at very first chance, often bypassing a quality line sitting in the right seat so he/she can sit in the left seat. If the company mandates the wearing of hats*, you can bet this person's cap is on low and tight, exactly per regs. Almost certainly carrying a firearm, it is always within easy reach and they are instantly ready and mentally prepared to defend their aircraft. You could cut glass with the crease in their uniform shirt and, rumor has it there is a reward offered if you ever catch them smiling. They will often complain about having to wear a uniform instead of a flight suit.

Standard briefing: 15-minute detailed monologue encompassing every foreseeable aspect of the flight with emphasis on company SOP's.

Flight Bag: Covered with military squadron and union stickers. If flying a wide-body jet, they may also display equipment stickers [e.g.: B-767, B-747]

The Casual "Type B" Personality

This pilot is out of shape, the last calisthenics having been performed the night before at the hotel bar repeatedly raising 12 ounces of adult beverage to their lips. Usually their 'beer belly' is found hanging over their baggy uniform pants, the sole saving grace is that a tattered belt holding them up could be located only after a diligent search [you're on your own there]. Their uniform shirt is wrinkled, half untucked and graced by a coffee stain obtained during the Day 2 breakfast of a 4-day trip. This person may, or may not, be wearing regulation white socks under their scuffed black regulation shoes. This person is always looking for 'snacks', usually nabbed from the FO's snack basket without asking.

Standard briefing: "Coffee, 3 creams, 5 sugars."

Flight Bag: Falling apart, usually decorated with Harley-Davidson stickers.

The 'Dude'

This mellow guy is one of the favorites, thinking nothing of reporting for duty without a hat*, no matter how crazy this makes the Military Type A Pilot. He's less concerned with following rules & regulations than he is with making work 'fun'. He is vigilant about what matters [safety] and 'chill' about everything else. This person is in the industry for one thing and one thing only - time off - which he usually spends chasing "bitchin' waves" around the globe. They usually take off the entire months of July and February to ski and/or surf in Tahoe and/or Chile during their respective summers or winters.

> **Standard Briefing:** "We're all in this together; just let me know what I can do to make your job easier."
>
> **Flight Bag:** Stickers from everywhere he's been that was 'cool', from the Maldives to Nepal.

The 'Disappearer'

This recluse shuts himself up in the cockpit at the first opportunity; not one for small talk, tis person has neither time nor inclination for acknowledging needs of fellow crew. One could hypothesize he/she has been burned in a relationship with a fellow crewperson; but for this theory to be proven true one must make the assumption they were once NOT like the Disappearer enough to actually talk to a fellow crewperson. One never hears the proverbial peep from them; they never ask for anything, ever, even for a bathroom break during a Transcon. After the flight, they are off the airplane and halfway up the jetway before the first passenger has a chance to deplane.

Standard Briefing: "Everything standard."

Flight Bag: No-one has ever seen it, except as a blur up the jetway.

The 'Tekkie' Nerd

Long before 'smart phones', there were 'smart watches'. They were huge and could calculate arrival times down to fractions of a nanosecond, predict the weather at one's destination half a world away, order a particular crew meal three days in advance and monitor where their spouse/significant other was at any particular time. All the 'cool' pilots had one, or so the Nerd thought; these are the pilots who really do use pocket protectors and use the watch during layovers to calculate down to the penny/farthing/centavo/pfennig the share of each crewperson for the meals and/or drinks [stiffing the servers, of course]. Need a quote, let alone company interpretation of FAR 121.24 (b)3.1.2(d)? This is your go-to guy; if he's having an off day and cannot recall the exact verbiage, no worries! There's an app on the watch immediately available to look it up.

> **Standard Briefing:** Doesn't matter, no-one is going to get through one without glazing over.
>
> **Flight Bag:** Standard issue, unadorned. Full of protractors, mechanical pencils, spare batteries and a roll of duct tape.

THE RIGHT CAP

This was sent to me by a buddy from the Southeast Asia War Games. He swears the story is true. Knowing his predilection for practical and impractical joking around, I submit this with a rather hefty shaker of sodium chloride [salt, for those of you ... ahhh ... chemically impaired]. As most of the original cast of that production is now retired, I pass this along as something to do when boredom overcomes the inclination to play the same nine holes again.

Have fun ... and wear the right cap [heh heh heh].

Yesterday, I wore my Vietnam Veteran cap to Wal-Mart. There was nothing in particular that I needed at the world's largest retailer, but since I'm retired trips to "Wally World" to look at the 'Walmartians' * is always good for some entertainment and comic relief. Besides, I always feel normal after seeing some of the people that frequent the establishment. But I digress - enough of my psychological fixations ...

While standing in line to check out, the guy in front of me, probably in his early thirties, asked, "Are you a Viet Nam Vet?"

"No," I replied.

"Then why are you wearing that cap?"

"Because I couldn't find the one from the War of 1812."

I thought it was a snappy retort.

"The War of 1812, huh?" the Walmartian queried, "When was that?"

God forgive me, but I couldn't pass up such an opportunity; "1946"

I answered as straight-faced as possible.

He pondered my response for a moment and responded, "Why do they call it the War of 1812 if it was in 1946?"

"It was a Black Ops Mission. No one is supposed to know about it."

This was beginning to become fun!

"Dude! Really?" He exclaimed. "How did you get to do something that COOOOL?"

I glanced furtively around, leaned toward the guy and in a low voice said, "I'm not sure. I was the only Caucasian on the mission."

"Dude," he was really getting excited about what he was hearing, "That is seriously awesome! But, didn't you kind of stand out?"

"Not really. The other guys were wearing white camouflage."

The moron nodded knowingly.

"Listen man," I said in a very serious tone, "You can't tell anyone about this. It's still classified 'Top Secret' and I shouldn't have said anything."

"Oh yeah?" he gave me the 'don't threaten me look.'

"Like, what's gonna' happen if I do?"

With a really hard look I said, "You have a family, don't you? WE wouldn't want ANYTHING to happen to them, WOULD we?"

The guy gulped, left his basket where it was and fled through the door.

The lady behind me started laughing so hard I thought she was about to have a heart attack. I just grinned at her. After checking out and going to the parking lot, I saw dimwit leaning in a car window talking to a young woman.

Upon catching sight of me, he started pointing excitedly in my direction.

Giving him another 'deadly' serious look, I made the 'I see you' gesture.

He turned kind of pale, jumped in the car and sped out of the parking lot.

And these people VOTE! AND have children! OMG!!!

I had a <u>great</u> time! Tomorrow I'm going back, wearing my Homeland Security cap. Then the next day I will go to the driver's license bureau wearing my Border Patrol hat and see how long it takes to empty the place.

Whoever said retirement is boring? You just need to wear the right kind of cap!

 See you guys at Walmart!!

---

 * **www.peopleofwalmart.com**   Log in and then be amazed at the range, width and lack of depth of the Walmart community. NOT saying it's the fault of that great business, but – oh, wow!

THE RULES AS PERTAINING TO FLIGHT –
EXCEPT HELICOPTERS

I received these rules courtesy of John Clare-Paton, RAF [retired], one of a handful of foreign pilots seconded to US forces to fly combat during the Southeast Asian War Games [1963-1973], now chief pilot of Peak Aviation at the Colorado Springs, Colorado airfield and aviation playground.

Whenever the 'PILOT' is mentioned it is inferred we are speaking also of the Captain and/or the 'Aircraft Commander' and whenever the 'CO-PILOT' is mentioned we are inferring to that barely sentient body sitting in the right seat awaiting the beck and call [orders] of the Captain and/or the AC. All else remains factual and true.

FAR 91.3 The PILOT IN COMMAND is directly responsible for, and is the final authority as to, the operation of an aircraft.
That means the PIC is the King or Queen of the skies. It also means that no matter what happens, it's all on your shoulders [e.g. "State your name, rank and serial number for the Board of Inquiry"]

- The PILOT always makes the rules.

- The rules are subject to change at any time without prior notification.

- No CO-PILOT can possibly know all the rules.

- If the PILOT suspects the CO-PILOT is getting familiar with the rules, the PILOT must immediately change, alter and/or amend the rules.

- The PILOT is never wrong.

- If it is suspected that the PILOT is/was wrong, it most certainly is due to a misunderstanding which was a direct result of something the CO-PILOT said and/or did or did not do.

- The CO-PILOT must therefore apologize IMMEDIATELY for causing said misunderstanding.

- The PILOT can/will/may change his or her mind at any time.

- The CO-PILOT can/will/may change his or her mind ONLY with the express written consent of the PILOT.

- The PILOT retains every, and all rights to be angry and/or upset at any time for any reason.

- The CO-PILOT must always remain calm unless the PILOT specifically allows him or her to become angry, upset, or panicky.

- The CO-PILOT is always always expected to read the mind of the PILOT.

- The PILOT is ready when he/she is ready.

- The CO-PILOT must always always be ready.

Any attempt to document these rules shall result in bodily harm and/or mental anguish. *

The CO-PILOT who does not abide by the rules - whatever they may be - shall be grounded until displaying the appropriate level of contrite sincerity as to the error of their ways.

Since I - "Captain Emeritus" [otherwise known as 'His Most Exalted Airworthiness'] am no longer, by dint of age, experience, and authority, subject to any or all form of 'the rules', I share them with my loyal subjects as a public service. I am not afraid of any retribution because here, in my high mountain ~~lair, hideout~~, abode I have plenty of food, plenty of booze, plenty of TP, plenty of ammunition and clear fields of fire. So, come get me ... if you dare.

"We have our clearance, Clarence. Roger, Roger. What's our vector, Victor?"
- from the movie <u>AIRPLANE</u>

THE RULES AS PERTAINING TO HELICOPTER FLIGHT

I have flown helicopters under the [extremely] watchful gaze of those individuals properly trained and certificated to gaze watchfully at those attempting vertical ... *ahem* ... 'flight'.

I must admit looking down at the flight instruments to see airspeed at zero, a pinnacle approach and landing, 'hovering' and other such aberrations of 'flight' have a morbid fascination for those of us who grew up thinking "Airspeed is Life: Altitude is Life Insurance." The following was obviously penned by someone with that morbid sense of curiosity who then unfathomably, went to a helicopter school for their first ... and apparently only ... lesson.

Although flying a helicopter may seem very difficult, the truth is that if you can drive a car, you can, with just a few minutes of instruction, take the controls of one of these amazing machines. Of course you would immediately crash and die.

Therefore you need to remember:

RULE ONE OF HELICOPTER PILOTING:

Always have somebody sitting right next to you who actually knows how to fly the helicopter and can snatch the controls away from you. Because the truth is that helicopters are nothing at all like cars. Cars work because of basic scientific principles that everybody understands, such as internal combustion and parallel parking. Whereas scientists still have no idea what holds helicopters up. "Whatever it is, it could stop at any moment," is their current feeling. This leads us to:

RULE TWO OF HELICOPTER PILOTING:

Maybe you should forget the entire thing. This was what I was thinking on a recent Saturday morning as I stood outside a small airport in South Florida, where I was about to take my first helicopter lesson. This was not my idea. This was the idea of Pam Gallina-Raissiguier, a pilot who flies radio reporters over Miami during rush hour so they can alert drivers to traffic problems ("Bob, we have a three-mile backup on the interstate due to an overturned cocaine truck").

Pam is active in an international organization of women helicopter pilots called - Gloria Steinem; avert your eyes - the "Whirly Girls." She thought it would be a great idea for me to take a helicopter lesson. I began having severe doubts when I saw Pam's helicopter. This was a small helicopter. It looked like it should have a little slot where you insert quarters to make it go up and down. I knew that if we got airborne in a helicopter this size in South Florida, some of our larger tropical flying insects could very well attempt to mate with us.

Also, this helicopter had no doors. As a Frequent Flyer, I know for a fact that all your leading U.S. airlines, despite being bankrupt, maintain a strict safety policy of having doors on their aircraft.

"Don't we need a larger helicopter?" I asked Pam. "With doors?"

"Get in," said Pam.

You don't defy a direct order from a Whirly Girl.

Now we're in the helicopter, and Pam is explaining the controls to me over the headset, but there's static and the engine is making a lot of noise.

"... Your throttle (something)," she is saying. "This is your cyclic and (something) your collective."

"What?" I say.

"(something) give you the controls when we reach 500 feet," Pam says.

"WHAT?" I say.

But Pam is not listening. She is moving a control thing and WHOOAAA we are off the ground, hovering, and now WHOOOOAAAAAA we are shooting up in the air, and there are still no doors on this particular helicopter.

Now Pam is giving me the main control thing.

RULE THREE OF HELICOPTER PILOTING:

If anybody tries to give you the main control thing, refuse to take it. Pam says: "You don't need hardly any pressure to . . ." AIEEEEEEEEEEEEEE.......

"That was too much pressure," Pam says.

Now I am flying the helicopter. I AM FLYING THE HELICOPTER. I am flying it by not moving a single body part, for fear of jiggling the control thing. I look like the Lincoln Memorial statue of Abraham Lincoln, only more rigid.

"Make a right turn," Pam is saying.

I gingerly move the control thing one zillionth of an inch to the right and the helicopter LEANS OVER TOWARD MY SIDE AND THERE IS STILL NO DOOR HERE. I instantly move the thing one zillionth of an inch back.

"I'm not turning right," I inform Pam.

"What?" she says.

"Only left turns," I tell her. When you've been flying helicopters as long as I have, you know your limits.

After a while it becomes clear to Pam that if she continues to allow the Lincoln statue to pilot the helicopter, we are going to wind up flying in a straight line until we run out of fuel, possibly over Antarctica so she takes the control thing back. That is the good news. The bad news is, she's now saying something about demonstrating an "emergency procedure."

"It's for when your engine dies," Pam says. "It's called "auto-rotation.' Do you like amusement park rides?"

I say: "No, I DOOOOOONNNNN . . ."

RULE FOUR OF HELICOPTER PILOTING:

"Auto-rotation" means "coming down out of the sky at about the same speed and aerodynamic stability as that of a forklift dropped from a bomber."

Now we're close to the ground (although my stomach is still at 500 feet), and Pam is completing my training by having me hover the helicopter.

RULE FIVE OF HELICOPTER PILOTING:

You can't hover the helicopter. The idea is to hang over one spot on the ground. I am hovering over an area approximately the size of Australia. I am swooping around sideways and backward like a crazed bumblebee. If I were trying to rescue a person from the roof of a 100-story burning building, the person would realize that it would be safer to simply jump. At times I think I am hovering upside-down. Even Pam looks nervous.

So I am very happy when we finally get back on the ground. Pam tells me I did great, and she'd be glad to take me up again. I tell her that sounds like a fun idea.

RULE SIX OF HELICOPTER PILOTING:

Sometimes you must lie.

"I never liked riding in helicopters because there's a fair probability the bottom part will get going around as fast as the top part.
- Lt. Col. John Wittenborn, USAF

TOP 10 REASONS TO FLY AT AURORA AIRPARK

The Aurora Airpark sadly has disappeared into the haze of history and memory ["There used to be an airport here."]. Out on the prairie east of Denver, Colorado one felt like they were driving to western Kansas just to get there; nowadays 'civilization' is edging closer and closer to the remains. At first the flight paths of the old Stapleton International Airport put a damper on available airspace in which to commit aviation. The arrival of Denver International put the kybosh on any remaining operations. The few tenants departed, the old hangars - some indistinguishable from pioneer outbuildings - were torn down and the dilapidated runway now provides straightaways only for jackrabbits practicing their quick starts and getaways. Lest we forget ...

10. You can practice turns around a point avoiding antelope on the runway.

9. While legally flying in the pattern, you can annoy airline flight crews by setting off their TCAS and traffic alert warnings.

8. Complimentary week-old doughnuts always available.

7. The grass runway is maintained by herds of cottontails and antelope.

6. It is a refuge for pilots with A.I.D.S. [Aviation Induced Divorce Syndrome]

5. Free hangar-flying instruction from anyone in attendance. [Endorsements extra]

4. The pilot lounge is always accepting used furniture.

3. It is a place where no airplane is "too ugly to fly".

2. If you forget to follow the FARs and area SOPs, a lady from the trailer park nearby will call and enlighten you.

1. It is the airport your instructor warned you about.

R.I.P. Aurora Airpark, Watkins, Colorado

Shared with the author by 'Captainette' Christine Wolff

THINKING OUTSIDE THE BOX

An interesting treatise of history which ends up in a completely different place than what was envisioned. Just shows that if the answer doesn't jive with the postulates, change the postulates.

During WWII, the Navy tried to determine where they needed to armor their aircraft to ensure they came back home. They ran an analysis of where planes had been shot up, and came up with this.

Obviously the places that needed to be up-armored are the wingtips, the central body, and the elevators. That's where the planes \vere all getting shot up.

Abraham Wald, a statistician, disagreed. He thought they should better armor the nose area, engines, and mid-body. Which was crazy, of course. That's not where the planes were getting shot.

Except Mr. Wald realized what the others didn't. The planes were getting shot there too, but they weren't making it home. What the Navy thought it had done was analyze where aircraft were suffering the most damage. What they had actually done was analyze where aircraft could suffer the most damage \vithout catastrophic failure. All of the places that weren't hit? Those planes had been shot there and crashed. They weren't looking at the whole sample set, only the survivors.

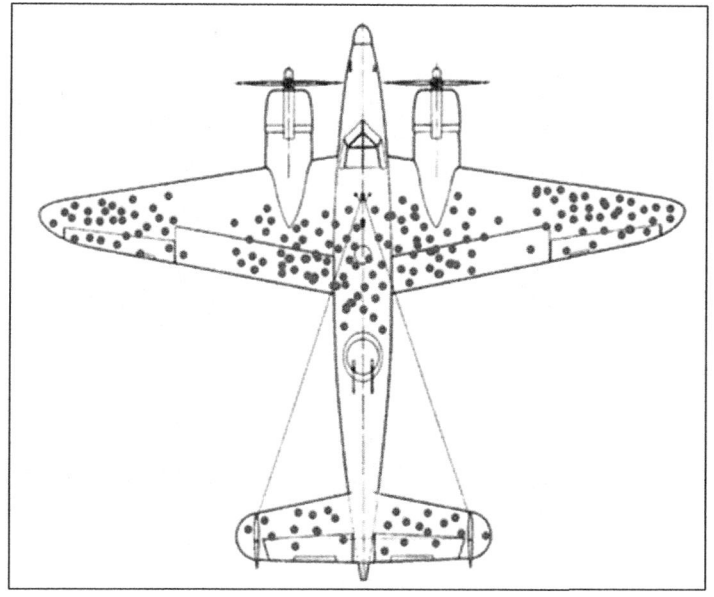

TO ALL CO-PILOTS

I found this note to co-pilots somewhere in my deep, dark, dank, damp, dismal, and distant past. Written by the Operations Manager [one Jerry Marshall] of the Southern Division of American Airways, Inc. on October 25, 1930 (!) it details the duties, responsibilities and mindset expected of all co-pilots of that time. Recall the airlines of the day were flying loud, noisy, unpressurized airplanes such as the Ford Trimotor, cabin biplanes [DeHaviland Rapides] and DC-2's. The authority of the 'First Pilot' [Captain] most likely had yet to be formalized as such [such as found in current FAR 91.3], yet was regarded by all such as the Captain of a sailing vessel - when out of port the Captain was God. There must have been some event(s) which prompted this letter - unknown now in the mists of distant past - however the words in this letter live on. Heed them well, ye co-pilots/first officers/right-seaters! For the truth lies with them.

To: All Co-pilots

October 25, 1930

Every man in an organization has a certain part to play and duty to perform. To the First Pilot is delegated the responsibility of flying the ship; the service crew has the responsibility of keeping the ship in safe flying condition; the traffic department has the responsibility of supplying the passengers, and the operations department has the responsibility of ordering the ships in and out and making certain that everyone in the operations department performs his duty.

Even with all this division of authority into the above-named competent departments, there are still many SMALL CHORES which have been left undone, and for this reason and none other, there has been created in the aviation industry a demand for THE CO-PILOT. There are now fourteen co-pilots in the Southern division of American Airways, Inc. whose flying times range from 400 hours to 2,500 hours.

Regardless of how much flying time a co-pilot has, it is necessary that all co-pilots be regarded alike by their superiors, which is THE FIRST PILOT. Your job is to do the many things which other employees do not wish to do. Your immediate superior is the FIRST PILOT; his wants are your orders - he is the King - you are his faithful and alert servant. You are on probation always; your working hours are from now on and your pay is small. Your advancement is uncertain and there are thousands of other First Pilot aspirants striving to get your job at even less money and more work. You are not employed because of your flying ability; your employment is not assurance of having a run of your own as First Pilot.

The pilot with whom you now have the privilege of flying largely controls your destiny. If you handle the many details assigned you, many of which may be unpleasant, and if you prove to be of value to him and to others, you may assume you will have the privilege of remaining as his co-pilot for some years to come, at which time you will have learned much from your association and flying experiences with him; and you will have won for yourself recognition by the company and all, as a gentleman and as an experienced co-pilot worthy of promotion.

You were not employed to do the flying, not only because you are not considered capable but because far better pilots, the finest in the world, have been employed for that work and if you are permitted to take the controls at any time you may consider this a special favor on the part of the First Pilot. A co-pilot who does his job well, makes very little noise and listens attentively to his superiors will in time receive recognition for his services.

As co-pilot, there is something which really is worth working for and which can be attained, but first IT MUST BE EARNED. As long as you do your work well and conduct yourself strictly as a co-pilot, this company will regard you really as an important member of this organization and you will find many very good friends among those with which you are working. You are going to be asked to perform personal favors for older pilots but always keep in mind that these same older pilots are at some time later going to be in a position to do many and greater favors for you.

If you know yourself to have an excess of pride, swallow it; if you have personal faults, overcome them: always make a neat and pleasant impression on your passengers and upon those with whom you work and live.

I am trusting you will become successful in your enterprise of becoming A GOOD CO-PILOT.

Sincerely yours,

JERRY MARSHALL
OPERATIONS MANAGER
CC - All pilots

UAL TO STOP HIRING NAVY & MARINE CORP PILOTS

Go to www.Youtube.com; enter 'Naval Aviation', 'Aircraft Carrier Landings' or something along those lines. Then sit back and peruse [fancy word alert! Look it up] the way Navy planes conduct 'controlled crashes' on aircraft carrier decks. Once thoroughly amazed, look up the same subject but add the word 'night' to the search. 'Flabbergasted' [another fancy word] and 'flabbergastation' will ensue: Throughout this you might see where the 'landing area' [aircraft carrier deck] is not only pitching up and down 60 feet or more but also rolling an inordinate number of degrees. If that weren't enough, the entire ship might then also be heaving [rising and descending enmasse] as the ship plows through rough seas. Got to admit, the men and women who land on carriers under any and all adverse conditions are the best in the world ... unfortunately that skill doesn't transfer well to civilian operations -

CHICAGO, IL.

New airplane liveries aren't the only change coming to United Airlines. Amid a vast airline pilot shortage, United Airlines spokeswoman Janine Davidson announced earlier today that the airline is considering not offering new pilot positions to former Navy and Marine Aviators. This comes in the wake of last week's incident involving United Flight 2921 from Orlando to Milwaukee that left two passengers hospitalized and dozens of others stunned. The United Airlines Boeing 737 was piloted by two former Naval Aviators—an F/A-18C and E-2D pilot.

"The plane came down so hard, I soiled myself," reported passenger Dale Gordons of Lake Okeechobee, FL. United Flight Attendant Stacie Sommers, working aboard Flt 2921, recounts: "There was a 29-year-old college student in 12B who was crying hysterically. I went over to help and noticed that his comfort gerbil was crushed under the weight of the obese man next to him when the plane touched down. The other flight attendant rushed to the flight deck to see what happened and as the door opened, the pilots were high-fiving and making 'one-wire' jokes."

United Airlines Chief Pilot, Jack McCann, understands that Naval Aviators fly jets that regularly touch down in excess of 800 feet per minute aboard their aircraft carriers. "These rates of descent are just too hard on our passengers and too hard on our planes. We try to train these tendencies out of them, but it's a culture thing. They're brainwashed and it's hard to teach old dogs new tricks."

This seems to be the final straw to break the camel's back at United. Last month, United Airlines maintenance workers filed a formal grievance against seven pilots, all former Naval Aviators, who were caught opening panels and pre-flight inspecting their airplanes before their flights. "It's a clear gesture of distrust," stated United Airlines Aircraft Mechanic Jason Dant. Passengers are also becoming worried about safety practices when they see pilots clambering over their airplanes and inspecting them. Shannon Kelsey, of Laguna Beach, CA doesn't feel comfortable seeing airline pilots concerned over the plane's status. "It's like seeing the barista at Starbucks sip your drink before serving it to you to make sure it's actually a Java Frappuccino with vegan almond milk. It makes me uncomfortable and a little offended."

Former Marine Aviator Mike Highway just wants to make sure his aircraft is safe. "I'm not sure what these freakin' snowflakes are whining about. How would you like to fly in a plane that's probably been inspected by some 12-year-old that just graduated from Embry Riddle, makes $9 an hour and lives with his mom? I'm not signing for that s**t without double checking it. I didn't do it in the Fleet, and I ain't doing that s**t now."

As far as recruiting former military aviators, Davidson says she is encouraging more Air Force pilots to apply. "Former Air Force pilots have been shown to gently guide their aircraft through the sky and squeak it on. They use the autoland flight control assistance capabilities on our planes more regularly, but always when they haven't yet finished their in-flight meals. They aren't accustomed to performing hard carrier landings so cost our company fewer medical expenses in treatment of varicose veins and hemorrhoids.

"Air Force pilots also don't perform pre-flight inspections and tend to be more team-oriented. We prefer a trusting relationship between members of the United Airlines Team and show our valued passengers that our pilots are just as comfortable boarding alongside them from the airport jetways."

Fleet Aviation Gazette is awaiting comment from the Pilot's Union currently.

"We do not consider that aeroplanes will be of any possible use for war purposes."
- British Secretary of War, 1910

"Aeroplanes are interesting toys but of no military value."
- Marshall Ferdinand Foch, French War College, 1911

URBAN LEGEND... OR?

An investigation into the veracity of this story indicates it is either urban legend or was produced under the category of 'Satire'. In either case it creates a picture in the mind of the reader "Man, wish I could do that to ..." [Washington, DC immediately comes to mind]. Notwithstanding the many FAR infractions, the civil laws broken and other such violation(s) of miscellaneous and sundry regulations, I'll wager next years' flower beds and vegetable gardens in that city will produce a bumper crop.

SHIT FALLS FROM THE SKY OVER CLORADO TOWN

DRUNK CROPDUSTER PILOT SPREADS 4 TONS OF LIQUID MANURE ON CITY!

Watkins, Colorado (Courtesy of the Denver Post)

A local agricultural airplane pilot made a serious mistake this afternoon while operating his airplane under the influence of alcohol, 'accidentally' dumping several tons of liquid manure over cars, houses, and residents. According to police, 67-year-old Tom Burlace had a blood alcohol concentration (BAC) of 0.48% when arrested. This is six times the legal limit allowed to drive a motor vehicle and 12 times the legal limit allowed to operate a plane.

 He was supposed to spread his cargo over fields belonging to Burt Eaton, a local 'gentleman farmer' and businessman, but his capacities were just too impaired. Reports from the scene indicate he was so drunk he had urinated on himself and couldn't stand up when deputies arrived minutes after he landed. It seems he made his approach to the correct field just east of town but turned the wrong way, heading over the city before dropping his smelly load.

Residents of this farming and ranching town were taken off guard as tons of liquid manure began raining down on the city causing several car accidents and entirely ruining an outdoor wedding ceremony. Adams County Sheriff's Office spokesperson, Lt. Spencer Mamber, says the 911 emergency call center had over 350 calls and was entirely jammed for at least one-half hour. Dennis Koontz, a retired airline captain and his wife Celeste witnessed the entire event, commenting: "Everyone was freaking out, what with all that shit falling from the skies. We were fearful of a biological attack by Islamic terrorists; either them or the Democrats."

"We're a small community," said Ms. Christine Wolff, a well-known local 'personality', "We all knew Tom drank but he could do some amazing things with that airplane. He could really put on a show. We've just never seen him fly so loaded before."

Mr. Burlace, it is estimated, will now face a total of 269 criminal and civil charges including unauthorized dispersal of effluent, aggravated assault, and damage to property. In addition the FAA is still counting the number of 'infractions' Mr. Burlace committed. Mr. Brian Richardson, a senior inspector with the FAA, said "I don't mean to be flippant, but he's facing a shit-load of charges."

If found guilty, Mr. Burlace faces a total of 1,250 years in prison, a fine of $2,350,217.59, and restitution of an undetermined amount. His pilot certificate will likely be revoked for flying under the influence of alcohol, careless and reckless operation of an airplane and other and sundry Federal Air Regulation violations.

His trial is scheduled for June third at the Adams County courthouse.

"There will be those who will pressure you into doing things that may be unsafe. Use your good judgement and tell them "I would rather be laughed at than cried over."
- George MacDonald

WHAT WE HAVE HERE... IS FAILURE TO COMMUNICATE

That very famous line came from a movie released in 1967 titled 'Cool Hand Luke' starring Paul Newman; he starred as a societal rebel convicted of misdemeanors and sentenced to a work camp in the Deep South. He was constantly bucking the system and attracting the negative attention of the authorities, concluding with his ultimate demise.

The point I wish to make herein is particularly addressed to flight instructors and those who must communicate with student pilots and those they are attempting to instruct. As a DPE who is authorized to examine CFI candidates, I have heard these applicants use some - shall we say - 'creative terminology' trying to teach the principles and techniques of aviation.

I will present what CFI candidates have actually said in front of me during their flightcheck, then adjacent that, what I infer they meant to say. More comments then will follow.

What was said	What they meant [and some smart-aleky commentary]:
"Bump the throttle"	Add some more power [How hard do you want me to 'bump' it?]
"Chop the throttle"	Reduce power to idle [Like maybe a karate chop, or what?]
"Get rid of the gear and flaps"	Raise the gear and flaps [You want me to jettison the gear and flaps?]
"Pull the engine back"	Reduce the power *(how much?)* [I can't reach the engine from here}
"Bleed off some airspeed"	Allow the airplane to slow down [Which artery do I cut to let it bleed?]
"We want to fly normally"	[WTF does that mean?]
"Pitch the nose forward"	Pitch the nose down [Pitching is either 'up' or 'down', get it? We do that by either pushing the yoke forward or pulling the yoke back.]

"Dirty it up"	Extend the gear and/or flaps
	[I washed the plane yesterday; I don't want it to get dirty so soon after that!]
"Pitch over"	*[WTF does that mean?]*
	[I say again, pitch is either up or down, which way is 'over'?]
"Pitch back"	*[Okay, let's get this straight once and for all - Do you mean 'Pitch up' ... or 'pull back on the yoke'?]*
"Pull the plane back into a stall"	Increase the back pressure on the yoke
	[I can't pull the airplane 'back', it's 'way too heavy]
"Pull the power"	Reduce power *(How much?)*
"Throw in some flaps"	Extend the flaps *(how far?)*
	[So, we can throw flaps out?]
"Save some juice"	*[WTF does that mean?]*
"Pop your door"	Open your door prior to an off-airport landing
	[How does one 'pop' a door?]
"Clock into the freq"	Change the radio frequency to
	[Just where on the clock can I adjust radio frequencies? And at what time do I 'clock' it?]

"Drain the airspeed"	Decrease airspeed to
	[Do we have a bucket large enough into which we can drain all this airspeed?]

Instructors - are you getting the picture?

DO <u>NOT</u> USE SLANG, JARGON, OR AVIATION 'COOL' WORDS WHEN YOU ARE TEACHING!!!

*You **must** use the words, phrases, terminology, and verbology the student reads in their textbooks, manuals, handbooks, and study aids! That which they study is a 'building block of knowledge'. When you use the same words and phrases they read in their manuals, you are building -strongly and solidly - upon that which they've already studied. Building block upon building block raising under your guidance and tutelage a strong and solid structure of knowledge and skill(s) in the mind and hands of your student.*

Experienced pilot to experienced pilot, we know what those phrases and slang words mean - students do not. You MUST speak - and instruct - with precise language a student [who is just now beginning to learn the language of aviation] can easily understand. ANY of the phrases mentioned above require the student to use up time and effort to decipher what the instructor means. THAT is a huge break in the communication chain. Speak exactly what you want to say using precise language a student can easily understand. They will learn the slang and jargon on their own as they progress - but not from you. It will require some diligence on your part to speak like a professional; that means an instructor who knows what they're talking about. In the end your student(s) will learn faster and understand more exactly what you are attempting to convey to them.

For example: Years ago while teaching the wife of a buddy to fly, we were in Slow Flight and sagging out of our altitude. I told her "C'mon, Sara, raise your nose." She got this weird expression on her face and then - I kid you not - tilted her head back and 'raised her nose' [the physical, on the front of her face, nose!]. It was all I could do to keep from laughing out loud. But I thought about it; realizing the meaning she attached to the words she heard was NOT the meaning I intended when I sent those words forth. So I came up with this instructional formula which I will happily share with all you instructors - especially newer ones - out there:

Tell your student:

- WHAT TO DO

- HOW TO DO IT

- WHAT THEY SHOULD SEE OR EXPERIENCE

So - "Sara, raise your nose." Became:

"Raise the nose of the airplane

By pulling back on the yoke

Until the cowling rises to just above the horizon

ANY ambiguity or communication confusion? Nope! Your student now knows exactly what you want them to do, how to do it and what the result should be or look like. Try it and see how faster your student(s) understand what you mean to say and how much quicker they catch on. Using this technique I was sending students to the checkpilot hours before my peers were. My compadres were in awe and were always asking how I did it. Of course, the usual answer was:

"Well, I'm just a far more superior instructor pilot than you are."

THAT got a LOT of 'after-hours discussions' going - usually including adult beverages [aka: Safety Awards] with aviation slang and jargon which everyone understood all too well flying around the room [among other things].

"Learning should be fun. If you don't have fun in aviation then you don't learn; and when learning stops, you die."
- Pete Campbell, FAA

[THIS from a FED! Believe it or not! - Ed.]

USAAC WWII Flight Surgeon wings.

WHEN MEN WERE MEN
& DC-8'S, 707'S, P2VS, F8 CRUSADERS AND F-4 PHANTOMS ROAMED THE EARTH

Another homage to 'the way things were then.' Those who were there will read this and then stare off into the distance remembering the days of their youth and may recall some things they did back then [some relatable only in gatherings of fellow survivors – most not told in mixed company or around 'easily offended' sensitive individuals (snowflakes). But ... it WAS a time, wasn't it?

Those were the good ole days. Pilots back then were men that didn't want to be women or girly men. Pilots all knew who Jimmy Doolittle was. Pilots drank coffee, whiskey, smoked cigars and didn't wear digital watches. They carried their own suitcases and brain bags, like the real men they were.

Pilots didn't bend over into the crash position multiple times each day in front of the passengers at security so that some previously-unemployed 'Govmint' agent could probe for tweezers or fingernail clippers or too much toothpaste.

Pilots did not go through the terminal impersonating a caddy pulling a bunch of golf clubs, computers, guitars, and feed bags full of tofu and granola on a sissy-trailer with no hat and granny glasses hanging on a pink string around their pencil neck while talking to their personal trainer on their cell phone!

Being an airline Captain was as good as being the King in a Mel Brooks movie. All the Stewardesses (aka Flight Attendants) were young, attractive, single women that were proud to be combatants in the sexual revolution. They didn't have to turn sideways, grease up and suck it in to get through the cockpit door. They would blush, and say thank you, when told that they looked good, instead of filing a sexual harassment claim. Junior Stewardesses shared a room and talked about men … with no thoughts of substitution.

Passengers wore nice clothes and were polite; they could speak AND understand English. They didn't speak gibberish or listen to loud gangsta rap on their IPods. They bathed and didn't smell like a pile of garbage in a jogging suit and flip-flops.

Children didn't travel alone, commuting between trailer parks.

There were no Biggest Losers asking for a seatbelt extension or a Scotch and grapefruit juice cocktail with a twist.

If the Captain wanted to throw some offensive, ranting jerk off the airplane, it was done without any worries of a lawsuit or getting fired.

Axial flow engines crackled with the sound of <u>freedom</u> and left an impressive black smoke trail like a locomotive burning soft coal. Jet fuel was cheap and once the throttles were pushed up they were left there. After all, it was the jet age and the idea was to go fast.

"Economy cruise" was something in the performance book, but no one knew why or where it was. When the clacker went off, no one got all tight and scared because Douglas & Boeing built it out of iron. Nothing was going to fall off and that sound had the same effect on real pilots then as Viagra does now for these new age guys.

There was very little plastic and no composites on the airplanes (or the Stewardesses' pectoral regions). Airplanes and women had eye-pleasing symmetrical curves, not a bunch of ugly vortex generators, ventral fins, winglets, flow diverters, tattoos, rings in their nose, tongues and eyebrows.

Airlines were run by men like Howard Hughes, Eddie Rickenbacker, C.R. Smith, Juan Trippe, William Patterson, Jack Frye, and Bob Six, who had built their companies virtually from scratch, knew most of their employees by name, and were lifetime airline employees themselves, not pseudo financiers and bean counters who flit from one occupation to another for a few bucks, a better golden parachute or a fancier title, while fervently believing that they are a class of beings unto themselves.

And so it was back then ... and never will be again!

"My father had been opposed to my flying from the first and had never flown himself. However, he had agreed to go up with me at the first opportunity, and one afternoon he climbed into the cockpit, and we flew ... together. From that day on I never heard a word against my flying, and he never missed a chance to ride in the plane."
- Charles Lindbergh, 1928

WHEN NATURE CALLS IN THE COCKPIT

A true story ... *[I'm told]*

This was sent to me by a lady friend - whose name will not appear in this story – about the experience of another pilot I know – identity also redacted for matters of personal safety [mine] – while on a cross-country flight. Long x/c flights can be physiological endurance sessions and we male pilots have a certain ... ahhh ... 'ability' to cope therewith which is unavailable to our female compatriots. There IS a downside, however ...

On a long cross-country flight in a vintage Stearman biplane, the pilot in the rear seat began to feel the need to "drain the sump": This term [for the uninitiated] means to relieve 'pressures in the bladder.' The empty water bottle on the floor looked like an excellent vessel in which to collect the wastewater, and its opening appeared large enough to comfortably accommodate the ... ahhh ... equipment.

Rather than interrupting the trip to make a rest stop landing, the pilot asked his front-seater to take the controls for a spell. Then with safety harness released and flight suit unzipped, he began the process of carefully positioning and filling said bottle.

But then things went terribly wrong ...

Whether it was the warm breeze circulating about the open cockpit or the novelty of being, well - surrounded by the aperture of the bottle will never be known, but the effect was none-the-less cause for great concern: The fit of the bottle quickly became too tight for withdrawal once the original mission was completed.

The bottle's mouth had a hard, slightly sharp edge so his attempt to pull it off resulted in an immediate and painful abrasion. He tried twisting it off, but that produced a sensation which felt like a slow amputation...

What to do, what to do???

The ONLY thing a guy could do in a situation like that; he stopped staring at it, quit thinking about it, and just "waited it out."

That's his story and he's sticking to it.

[A certain ... *ahem* ... person connected with this book can, in the first person, relate how it IS possible to use an empty beer bottle for the same purpose while piloting an O-1 Birddog ... while wearing a flight suit ... with a back-seater who could hardly speak English ... and who didn't know the first thing about flying ... in turbulence ...]

Have confidence in yourself and tell yourself "I can" twice for every time you are told "you can't". Confidence that you can succeed is everything; take every negative remark as a challenge to achieve. You can do anything you believe you can do - heck, you might even surprise yourself.

WHEN THE MUSIC STOPPED

For those who are unaware: At all military base theaters, the National Anthem is played before the movie begins. This was written by a Chaplain in Iraq. I include it without comment – it stands for itself ... and everything I believe in.

I recently attended a showing of 'Superman 3' here at LSA Anaconda. We have a large auditorium that we use for movies as well as memorial services and other large gatherings. As is the custom at all military bases, we stood to attention when *The National Anthem* began before the main feature. All was going well until three-quarters of the way through the music stopped.

Now, what would happen if this occurred with 1,000 18-to-22-year-olds back in the States? I imagine that there would be hoots, catcalls, laughter, a few rude comments, and everyone would sit down and yell for the movie to begin. Of course, that is, only if they had stood for *The National Anthem* in the first place.

Here in Iraq 1,000 soldiers continued to stand at attention, eyes fixed forward. The music started again, and the soldiers continued to quietly stand at attention. Again, though, at the same point, the music stopped. What would you expect 1,000 soldiers standing at attention to do? Frankly, I expected some laughter, and everyone would eventually sit down and wait for the movie to start.

No! You could have heard a pin drop while every soldier continued to stand at attention.

Suddenly, there was a lone voice from the front of the auditorium, then a dozen voices, and soon the room was filled with the voices of a thousand soldiers, finishing where the recording left off: "And the rockets' red glare, the bombs bursting in air, gave proof through the night that our flag was still there. Oh, say, does that Star-Spangled Banner yet wave, o'er the land of the free, and the home of the brave."

It was the most inspiring moment I have had in Iraq and I wanted you to know what kind of U.S. Soldiers are serving you! Remember them as they fight for us!

Pass this along as a reminder to others to be ever in prayer for all our soldiers serving us here at home and abroad. Many have already paid the ultimate price.

Chaplain Jim Higgins
LSA Anaconda is at the Ballad Airport in Iraq, north of Baghdad.

GOD BLESS AMERICA

Land that I Love
Stand beside her and guide her
Through the night with a light from Above.
From the mountains
To the praries
To the ocean white with foam
God Bless America
My home, sweet home.
God bless America
My home, sweet home

Photo taken by the author at an airshow, somewhere.

In 1938, The 'biggest star' in Hollywood, Kate Smith – someone today we'd call a 'plus-sized' woman but who had a voice unmistakable and unmatched – asked songwriter Irving Berlin for a patriotic song she could sing during her radio program. The times then were dark around the world, with the rise of Nazi Germany, Fascist Italy, Communist Russia, and Imperial Japan. Irving reached 20-some years in the past and submitted "God Bless America" to her, which she then sang on her show, introducing it to the country.

In the YouTube link below, you'll hear her version as depicted in a patriotic movie of the time, the name escapes me. At 4:20 into the 5 ½ minute clip, you'll see – those of you over 50 – a familiar face.

https://www.youtube.com/watch?v=_zF7a0wB-Lg

WHERE AIRPLANE PILOTS COME FROM

This rather unscientific treatise comes from the days when aviation was a male-dominated endeavor and thus must be viewed through the wrong end of the telescope, historically speaking. It still explains a lot but in the years since the mid- to late- 1960's the level[s] of the playing field have, shall we say, been altered. I would submit these changes – mostly – are for the good of the industry but there is much that will be missed, never to be seen and/or experienced again. Those of us who, metaphorically-speaking, ran into walls with buckets on our heads [see below] will forever treasure the days when we could do that with the only ramification being we were admonished [accompanied by the shaking of the admonishers head and/or wagging of a singular finger digit] of either 'showing off' [whatever that means] or inciting an innocent party [see: 'Nugget' and/or 'FNG'] to follow our lead.

All babies start out with the same number of raw cells which, over nine months, develop into a complete female baby. The problem occurs when cells are instructed by the little chromosomes to make a male baby instead. Because there are only so many cells to go around, the cell necessary to develop a male's reproductive organs have to come from cells already assigned elsewhere in the female.

Recent tests have shown that these cells are removed from the communications center of the brain, migrate lower in the body and develop into male sexual organs. If you visualize a normal brain to be similar to a full deck of cards, this means that males are born a few cards short, so to speak, and some of their cards are in their shorts.

This difference between the male and female brain manifests itself in various ways. Little girls will tend to play games like 'house' or learn to read. Little boys, however, will tend to do things like placing a bucket over their heads and run into walls. Little girls will think about doing things before taking any action. Little boys will just hit or kick something then will look surprised if someone asks them why they just punched their little brother who was half asleep and looking the other way.

This basic cognitive difference continues to grow until puberty, when the hormones kick into action and the trouble really begins. After puberty, not only the size of the male and female brains differs, but the center of thought also differs. Women think with their heads. Male thoughts often originate lower in their bodies where their ex-brain cells reside.

Of course, the size of this problem varies from man to man. In some men only a small number of brain cells migrate, and they are left with nearly full mental capacity, but they tend to be rather dull, sexually speaking. Such men are known in medical terms as Lawyers, Accountants, Engineers, Scientists, Doctors, and "Blackshoes."

Other men suffer larger brain cell relocation.

These men are medically referred to as "Pilots."

WHERE HELICOPTER PILOTS COME FROM

You have just read "Where Airplane Pilots Come From" and while there are many similarities between the two, there is one salient and outstanding difference between airplane and helicopter pilots. Budding helicopter pilots can be discerned at a much earlier age: Scientifically speaking, it is due to the migrating brain cells referred to in the preceding chapter commencing said journey much earlier in life. This 'jumping of the gun' – so to speak – increases the velocity of the cells' migratory journey; the result of which can be explained by the following algorithm –

$$KE = \underline{Mass \ x \ Velocity} \ 2$$

… *That is to say: Kinetic Energy is equal to the square of mass times velocity.*

In laymen's' terms, it means in budding helicopter pilots the cells' migration begins earlier, more of them depart on said migration than what could be considered 'normal' and when the migration reaches it terminus, said cells arrive with much more force ['kinetic Energy'], creating a larger … ahhh … impact area. It is medically unclear what causes this cellular aberration; however its onset can be readily observed by behavioral symptoms easily identifiable to the casual observer. For example, one young man in this elementary school class from 1955 went on to retire from Army Aviation as a Warrant 5. He is easily picked out of this [Catholic School, even!] class picture.

A PILOT'S PRAYER

God, Grant me the eyes of an Eagle,
The judgment of an Owl,
The quickness of a Hummingbird,
The reflexes of a Cat,
The radar of a Cave Bat,
The heart of a Bull, and
The balls of an Army helicop-ter pilot
~Annonymous

A WOMAN'S BEST FRIEND

A real man is a woman's best friend.
He will never stand her up and never let her down.
He will reassure her when she feels insecure
And comfort her after a bad day.
He will inspire her to do things she never thought she could do.
To live without fear and forget regret.
He will enable her to express her deepest emotions and
Give in to her most intimate desires.
He will make sure she always feels as though she's
The prettiest woman in the room and
Will enable her to be the most confident, sexy, and invincible…
… ahhh … wait a minute …
SORRY
I'm thinking of Wine.
It's wine that does all that shit.
Never mind …

PS: Dear Wine: We had a deal; you were going to make me funnier, sexier, smarter and a better dancer. I saw the video – we need to talk.

WINGLESS PLANE AT THE PUB – CRIKEY MATE!

As we have all learned over our lifetime(s), fact is truly stranger than fiction. This news story from Australia certainly keeps that line of thought alive because it is both one of the funniest and outside-the-box things we have read in a long time. The funny part arises when a guy buys a clapped-out plane with no wings and decides the way to get it home is to taxi it there on the public roads. We're not certain how large the city of Newman is but apparently, they didn't take kindly to the idea of someone driving an airplane around on their byways. Secondly, the fact that the guy figured he'd have time to stop at the bar and have a couple of drinks before completing his trip also made us laugh. We're reasonably certain that the airplane is not equipped with reversers, so imagine the scene: He exits the bar in a mellow mood, collects the cones he had put out to forewarn people of the prop, pushes the thing backwards out of its parking space, fires it up in the parking lot and then goes rumbling off down the road.

I have seen some great entrances into – and even greater exits from - local watering holes before [even performed a few myself!], but this one takes the matter to a higher level never considered! The news story is below and the level of unintentional humor factor in it is high because it reads like a *police report. ["Just the facts, ma'am ... just the facts."] And what could they charge him with? He was 'operating an aircraft' but with no wings there certainly was no intention to commit an aviation activity. Perhaps an 'unlicensed motor vehicle' operated on a highway? Too thin. Sooo ... then what?*

Oh, one more thing. Can we agree that the guy who drove the plane in would probably be a fun ~~dude~~ bloke to have a beer with? Fair dinkum, mate – and put some shrimp on the Barbie while you're up!

Newman, W.A. *[Western Australia – Ed.]*

A 37-year-old man was charged today in relation to him taxiing a propeller driven Beechcraft 2-seater aircraft (minus wings) through Newman to the Newman Hotel's Purple Pub on Friday 31 October 2014 at about 2.10pm.

It will be alleged that he had just bought the aircraft from a private residence and was taking it home on the other side of the town, but stopped at the pub.

On examination it was found to have an exposed fuel line hanging from the side of the aircraft attached to an unsecured jerry can inside the cabin to enable the engine to run. On stopping the aircraft the accused left the engine in a potentially dangerous condition with the ignition on. *[Mag switch - ON? – Ed.]*

The accused does not hold a pilot's license and the roads were busy with other vehicles and pedestrians at the time.

The accused has been charged with the Endangerment of Life, Health or Safety of a Person and is due to appear in the Newman Magistrates Court on 18 November 2014.

The three biggest lies in Army Aviation:
1. You're the only crewman available
2. Don't ask me, I'm not the regular crew chief
3. Wait right here, sir. The crew bus should be here any minute

ZEN TEACHINGS FOR PILOTS

While not necessarily aviation-related, the following are offered as some of life's "Points of Order" [for you parliamentarians out there] or for the rest of you anarchists, some of "Life's Rules". Well, not so much 'rules' as 'guidelines.'

1. Do not walk behind me, for I may not lead. Do not walk ahead of me, for I may not follow. Do not walk beside me for the path is narrow. In fact, just leave me the Hell alone.

2. Sex is like air. It's not that important unless you aren't getting any.

3. No one is listening until you fart.

4. Always remember you're unique. Just like everyone else.

5. Never test the depth of the water with both feet.

6. If you think nobody cares whether you're alive or dead, try missing a couple of payments.

7. Before you criticize someone, you should walk a mile in their shoes. That way, when you criticize them, you're a mile away and you have their shoes.

8. If at first you don't succeed, skydiving is not for you.

9. Give a man a fish and he will eat for a day. Teach him how to fish, and he will sit in a boat and drink beer all day.

10. If you lend someone $20 and never see that person again, it was probably well worth it.

11. If you always tell the truth, you don't have to remember anything.

12. Some days you are the dog, some days you are the tree.

    Corollary: Some days you're the windshield, some days you're the bug.]

13. Don't worry; it only seems kinky the first time.

14. Good judgement comes from experience ... and most of that comes from bad judgement.

15. A closed mouth gathers no foot.

    [Corollary: It better to keep one's mouth shut and be thought a fool than to open it and remove all doubt.]

16. There are two excellent theories for arguing with women. Neither one works.

17. Generally speaking, you aren't learning much when your lips are moving.

18. Experience is something you don't get until just after you need it.

19. We are born naked, wet, hungry, then get slapped on the ass; after that things just keep getting worse.

20. Never, under any circumstances, take a laxative and a sleeping pill on the same night.

"In the case of pilots, it is a little touch of madness that drives us to go beyond all known bounds. Any search into the unknown is an incomparable exploration of oneself."
- Jacqueline Auriol

ZULU – CHARLIE: THE PAYOFF

In <u>The Aviator's Bathroom Reader volume I</u>, [available at my website and/or www.Amazon.com] the last story in the book was one of a one-each crusty old captain [COC] teaching an FNG about the ways of an aviator. In the following I include another such story – different people, different situations = same outcome, same lesson.

The lesson is – if you wish to become more than an 'Airplane Driver' [NOT a compliment, btw] and even more than just a pilot, you MUST strive to be the best there is. And that takes study, effort, work, sacrifice, and commitment. It doesn't matter whether you're flying a Piper Cub, Beech Baron, C-130, RJ or777; unless you are at your best doing that which you do you are only adequate, merely average, just doing your job.

Recall that old saying: "Aviation is not inherently dangerous ... but it is terribly unforgiving of carelessness, incapacity or neglect." If you are careless in what you do, you'll hurt an airplane. If you are incapable of doing what must be done, you'll hurt yourself or someone else. And if you neglect the precepts of safety in all matters, someone is going to die. Tell yourself "Not on my watch!"

ATTENTION TO DETAIL IS EVERYTHING!

Dedicated to: Captain Frank Crismon (1903-1990)
By: Captain G. C. Kehmeier (United Airlines, Ret.)

"I ought to make you buy a ticket to ride this airline!"

The chief pilot's words were scalding. I had just transferred from San Francisco to Denver. Frank Crismon, my new boss, was giving me a route check between Denver and Salt Lake City.

"Any man who flies for me will know this route," he continued. "'Fourteen thousand feet will clear Kings Peak' is not adequate. You had better know that Kings Peak is exactly 13,498 feet high. Bitter Creek is not 'about 7,000 feet.' It is exactly 7,185 feet, and the identifying code for the beacon is dash dot dash. "I'm putting you on probation for one month, and then I'll ride with you again. If you want to work for me, you had better start studying!"

Wow! He wasn't kidding!

For a month, I pored over sectional charts, auto road maps, Jeppesen approach charts, and topographic quadrangle maps. I learned the elevation and code for every airway beacon between the West Coast and Chicago. I learned the frequencies, runway lengths, and approach procedures for every airport. From city road maps, I plotted the streets that would funnel me to the various runways at each city. A month later, he was on my trip.

"What is the length of the north-south runway at Milford?"

"Fifty-one fifty."

"How high is Antelope Island?"

"Sixty-seven hundred feet."

"If your radio fails on an Ogden-Salt Lake approach, what should you do?"

"Make a right turn to 290 degrees and climb to 13,000 feet."

"What is the elevation of the Upper Red Butte beacon?"

"Seventy-three hundred."

"How high is the Laramie Field?"

"Seventy-two fifty."

This lasted for the three hours from Denver to Salt Lake City. "I'm going to turn you loose on your own. Remember what you have learned. I don't want to ever have to scrape you off some hillside with a book on your lap!"

Twenty years later, I was the Captain on a Boeing 720 from San Francisco to Chicago. We were cruising in the cold, clear air at 37,000 feet. South of Grand Junction, a deep low-pressure area fed moist air upslope into Denver, causing snow, low ceilings, and restricted visibility. The forecast for Chicago's O'Hare Field was 200 feet and one-half mile -- barely minimums. Over the Utah-Colorado border, the backbone of the continent showed white in the noonday sun. I switched on the intercom and gave the passengers the word: "We are over Grand Junction at the confluence of the Gunnison and Colorado Rivers. On our right and a little ahead is the "Switzerland of America" -- the rugged San Juan Mountains. In 14 minutes, we will cross the Continental Divide west of Denver. We will arrive O'Hare at 3:30 Chicago time."

Over Glenwood Springs, the generator overheat light came on. "Number 2 won't stay on the bus," the engineer advised. He placed the essential power selector to number 3. The power failure light went out for a couple of seconds and then came on again, glowing ominously. "Smoke is coming out of the main power shield," the engineer yelled. "Hand me the goggles."

The engineer reached behind the observer's seat, unzipped a small container, and handed the copilot and me each a pair of ski goggles. The smoke was getting thick. I slipped the oxygen mask that is stored above the left side of the pilot's seat over my nose and mouth. By pressing a button on the control wheel, I could talk to the copilot and the engineer through the battery-powered intercom. By flipping a switch, either of us could talk to the passengers.

"Emergency descent!"

I closed the thrust levers. The engines that had been purring quietly like a giant vacuum cleaner since San Francisco spooled down to a quiet rumble. I established a turn to the left and pulled the speed brake lever to extend the flight spoilers. "Gear down. Advise passengers to fasten seat belts and no smoking." I held the nose forward, and the mountains along the Continental Divide came up rapidly. The smoke was thinning. "Bring cabin altitude to 14,000 feet," I ordered.

At 14,000 feet over Fraser, we leveled and retracted the gear and speed brakes. The engineer opened the ram air switch and the smoke disappeared. We removed our goggles and masks.

Fuel is vital to the life of a big jet, and electricity is almost as vital. The artificial horizon and other electronic instruments, with which I navigated and made approaches through the clouds, were now so much tin and brass. All I had left was the altimeter, the airspeed, and the magnetic compass -- simple instruments that guided airplanes 35 years earlier.

"Advise passengers we are making a Denver stop."

"The last Denver weather was 300 feet with visibility one-half mile in heavy snow. Wind was northeast at 15 knots with gusts to 20," the copilot volunteered.

"I know. I heard it."

The clouds merged against the mountains above Golden. Boulder was in the clear. To the northeast, the stratus clouds were thick like the wool on the back of a Rambouillet buck before shearing. I dropped the nose and we moved over the red sandstone buildings of the University of Colorado. We headed southeast and picked up the Denver-Boulder turnpike.

"We will fly the turnpike to the Broomfield turnoff, then east on Broomfield Road to Colorado Boulevard, then south to 26th Avenue, then east to Runway 8."

The copilot, a San Francisco reserve, gave me a doubtful look. One doesn't scud-run to the end of the runway under a 300-foot ceiling in a big jet. Coming south on Colorado Boulevard, we were down to 100 feet above the highway. Lose it and I would have to pull up into the clouds and fly the gauges when I had no gauges. Hang onto it and I would get into Stapleton Field. I picked up the golf course and started a turn to the left. "Gear down and 30 degrees."

The copilot moved a lever with a little wheel on it. He placed the flap lever in the 30-degree slot. I shoved the thrust levers forward.

"Don't let me get less than 150 knots. I'm outside."

I counted the avenues as they slid underneath -- 30th, 29th, and 28th. I remembered that there was neither a 31st nor a 27th. I picked up 26th. The snow was slanting out of the northeast. The poplar trees and power lines showed starkly through the storm. With electrical power gone, we had no windshield heat. Fortunately, the snow was not sticking.

"Let me know when you see a school on your side and hack my time at five-second intervals from the east side of the school yard."

Ten seconds.

"There it is. The yard is full of kids. Starting time now!"

Good boy. Smiley faced Holly. From the east side of the school yard, I counted Kearney, then Krameria, Leyden, Locust. Remember the double lane for Monaco Parkway. Then Magnolia, Niagara, Newport. Time the speed at 130 knots. Only eight blocks to the end of the runway. Oneida, Olive, Pontiac, Poplar. From Quebec to Syracuse, the cross streets disappear; figure eight seconds. Keep 26th Avenue under the right side of the nose.

"Full flaps."

Dead ahead, glowing dimly in the swirling snow, were the three green lights marking the east end of Runway 8. We crossed 20 feet above the center green light and touched down in a crab to the left. I aligned the nose to the runway with the right rudder, dropped the nose wheel, popped the speed brakes, and brought in reverse thrust.

It took us 10 minutes to find the terminal in the swirling whiteout. We saw the dim, flashing red light atop the building indicating the field was closed to all traffic. A mechanic materialized out of the snow carrying two wands. He waved me into the gate. I set the parking brake.

"We have ground power," the engineer advised.

"Cut the engines." The bagpipe skirl of sound spiraled down to silence.

"My hat is off to you, skipper. I don't know how you ever found this airport."

"I used to fly for an ornery old chief pilot who made me learn the route," I replied as I hung up my headset and scratched the top of my head where it itched.

Frank Crismon passed away at his home in Denver on 25 Jan 1990.

Editor's note: *Professionalism, readiness, and knowledge can never be replaced by all the electronic gadgets in the world. It makes no difference what you fly, you are the Pilot-in-Command - the CAPTAIN OF THAT SHIP. Nothing beats knowing your capabilities and those of your machine and knowing where you are at all times. It's hard to come up with options if you don't know what's going on.*

The reader can infer from information herein just about when all this happened; Frank Crismon would have had to retire from the airlines at age 60, which would have been in 1963. So Captain Kehmeier, the pilot relating this story, would have been hired by United in the early 1960's – and is long ago retired and hopefully still with us to read this. Beacon codes, Boeing 720s, smoking in airplanes and flight engineers are now long-gone from aviation but the lessons remain.

All we must do is heed and abide by them.

Thus endeth the lesson for today.

END PIECE & AFTERWORD

As a final comment, I commend all you aviators to accomplish some form of training and/or proficiency exercise each and every time you fly.

Give yourselves a task out of the PTS appropriate to your certificate and ratings…and **practice precision.**

Choose a runway stripe and practice until you can land, full stall, centered over the centerline, drift corrected, on that exact stripe.

Choose a heading, then practice stalls and recoveries so the Heading Indicator hardly wavers.

Choose an altitude and transition from cruise airspeeds to Vso and back all within 100'. Then add heading control as above to the mix.

Practice instrument approaches until you think the localizer and glideslope needles are broken and frozen in the crosshairs.

Practice partial-panel approaches until they can be done with 'no sweat'.

Dust off those old textbooks, manuals and yes, the FAR/AIM and read, inquire, study and relearn all you learned those many years ago to get where you are now.

And if you need assistance or advice in polishing your knowledge and skills a little, employ your local CFI for a few hours of scrapping off the rust.

Remember:

You are an Aviator, not just a fly-boy.

Always plan to do your best.

Blue Skies & Tailwinds!

Drew Chitiea
Designated Pilot Examiner - Retired
Master Flight Instructor - Emeritus
Centennial, Colorado
2022

"It is possible to fly without motors, but not without knowledge and skill."
- Wilbur Wright, 1901

APPENDIX

ABR Pithy One-Liners

We find these truths to be self-evident, that all pilots are NOT created equal. Only through hard work, study and practice may they join the elite fellowship privileged to be known as 'Aviators'. Truths are seldom wordy ramblings inducing slumber in the reviewer while comfortably reclined in their ... ahhh ... recliner. Most truths may be summarized in a mere sentence, perhaps two, eliciting from the recipient of such wisdom a comment somewhat along the lines of "Wow, that's pithy." Presented herein are many of the piths known, if not precisely followed, by pilots everywhere.

1. If God had meant for Man to fly, he would have made his bones hollow – not his head.
2. Flying is not dangerous – crashing is dangerous.
3. Aviation is not so much a profession as it is a disease.
4. Always keep an 'out' in your back pocket.
5. The worst day of flying beats the best day at work.
6. You cannot be lost if you don't care where you are.
7. Let's do a 360 and get the hell outa here!
8. The medical profession is the natural enemy of the aviation profession.
9. What you know is not so important as what you do with it.

10. Do not spin this aircraft! If a spin occurs, it will return to earth without further attention on the part of the aeronaut.

11. Never trade skill for luck.

12. You will never do well if you stop doing better.

13. The most dangerous part about flying is the drive home from the airport.

14. Luck may stand in for skill occasionally, but not consistently.

15. Any comment regarding how well things are going – or in regards to tailwinds of any velocity – will immediately get things going in the opposite direction.

16. Airspeed, altitude, Brains: Any 2 are required for a successful flight.

17. Keep the aeroplane in such an attitude that the air pressure is directly in the pilot's face.

18. Aviate, navigate, and communicate – in that order.

19. Truly superior pilots are those who use their truly superior judgment to avoid those situations requiring their truly superior skills.

20. Keep flying the airplane until all the moving parts have stopped moving.

21. Death is a small price to pay for looking 'Shit Hot'.

22. There are three simple rules for making good landings – unfortunately, no-one knows what they are.

23. Airspeed is Life – Altitude is Life Insurance.
24. It is far better to break ground and fly into the wind than the other way around.
25. When a flight is going incredibly well, something was forgotten.
26. "IFR" flying – I Follow Roads, Rivers & Railways.
27. Aviation rule #1: First and Foremost – Always fly the plane.
28. 'Tis best to keep the pointy end going forward and the greasy side down.
29. Given a choice, always go for the more conservative option.
30. And so, at the beginning of each day, consider that ATC, the weather-guessers, mechanics, supervisors…and birds…are all trying to kill you. Your job is to not let them.
31. The future is aviation is the next 30 seconds. Long-term planning is the next hour and a half.
32. Much of what you think you know is incorrect.
33. "Happy Hour Landing" – two for the price of one.
34. It has been said that two wrongs don't make a right – but two Wrights can make an airplane.
35. Without fuel, pilots are just pedestrians.
36. To err is human, to forgive divine – neither of which is corporate policy.

37. It is better to die than to look bad; but it is possible to do both.

38. I knew I was in trouble when the tower asked me to climb to field elevation.

39. Flying is not a Nintendo game: You cannot push a button and start over.

40. Murphy's Law of Flight Instruction: If a student can do the wrong thing at the wrong time, he will.

41. FAA regulations prohibit drinking within 8 feet of the airplane and smoking within 50 hours of the flight; or is it the other way around?

42. If you crash because of bad weather, when they bury you it will be beautiful, clear and calm.

43. There is no financial reason in the world why you cannot pass your next flightcheck.

44. Learn from the mistakes of others; you will never live long enough to make them all yourself.

45. Better higher than lower; better faster than slower.

46. The survivability of the landing is inversely proportional to the angle of arrival.

47. You have never been lost until you have been lost above Mach 3.

48. Hovering is for pilots who love to fly but have nowhere to go.

49. Asking a pilot what he thinks of the FAA is like asking a fire hydrant what it thinks of a dog.

50. Never trust a fuel gauge.

51. If you must make a mistake, try to make it a new one.

52. FARs are worded either by the most brilliant lawyers in Washington – or the most stupid.

53. An airplane flies because of a principle discovered by Bernoulli, not Marconi.

54. Good judgment comes from experience: Experience comes from bad judgment.

55. Dyslexic atheist – doesn't believe in dog.

56. Forget all that stuff about Lift, Weight, Thrust & Drag - an airplane flies because of money.

57. The Law of Gravity is not a generalized rule.

58. In thrust I trust [put another way: I feel the need for speed]

59. It is better to be on the ground wishing you were flying than flying wishing you were on the ground.

60. A light twin defined is that airplane when one engine fails the other gets you to the scene of the crash.

61. It is always better to have C_{sub-t} greater than C_{sub-d}. Simply put, thrust should always exceed drag.

62. Passengers prefer old captains and young flight attendants.

63. A fool and his money are soon flying more airplane than he can handle.

64. A helicopter is a collection of rotating, oscillating & reciprocating parts going 'round and 'round & up and down – all of them attempting to become simultaneously random in motion.

65. Fighter pilots make movies; attack pilots make history.

66. If it ain't broke, don't fix it. If it ain't fixed, don't fly it.

67. A mechanic's favorite: "It's not a leak…it's a seep."

68. Be nice to your First Officer – he just might be your captain at the next airline.

69. For those who don't care, fly Military Air.

70. The next time war is decided on how well you can land on a carrier, the Navy will clean up. Until then, I'll worry about who spends their training time flying and fighting.

71. Experience is the knowledge that enables you to recognize a mistake when you make it again.

72. Never let an airplane take you anywhere your brain hasn't been to at least 5 minutes prior.

73. Always remember: You fly with your head, not just your hands.

74. If it doesn't work, rename it. If it still doesn't work, the new name isn't long enough.

75. One of the most important skills a pilot must master is ignoring those things in an aircraft which were put there by non-fliers to get the pilot's attention.

76. Out on the line, all the girls are looking for husbands…and all the husbands are looking for girls.

77. A good simulator checkride is like successful surgery on a cadaver.
78. Please don't tell Mother I'm a pilot – she thinks I'm a piano player in a whorehouse.
79. You know you've landed gear up when it takes full power to taxi.
80. Trust in your captain…but keep your seatbelt securely fastened.
81. The owners' guide that comes with a $1,000 refrigerator makes more sense than the one that comes with a $100 million dollar airliner.
82. A 'greaser' landing is 50% luck, two in a row is 100% luck, and three in a row means someone is lying.
83. "Come see me" notes from the Chief Pilot are always distributed on Friday afternoons…after office hours.
84. A kill is a kill.
85. Experience is a tough teacher: First comes the test, then the lesson.
86. Pilots believe in clean living – they never drink whiskey from a dirty glass.
87. Flying is the perfect vocation for the man who wants to feel like a boy – but not for one who still is.
88. Nothing flies without fuel – so let's have some coffee!
89. Fuel in the tanks is limited – Gravity is forever.
90. Assumption is the mother of all screw-ups.

91. There are no atheists in the foxholes.

92. The three most common things heard on the CVR are "Was that for us?", "What did he say?" and "Oh, shit!" since computers are now onboard airplanes, a fourth and a fifth have been added: "What's it doing now?" and "Why is it doing that?"

93. If God had meant for Man to fly, He would have given him green, baggy Nomex skin and full wallets.

94. When you are sitting in the rubber raft looking up at where your airplane used to be, it's too late to check the weather, flight plan or wonder where the emergency checklist is.

95. Flying a twin doesn't make you twice as safe – it merely doubles the chances of suffering an engine failure.

96. The main thing is to take care of the main thing.

97. Every pilot knows the definition of a good landing is one you can walk away from. A great landing is when you can use the airplane again without major maintenance.

98. "It was my ex-wife who drove me to drink. It's the only thing I'm grateful to her for." - W.C. Fields.

99. There will be a day when you walk out of an airplane and two things will be true: You will either know it's your last flight in an airplane, or you won't.

100. "I ran out of altitude, airspeed and ideas all at the same time." Attributed to just about every test pilot who ever survived a crash.

101. Helicopters don't fly – they beat the air into submission. Sometimes the air wins.

102. Tell someone you work for a different airline than the one you really work for, and they'll tell you how much better yours is.

103. One problem is a problem; two problems are a hazard, three problems create accidents.

104. Any attempt to stretch fuel is guaranteed to increase headwinds.

105. The nicer an airplane looks, the better it flies.

106. The sharpest captains are the easiest to work with.

107. Never ask a man if he's a fighter pilot. If he is, he'll let you know. If he isn't, don't embarrass him.

108. How come every ground school class I've ever been in has one ass who, 5 minutes before the end of the day, asks a question requiring a 20-minute answer?

109. Sure, the money is better in the private sector...But then, you can't call in airstrikes.

110. Everything in aviation is accomplished through teamwork until something goes wrong - then one pilot gets the blame.

111. When in doubt, hold on to your altitude; no-one has ever collided with the sky. BUT – did you check about mountains along your route at 'your' altitude?

112. One who flies with fear encourages fate.

113. Any pilot who does not privately consider himself the best in the game is in the wrong game.

114. I hate to wake up and find my co-pilot asleep.

115. A thunderstorm is Nature's way of saying "Up Yours!"

116. Definition of 'Pilot': The first one to the scene of an aircraft accident.

117. When a weather forecaster talks about yesterday's weather, he's a historian. When he talks of tomorrow's weather, he's reading tea leaves.

118. Regarding engine power: Lots is good, more is better & too much is just about right.

119. When beginning an aviation career it is not unusual to be overwhelmed, terrified, suffer from lack of confidence and just plain old be scared. As experience grows, self-confidence replaces fear ... but after a time, when you think you have seen it all, you realize your initial reactions to flying were all too true.

120. The three best things in life are a good landing, a good shit and a good orgasm. A night carrier landing is one of the few opportunities to experience all three at the same time.

121. One peek is worth a thousand instrument crosschecks.

122. An airplane may disappoint a good pilot but it should never surprise him.

123. Your mind is like a parachute – it only works when open.

124. What separates Flight Attendants from the lowest form of life on earth? The cockpit door.

125. No-one ever collided with the sky.

126. If you don't gear up your brain before takeoff, you'll probably gear up your airplane upon landing.

127. It is far better to arrive late in this world than early in the next.

128. The most useless things in aviation: Altitude above you, runway behind you, fuel in the truck [air in the fuel tanks], approach plates in the car, the airspeed you don't have, half a second ago, a navigator

129. Fly the plane until the last part stops moving.

130. Trust your instruments but have a good cross-check procedure.

131. A flightcheck should be like a short skirt; short enough to be interesting but long enough to cover everything.

132. There are some flight instructors where the student is important, and there are some instructors where the instructor is important. Choose carefully.

133. First, listen to the question the student asked, then listen to the question the student didn't ask, then figure out the question they really meant to ask.

134. Speed is life. Altitude is life insurance.

135. Don't drop the airplane to fly the microphone.

136. Flying is not dangerous, crashing is dangerous.

137. Winds aloft reports are of incomparable value - to historians.

138. There are four ways to fly: the right way, the wrong way, the company way, and the captain's way. Only one counts.

139. Being an airline pilot would be a great job if it wasn't for all those trips.

140. A co-pilot is a knothead until he spots opposite direction traffic at 12 o-clock, after which he's a goof-off for not seeing it sooner.

141. Any attempt to stretch fuel is guaranteed to increase headwinds.

142. ANY comment on how well things are going is an absolute guarantee of trouble coming ... and soon.

143. A thunderstorm is never as bad from the inside as it appears from the outside: It's worse.

144. Don't trust nobody and don't do nothing dumb.

145. Trusting to luck alone is not conducive to a long career in aviation.

146. He is most free from danger who, even when he is safe, is still alert and on his guard.

147. Being flexible is too rigid; in aviation one must be fluid.

148. The future for a pilot is the next 30 seconds. Long-term planning is an hour and a half.

149. Some pilots will make an emergency out of a bad magneto check; others, upon losing a wing, will ask for lower altitude.

Miscellaneous Quotes That Didn't Make It To A Page Herein

While doing ... ahhh ... research for this book I came across many fine and truthful quotes worthy of serious contemplation all on their own. I found so many there were not enough pages to which they could be appended, and so must they be collated here; you might call this a "Gaggle of Quotes" [look up 'gaggle' in the dictionary section]. Much has been spoken and written regarding aviation, flying, and pilots. You of course won't find everything here, but you will find most of the best. Enjoy! - Ed.

The air up there in the clouds must be very pure and fine, bracing, and delicious. And why wouldn't it be? It is the same the angels breathe.
- Mark Twain, in *Roughing It* – 1886.

Man must rise above the earth - to the top of the atmosphere and beyond - for only thus will he fully understand the world in which he lives.
– Socrates.

Don't let the fear of falling keep you from knowing the joy of flight. - Lane Wallace, 2001.

We who fly are going to get to know the Great Flying Boss in the sky better and better.
- Colonel Robert L. Scott in his book *God is My Co-pilot*, 1943.

More varied than any landscape was the landscape in the sky, with islands of gold and silver, peninsulas of apricot and rose against a background of the many shades of turquoise and azure blues.
- Cecil Beaton, 1985.

All was glorious - a cloudless sky above, a most delicious view all around. How great is our good fortune! I care not what may be the condition of the earth; it is the sky that is, for me, now.
- Jacques Alexandre Cesare Charles, 1783. Upon the first free flight in a manned hydrogen balloon.

I am with the angels and just completely happy.
- Bertrand Piccard, 1999, Swiss pilot of first around-the-world balloon flight.

I live for that exhilarating moment when I'm in an airplane rushing down the runway, pulling back on the stick, feeling the lift under the wings. It's a magical feeling to climb towards the heavens, seeing objects and people on the ground grow smaller and e insignificant. You have left the world beneath you. You are inside the sky.
- L. Gordon "Gordo" Cooper, 2000, one of the original Mercury 7 astronauts.

This plane can teach you more things and give you more gifts than I ever could. It won't get you a better job, a faster car or bigger house. But if you treat it with respect and keep your eyes open, it may remind you of things you used to know - that life is in the moment, joy matters more than money, the world is a beautiful place, and dreams really, truly are possible. And then, because airplanes speak in a language beyond words, I'll take him up in a summers evening sky and let the airplane show him what I mean.
- Lane Wallace, 2000, *Eyes of a Child*.

The obligation and responsibility each of us who fly has is to introduce the sky to those young ones coming along who have yet to venture aloft.
- Ed.

The engine is the heart of an airplane, but the pilot is its soul.
- Sir Walter Alexander Raleigh, 1910.

I might have been born in a hovel, but I determined to travel with the wind and the stars.
- Jacqueline Cochran, first woman to break the sound barrier.

One cannot contemplate the sea without wishing for the wings of a swallow.
- Sir Richard Burton.

Any pilot can describe the mechanics of flying. But what it does for the spirit is beyond description.
- US Senator Barry M. Goldwater.

The Americans cannot build aeroplanes. They are very good at refrigerators and razor blades.
- Herrmann Goering, 1940, in a report to Hitler.

He who has height controls the battle.
He who has the sun achieves surprise.
He who gets in close shoots them down.
- WWI advice to fighter pilots

The thing I miss about Air Force One is, they don't lose my baggage.
- President George W. Bush.

It only takes five years to go from rumor and inuendo to Standard Operating Procedure.
- Anon.

There are but two reasons to sit in the last row of seats in an airplane. Either you have diarrhea or you're anxious to meet those who do.
- US former Secretary of State Henry Kissinger.

You land a million airplanes safely, then you have one little mid-air, and you never hear the end of it.
- opening line from the movie Pushing Tin.

I must place on record my regret the human race ever learned to fly.
- Sir Winston Churchill.

No-one can realize how substantial the air is, until he feels its supportive power beneath him. It inspires confidence at once.
- Otto Lilienthal

The regret on our side is, they used to say years ago "We are reading about you in science class." Now they say, "We are reading about you in history class.
- Neil Armstrong, 1999 first human on the moon.

Real confidence in the air is bred only by mistakes made and recovered from at a safe altitude, in a safe ship, and seated on a good parachute.
- Rodney H. Jackson, 1930 in his book A Lesson in Stunting.

Just remember, if you crash because of weather, your funeral will be held on a sunny day.
- Layton A. Bennett.

Fly with your head and not just your muscles. This is the way for a long life for a ... pilot. He who is all muscle, and no head will never live long enough to receive his pension.
- Colonel Willie Bats, West German Air Force [237 victories as a Luftwaffe pilot in WWII].

Flying is so many parts skill, so many parts planning, so many parts maintenance, and so many parts luck. The key for a long life is to reduce luck by increasing the others.
- David L. Baker.

My airplane is quiet and for the moment I am still an alien, still a stranger to the ground; I am home.
- Richard Bach, in his book *Stranger to the Ground*.

Dad, I left my heart up there.
- Francis Gary Powers, after his first flight at 14. He was a CIA U-2 pilot shot down over the Soviet Union in the early 1960's. After retirement he flew as a Skywatch traffic reporter for a radio station in Los Angeles and I was fortunate enough to fly with him on one of those missions. A great man and genuine US hero.

They shall mount up on wings as eagles.
- Isaiah 40:30.

You can always tell when a person has lost their soul to flying. The poor bastard is hopelessly committed to stopping whatever he is doing look enough to look up to make sure the aircraft purring overhead continues its course. It is also a bound duty to watch every aircraft within view take off and land.
- Ernest K. Gann, in his book *Fate is the Hunter*.

The following quote was penned in 1929 - almost a century ago - and directed at the distaff portion of the population. We've come a long way since then and so I will rewrite the original quote to approach the matter in a more universal and egalitarian way.

If you are coming to flying seeking stimulation, excitement, and flattery, you had better stay away from flying. But if you think flying will develop character; will teach you to be orderly and well-balanced; will give you an increasing wider outlook on life; discipline you, and destroy vanity and pride; enable to control yourself more and more under all conditions and circumstances; to think less of yourself and your personal problems, and more of sublimity and everlasting peace that dwells serenely in the heaven - if you seek these latter qualities and think exclusively on them, then yes - FLY!
- Margory Brown, 1929.

There are only two kinds of airplanes - fighters and targets.
- Doyle "Wahoo" Nicholson, USMC.

The duty of a fighter pilot is to patrol his area of the sky and shoot down any enemy airplanes found there. Anything else is rubbish.
- Baron Manfred Freiheer von Richthofen, "The Red Baron", 1917.

Yes, it really happened! BTDT!

ATC: *Raven One-One, say callsign of your wingman.*
Raven 11: *We're a single ship.*
ATC: *Oooh - kay, then. You have traffic.*
The airport runway is the most important main street in any town.
- Norm Crabtree, aviation director for state of Ohio

Drones will not: be late to briefings, start fights at happy hour, destroy clubs, attempt to seduce others' dates, purchase huge watches, insult other services, sing O'Leary's Balls, dance on tables, yell "Show us yer tits!!", or do all of the other things that we know win wars! I see no future in them.

- Squadron CO [Name & Squadron redacted out of the need for safety ... mine! - Ed.]

Aviation Acronyms

God knows there are plenty of these in Aviation – and those people who over-use acronyms just make me PO'd!

AC Aircraft Commander
The "HMFWHIC" of a military aircraft.

ADF Automatic Direction Finder
The flight instructor/instructor pilot.

AFM Aircraft Flight Manual
The book provided by the manufacturer where all the details of the aircraft are hidden. Required by S/N to be aboard the aircraft, usually missing the first page where the N-number and aircraft S/N are noted with revisions haphazardly inserted therein.

AGL Above Ground Level
The larger this number, the fewer chances there are of running into the edges of the sky: The upper edge of the sky may be defined as interstellar space; the lower edges are where all the houses, trees, barns, poles, silos, towers, etc. are found.

AIM Aeronautical Information Manual
The repository of arcane knowledge, procedures and policy written by lawyers for bureaucrats: Of passing interest to pilots.

| AME | Aviation Medical Examiner
The person you go to for your aviation medical color test: Red blood + green money = you pass. |

| AO | Area of Operations
In essence: "No matter where you find yourself, there you are." |

| AOG | Aircraft On Ground
The acronym used when ordering a part desperately needed for an aircraft grounded until the part arrives, usually insuring delivery by stagecoach and/or snail mail. |

| APF | Attempts Per Flight
Can be number of landing tries per approach, number of runway impacts per landing try, number of times the localizer/glide-slope CDI is pegged per instrument approach. Of interest primarily to statisticians and those who charge by the hour. |

| ASI | Air Speed Indicator
Gauge in the cockpit of dubious veracity and trustworthiness as there are many types of 'airspeed', all subject to interpretation depending on the state of sobriety of the interpreter. |

| ASOS | The gooey stuff poured onto pasta. |

| ATC | (1) Air Traffic Control (civilian) – A ground-based aerial surveillance system in which the operators guide the unsuspecting – and trusting - pilot towards

opposing traffic and/or the red zone(s) depicted on weather radar.

(2) Air Training Command (military) - The cadre in charge of turning snot-nosed civilians into rip-roaring angels of death.

BS   Bullshit
An extremely useful word with multiple purposes & meanings: Can be used as a noun, verb, adverb, adjective, declaratory statement, statement of opinion and of fact. Usable in polite society when disguised as a sneeze.
[See also: Au Contraire]

BSR   "Bang – Stare – Red"
The principle – usually in rotorcraft – that dictates the louder the 'Bang' in your aircraft the quicker your eyes will go to the gauges. The longer you stare at the gauges the quicker the indicators will go from green to red.

BX   Base Exchange
A location on a military base where such necessities and possibles one might need for basic existence may be purchased out of the paltry pay those in service receive from an overly-generous government.

C – 4   C – 4
A form of plastic explosive with multiple and myriad number of uses including livening up a dull day.

CAVU Ceiling And Visibility Unlimited
The rare and glorious type of flying day where, if you squinted hard, you can see the back of your own head.

CAFB Clear As a F***ing Bell
[See: CAVU]

CDI Course Deviation Indicator
A gizmo attached to the old-fashioned navigational radio which indicates to the pilot when the boundaries of the airway and/or approach path have been exceeded. These are unnecessary when the aircraft is equipped with a GPS as no-one looks at it anyway.

CFI Certificated Flight Instructor
A person who rides in an aircraft with someone who is trying to kill him. All the CFI must do is figure out how this attempt will be made (may be several attempts per flight) and head it off.

CIGARTIPS Controls, Instruments, Gas, Aircraft status, Run-up, Trim, Ignition, Propeller, Seatbelts & Systems.
A quick-n-dirty before takeoff check.

COC Crusty Old Captain
A member of the dying breed of aviators who knew their stuff AND expected you to know it as well or, in some cases, better than they did.

CRM Crew (or Cockpit) Resource Management
The concept that Co-pilots and First Officers have something valid to contribute to the flight.

CVR Cockpit Voice Recorder
A device used by accident investigators to use whatever was said in the last 30 minutes of a flight to prove an accident was pilot error.

DG Directional Gyro (aka 'Heading Indicator')
One of the 6 primary flight instruments (in the old '6-pack' steam gauges days) guaranteed to precess a degree per minute in VFR and at least twice that in IMC.

DOD Department Of Defense
Formerly (Civil War – WWII) known as the 'War Department', now a part of the "Military-Industrial complex" President Eisenhower warned about.

DP Departure Procedure
The routing ATC issues to you when you want to go this-a-way and they want you to go that-a-way.

DZ Drop Zone
The location where the airborne troopers or equipment were supposed to land: If dealing with both troops and equipment, these are mutually exclusive locations.

ER Efficiency Report
A regularly-scheduled review of one's capabilities in the performance of their duties. Can range from "Sets low standards for himself and then fails to achieve them" on up.

EVAL	Evaluation An estimation of pilot skills, knowledge and abilities by someone who used to be able to do all that stuff.
FA	Flight Attendant Formerly 'stewardesses' (female) but now could be anyone and/or anything.
FAA	Federal Aviation Administration 1. Really nice men and women from the government whose primary concern is your welfare and well-being as a pilot. 2. "Fear and Alarm."
FAR	Federal Air Regulations 1. Formerly written in blood, now written by blood-sucking lawyers for the edification of bureaucrats; the sole purpose of which is to confuse pilots. [See: NPRM – FARCA] 2. Opposite of NEAR. 3. What a pilot from southern states has when raw fuel is pumped into a hot engine nacelle.
FIGMO	F*** It, Got My orders Quaint old Anglo-Saxon expression used by 'short-timers' to tell the neophytes what to do, where to go and how to do it.
FITREP	Fitness Report Someone else's opinion on how you perform your duties. [See: Lies, Falsehoods and Fabrications]

FMB Fermented Malt Beverage(s)
E.g. Beers, ales, porters, stouts, lagers, and so forth.

FNG F**king New Guy [See: Nugget]
Persons allegedly holding pilot/crew credentials, new to the squadron, unit, outfit or company, who are not to be placed in any position of authority or responsibility until they can prove they're not going to get themselves killed, or get you killed, within the first few weeks of assignment, deployment or of being hired.

FO First Officer [See: Co-pilot]
One who laterally balances the cockpit and is never allowed to touch the flight controls unless the captain wants a nap or must exit the cockpit to perform a personal weight-and-balance check. *Oh, c'mon! You can figure that one out, right?*

FO F**k Off
An 'olde' Anglo-Saxon invitation to take yourself and your silly-assed ideas, thoughts and words to some inhospitable place far, far from where the exclaimer currently exists, resides or occupies.

FOM Flight Operations Manual
The repository of Management's policies and procedures which insure corporate profits and golden parachutes for those residing at company headquarters. It has no apparent direct correlation to flight safety, crew comfort, crew accommodations and the like. It can also be used as a doorstop.

FSS	Flight Service Station

The place where the specialists who give weather briefings work; a building with no windows.

FUBAR F**ked Up Beyond All Recovery

The third level of 'F**ked-up-edness' behind SNAFU and TARFU.

G The Force of Gravity

1. One 'G' is experienced just standing on the planet (Earth that is). Multiple G's are induced by acceleration forces created by maneuvering the aircraft. "I love the feel of G-forces in the morning!"
2. String worn by persons attempting to attract members of the opposite sex (c'mon, it is the 21st century now, ain't it? –ed.).

GIB Guy In Back

Anyone in an aircraft aft of the HMFWHIC.

GPS Global Positioning System

The latest whizzy-gizzy cockpit doo-dad that always indicates 'TO' where you're going. The old 'FROM' days of VOR navigation are gone…until those GPS satellites go Tango-Uniform and pilots must revert to ground-based navigational systems.

GUMPS <u>G</u>as, <u>U</u>ndercarriage, <u>M</u>ixture, <u>P</u>ropeller, <u>S</u>ystems & <u>S</u>eatbelts

A gouge to use for a pre-landing check until it is safe to use the official checklist.

HMFWHIC Head Mo-Fo What Him (or Her) In Charge
Usually that poor soul who, when all the fecal matter has been evenly distributed by the rotating oscillating air movement device, finds himself (or herself) up to their eyeballs in it.

IAP Instrument Approach Procedure
The procedure used when the weather conditions are less than "Clear and a million.
[See: North Pole Approach]

IFR Instrument Flight Rules
1. The rules and procedures to follow when you cannot see the ground or when wearing a 'view-limiting device'. The time to use the advice: "One peek is worth a thousand cross-checks".
2. Methodology for complying with definition 1. above: "I Follow Rivers, Roads & Railways."

IMC Instrument Meteorological Conditions
Where the advice given under 'IFR' doesn't work and your shit cannot be weak.

IOE Initial Operating Experience
Experience given to 'Nuggets' prior to actually being allowed to manipulate the flight controls of an aerospace vehicle.

IP Instructor Pilot
The military version of the civilian CFI; same duties and responsibilities except the IP gets to fly cooler aircraft and receives a steady paycheck.

LOX	Liquid Oxygen Something you don't want any form of spark or fire around.
LZ	Landing Zone The location where skids touch the ground: If reported 'cold', they will inevitably be 'hot' by the time you get there.
KMAG YOYO	Kiss My Ass Goodbye, You're On Your Own *Pretty self-explanatory if'n you ask me.*
MALF	Malfunction An event whereby the aircraft takes revenge on the pilot/aircrew by failing a critical instrument or equipment, usually at the worst possible time, thereby generating weighty & lengthy amounts of paperwork, usually after an 'event'.
MOA	Military Operating Area Airspace wherein there are only two kinds of aircraft: Fighters and Targets.
MTR	Military Training Route Published routes used by the U.S. Armed Forces where speed limits below certain altitudes do not apply. *I had 2 F-4's pass underneath me when I was but 500' AGL – quite a sight!*
NAVAID	Navigational Aid Usually a ground-based electronic navigational equipment placed either permanently or nearly-so by

those well-trained in map, compass and guesswork; relied upon by those overly-trusting souls piloting aircraft to get them within crawling distance of the local watering hole. [Also see: VOR, TACAN and - most relevant – NDB]

NDB Non-Directional Beacon
1. Fancy name for AM radio station.
2. You have **N**o **D**amn **B**usiness doing this kind of approach what with all the precision and GPS approaches around.

NOTAM Notice to Airmen
Important aeronautical information issued by the government the day after the planned event.

NTSB National Transportation & Safety Board
The governmental agency charged with determining how a particular aviation accident/incident was due to pilot error.

OEM Original Equipment Manufacturer
Maker of life-limited parts only they can replace.

ORI Operational Readiness Inspection(s)
Something that no combat-ready outfit has ever passed: A situation in which you stop doing what you were doing in order to simulate doing what you were doing so that you can show someone else that you can simulate doing what you were doing as well as you were doing it before you were interrupted.

OTS	Out of Service
	The appended identifier of the only airport for miles around when you need a close-by fuel or pit-stop.
P – 7	"Proper Prior Preparation Prevents Piss-Poor Performance"
	Never has a truer statement ever been made so succinctly for so many.
PA	Public Announcements
	Crew comments to the SLC's pointing out interesting things about the flight, such as "Out of the left side of the aircraft you can see Kansas, Oklahoma and the northern third of Texas."
PC	Proficiency Check
	A regularly scheduled event to prove to someone who doesn't fly regularly that you still can.
PC	Politically Correct
	A theory spread around the country that it's possible to pick up a turd by the clean end.
PIC	Pilot in Command
	The prime suspect when any event occurs.
PEBPAS	Problem Exists Between Panel and Seat
	[See also: Short Circuit Between the Headphones].
PIROOMA	Pulled It Right Out Of My Ass
	Where many rules, regulations, SOP's and company policies come from.

PLO   Permanent Latrine Orderly
Speaks for itself.

PMA   Parts Manufacturing Authority
The authorization given to those who want to make OEM parts, only cheaper

PO   Pissed Off
Meaning: Somewhat disappointed with the current state of affairs, conditions or situations.

POH   Pilot Operating Handbook
Mistakenly used by the uninformed as the last word in operating an aircraft [See: AFM]. While of good general knowledge, it is usually out-of-date with few-to-no revisions past the original publication date.

PTS   Practical Test Standards
The standards used to evaluate pilots in training: Written by office personnel who only see the sky when allowed outside by their supervisors or parole officer(s).

QA   Quality Assurance
Those people who look over the shoulders of those doing the work and tell them how they are not doing it correctly.

QNH   "Cue-En-Aich"
The altimeter setting over Great Britain and the Commonwealth nations given in milibars (Mb)

REMF	Rear-Echelon Mother F**ker A somewhat disparaging term used by those on the cutting edge for those in cushy jobs far from danger: Those who deal with the gear in the rear.
RNAV	Area Navigation What a pilot does on the first date.
RON	Remain Over Night Can mean exactly that to an extended stay. [Also see: TDY]
RPM	Rotations per Minute A number referring to the rotational disc either in front, above or behind the aircraft, in the old days (20thcentury) called a 'Fan'. A high number keeps the pilot cool; if the number is low or worse – zero – he begins to sweat profusely.
SLC	Self-Loading Cargo Passengers.
SHP	Sierra-Hotel-Papa Shit-hot Pilot (Aren't we all? –ed).
S/N	Serial Number The numbers placed on aircraft, aircraft parts and aircraft equipment to identify OEM and PMA approved parts. These numbers are usually placed in obscure and hard-to-get-to places.
SNAFU	Situation Normal – All F**ked Up The first status level followed by TARFU and FUBAR.

SOB   Son Of a Bitch
Either an endearing term of respect, or fightin' words.

SOG   Special Operations Group
A collection, gaggle or unit composed of individuals with 'special skills' who, when asked/commanded to perform feats of questionable legality and unquestionable daring, will have their existence denied if discovered, killed or captured by the opposition.

SOF   Supervisor of Flying
Someone charged with negating all the factors mentioned in "Fighter Pilot's Heaven."

SOP   Standard Operating Procedure
The techniques, methods, practices and procedures to fall back on when "just winging it" is found inadequate, unsuitable or downright dangerous. "When all else fails, read the directions."

STC   Supplemental Type Certificate
Authorization given to those who invent better and cheaper ways to circumvent the OEM/PMA cartels with 'new and improved' methods, addenda and miscellany about aircraft.

STFU   Shut The F**k Up
Self-explanatory request for silence.

SWAG   Scientific Wild-Ass Guess
A method of empirical observation with causal-dependent results when trustworthy data is lacking.

TACAN	Tactical Air Navigation Name for a military VOR. [See also: VOR & NAVAIDs]
TARFU	Things Are Really F**ked Up The status level between SNAFU and FUBAR.
TDY	Temporary Duty Originally meant as short-term duty stationing, it now can mean anything this side of the second deployment.
TLAR	That Looks About Right A means to determine if something – like an approach to landing – is within limits; can also be used as "TSAR" (That Sounds about Right) and "TFAR" (That Feels About Right). More precise than the 'SWAG' method.
TU	Tango-Uniform Otherwise known as "Tit's Up" (How bugs die…on their back with their T U). Otherwise known as 'Dead.'
UEI	Uniform & Equipment Inspection(s) Speaks for itself: Ironing just the outer sleeve showing in your locker doesn't pass anymore…they know this trick.
USAAC	United States Army Air Corps The flying arm of the US Army prior to WWI until 18 September 1947, when it became the (next entry).

USAF	United States Air Force Without munitions would just be an expensive flying club.
VFR	Visual Flight Rules Succinctly summarized in an old Confederate Air Force pre-airshow briefing: "Y'all stay above 5 feet and don't do nuthin' dumb."
VMC	Visual Meteorological Conditions Technically, when the cloud ceiling(s) are higher than 1,000' AGL and 3 miles visibility: Also, the conditions under which most mid-air collisions occur.
VOR	Very high frequency Omni-Range A ground-based navigational system from not only the last century but also the last millennium that has been confusing pilots and vexing the FAA Knowledge Test takers for years.
WSO	Pronounced 'Wizz-O' Weapons System Officer That unfortunate soul who, relegated to the back seat ["GIB" = Guy In Back] of a two-seat ship, must keep eyes and ears alert, monitoring 2 or 3 frequencies in one ear and 4 or 5 in the other, for targets of opportunity, hostile opposition, radio callouts/warnings/etc. while enduring the multiple-G-forces meanderings of the GIF ["Guy In Front"].
WTF	Whiskey Tango Foxtrot An expression of incredulity or bemused wonderment.

YGBSM   You Gotta Be Shitting Me!
Another expression of incredulity or bemused wonderment.

201 File   Personnel File
The repository of every complaint letter, FITREP (good & bad) and scrap of paper with your name on it produced by others and for which there is no appeal, excuse or redress.

Aviation Dictionary

How did the letters of the alphabet get in the order they are? Is it because of that song? And why is that song the same as "Twinkle, Twinkle, Little Star?" I <u>know</u> you just sang them to yourself – be I right?

Area Navigation
Done on the first date.

Aerial
[Also see: Antennae] That part of the airplane most frequently broken off by the pilot during the preflight inspection when ascertaining if anything is broken off.

Aero
That portion of the atmosphere which overlies Great Britain and any of the Commonwealth nations.

Aerodrome
Where aeroplanes alight on the ground under that portion of the atmosphere overlying Great Britain and any of the Commonwealth nations.

Airhead
Airplane lavatory.

Airport
Sweet red wine preferred by flight attendants and those not manly enough to drink Scotch Whiskey.

Airframe
What an FAA inspector is doing when he sends his kid out to ask a student pilot for a ride.

Airscrew
1. What the pilots in Great Britain and the Commonwealth nations call the propeller.
2. A flightcheck when the FAA Inspector rides along as an 'observer'.

Airspace Reservation
A geographical location set aside by the U.S. Government for the exclusive occupancy of airspace.

Airspeed
1. The speed of an aircraft through the air.
2. True airspeed plus 20% when talking to other pilots. Deduct 25% when speaking with retired fighter jocks.
3. Measured in furlongs-per-fortnight (FPF) when speaking with a Student Pilot.

Alternate Airport
An airport lying 20 minutes beyond the point of fuel exhaustion.

Altimeter Setting
The place where the altimeter is placed on the instrument panel – usually hidden by the control column when performing an instrument approach to minimums.

Approach
Asking that cute flight attendant out for dinner. [Also see: Departure]

Arresting Gear
Equipment used by the authorities to keep order at aviation-based parties.

ATC Control Center
Dark, drafty, ill-kept barn-like structures in which nefarious individuals gather for dubious reasons.

Au Contraire
("Oh con trair") From the French; an exclamation of disbelief. [Also see acronym: BS]

Autopilot
Someone who busted their flightcheck.

Bail Out
1. Any form of egressing an airplane while in flight.
2. Getting your friend out of the hoosegow after an all-night bender.

Bank
The folks who hold the lien on most pilots' cars.

Bar Bet
A wager whereby the individual making said wager knows the exact answer/outcome of the wager, thereby insuring obtaining a libation at someone else's expense.

Barrel Roll
 Getting the keg from the car to the hangar for the "safety meeting."

Blind Flying
 Having a date with someone you've never seen before.

Bloody Good Show
 Aka: "Well done!" as spoken in the British Commonwealth.

Brain Bag
 The container carried by pilots (all types) holding a rusted-out E6B, plotter, outdated charts, Dash-one (POH) 6 months out-of-date, pack of 12 year-old chewing gum (still good), cigarettes (or cigars), Hershey bars and three days dirty laundry.

Buzz Job
 (aka: "Buzzing") To fly extremely low, "Cut the grass'. The final maneuver by many pilots no longer with us.

Caged Gyro
 Not much less docile than a wild gyro.

Caging the Gyro
 Much easier with the domesticated species.

Captain
 Any airline pilot with four stripes on his sleeve; usually found holding his own hand.

Carburetor Icing
 A phenomenon mentioned in the report to the FAA/NTSB immediately after a pilot runs out of gas.

Center of Pressure
The location of the FAA knowledge (written) or practical tests.

Chart
1. A large piece of paper most useful for protecting cockpit surfaces from food and beverage stains.
2. A large piece of paper which, if folded and placed properly in the cockpit window, provides a passable sunscreen.

Chinese Landing
One wing low.

Chock
Pieces of wood or hard rubber which magically appear in the way of the nose wheel just before receiving taxi clearance. [Also see: Gremlin]

Circle-to-land
Maneuver fraught with peril, especially at closing time.

Clank Up
State of extreme agitation usually brought on by the recipient hearing such phrases as "Overseas", "Special Mission", "Flightcheck", "The C.O./Chief Pilot would like to see you in their office...NOW."

Clear
A warning to others shouted by the pilot two seconds after hitting the 'Start' button.

Clear the Prop
Moving all the admiring young ladies away from the front of the plane so the dashingly handsome pilot may gain access to same.

Cockpit
Where the pilot sits while trying to figure out where he/she is and/or where they are going.

Cone of Confusion
An area about the size of New Jersey, located above the final approach fix at any airport.

Contact
1. An archaic form of the word 'Clear!' also spoken two seconds after the starter is engaged.
2. Friend who can find 'cheap' aircraft parts.

Contact Approach
Not to be performed by anyone at any time unless approach clearance has been received and acknowledged. *If you know what I mean.*

Control Tower
A small shack on stilts inhabited by government pensioners who cannot hear; when they become blind they are sent to Centers.

Course
Popular alternate landing field marked by fairways and greens: Curiously, those who land here are said to be 'off course'.

Crab
1. The squadron Ops Officer or flight school chief pilot.
2. A technique used by pilots to compensate for crosswinds, usually without success.

Crash
To bed down for the night. [Also see: Suitable Landing Site]

Critical Altitude
Whatever AGL minus 6 feet.

Critical Engine
That part of the airplane which used to live under the cowling but now is in intensive care at the maintenance shop.

Cross Control
Angry tower operator.

Cross Country
Any student flight beyond eyeball acquisition of the home airfield.

Dead Reckoning
Navigational method: You reckon correctly, or you are.

Decision Height
Without a condom – 1 inch. N/A with condom.

Deicer
Aviation terms for hills, wooded slopes, apartment buildings and trailer parks.

Deicing Boots
Rubber inflatables designed to work under all weather conditions except icing.

Departure
What to do after a "Missed approach".

Destination
Geographical point 30 minutes beyond the pilot's bladder max pressure point.

Dive
Pilot's lounge and/or airport café.

Downwind
Direction of Student Pilot take-offs.

Downwind Leg
The one on the lee side when "seeing a man about a horse."

Drag
Enticing the IP back to the airplane to fly with you. [Also see: Induced Drag]

Dykes
Wire cutters. *Where did your filthy mind take you?*

Elevator
Device by which the tower raises or lowers the approach end of any runway. *Especially useful for playing with student pilots and Navy jocks.*

Engine Failure
A condition which occurs when all fuel tanks mysteriously become filled with low-octane air.

Event
1. An occasion used for the generation of paperwork.
2. An experience the PIC &/or aircrew did not wish to have.

Exceptional Flying Ability
A pilot who has logged an equal number of takeoffs and landings.

Fast
Describes the speed of any high-performance aircraft, especially military; lower-performance and training aircraft are described as "half-fast."

Final Approach
Asking out that cute flight attendant one last time.

Firewall
1. (Noun) Section of the aircraft specially designed to funnel heat and smoke into the cockpit.
2. (Verb) Act of pulling 65 inches of manifold pressure from an engine designed to give only 50.

Fixed Base Operator
Any male instructor after a vasectomy.

Flaps
Spirited discussion(s) between ATC and pilots usually brought on by the phrase "Advise when able to copy a phone number"

Flashlight
A device wherein pilots store dead batteries.

Flight Following
In-trail formation flight.

Flight Instructor
An individual of dubious reputation and sobriety, paid vast sums of money to impart knowledge of questionable value and who

has an amazing vocabulary concerning the coordination, intelligence and ancestry of student pilots.

Flight Line
Small diameter twine-like substance used to occupy 'Nuggets', e.g. "Go find me a ball of Flight Line." [Also see also: Bucket of prop wash]

Flight Service Station
1. The place wherefrom pilots obtain weather briefings prior to flight.
2. A building with no windows from which weather forecasts are issued.

Foxtrot-Oscar
See acronym "FO", 2nd definition.

Frost
Attitude shown by an uncooperative stewardess. [See: Horizontally Opposed]

Fuel
1) That substance which, if you take off without enough or fly to exhaustion, there are no words in the English language which can serve as an excuse for allowing to occur.

2) That substance carried on board the airplane which the only time you have too much of is if you're on fire.

Gaggle
(noun) A large number of anything headed in the same general direction in the same part of the sky.

Glide Distance
Half the distance from an airplane to the nearest suitable landing field at the point of engine failure.

Glider
Formerly 'airplane', prior to running out of fuel.

Gouge
An easy mnemonic, patois or saying that aids in memory & recall when one cannot remember the real thing.

Gravity
The principle that, given a collision between an aircraft and the planet, the planet always wins. *[Obey gravity; it's the LAW]*

Green Bag
Flight suit – so named for its fashionable color and fit.

Gremlins
Small invisible beings who enjoy tormenting pilots by putting chocks in front of nose wheels after everyone is aboard, kinking the vacuum lines during instrument flight, shifting weight/cargo to the furthermost aft position while inflight, and other such 'humorous' pranks as they can think of.

Gross Weight
Overweight pilot.

Ground Speed
Average speed from the airport to home and vice-versa.

Hangar
Sheltered area housing several cast-off couches, a comfy chair with no seat cushion support, a coffee pot (which hasn't been cleaned since the Nixon Administration) , coffee cups (ditto), numerous shelves with half-full cans, bottles and containers of gawd-knows-what, a work bench or two with no available flat surface upon which to work, old magazines and Trade-a-Planes ("Hey, here's a Cessna 185 for $35,000!"), a semi-classic old car awaiting restoration…and perhaps an airplane.

Headset
Not scanning for other traffic [Also see: 'midair' or 'near miss']

Heated Air Mass
Usually found in and about hangars, flight lounges, crew rooms, airport cafes and non-flying members of the opposite sex.

Helicopter
Thousands of parts flying in close formation surrounding oil leaks, waiting for metal fatigue to set in.

Hobbs Meter
The instrument which, when failed during dual instruction, brings the lesson to a screeching halt.

Holding Pattern
Term applied to the dogfight in progress over any navigational facility serving a terminal airport.

Hold Short
The order given by ATC when they want the aircraft to not go where they already are.

Hood Time
Logable flight time when aviating while not looking outside the airplane.

Horizontally Opposed
May be expressed in any of the following ways: "No!" "Hell, No!" or "Are you freakin' kidding me?!" [Also see: Frost]

Hovering
Flight for people who love to fly but have nowhere to go.

Hydroplane
An airplane designed to land long and fast on a short & wet runway.

Hyperventilation
Opening one or both windows at cruise airspeeds.

Ident
Asking if you're in the correct hotel room.

Induced Drag
Getting the instructor to fly with you again, usually by using a bottle of Scotch Whiskey as a lure.

Instrument Rating
A certificate indicating the holder has received enough training – and has all the knowledge, ability & awareness – to know when to stay on the ground.

Instrument Flight
The method of flying by needle, ball and ripcord.

Iron Compass
Railroad lines.

Junkers
1. Type of WWII German airplane.
2. A plane no-one can make airworthy.

Kilometer
Unit of measurement on aeronautical charts to further confuse those pilots who already have trouble with knots.

Land & Hold Short
See: Touch & Go.

Landing Flap
A 6,000 foot roll-out on a 5,000 foot runway.

Landing Gear
Those things that stick out from the bottom of the airplane which keep the propeller out of the dirt/concrete/asphalt after landing.

Lazy 8
The airport operator, his four mechanics and three lineboys.

Lean Mixture
Non-alcoholic beer.

Logbook
A small rectangular notebook used by a pilot to record lies ("Fly when you can, log what you need" - BC).

Loop

What a passengers' stomach does when subjected to unexpected aerial 'frivolity'. [Also see: Barf bag]

Max Gross Weight

Maximum permissible takeoff weight plus two suitcases, 10 oil cans, 4 sleeping bags, 4 rifles (with ammo), 8 cases of beer, a bottle of medicinal scotch, whisky and the groceries.

Mini Mag Lite

A device which supports the AA battery industry.

Missed Approach

When you lose the matchbook cover with that cute flight attendant's phone number.

Mixture Control

The Head Barkeep.

Motor

A word used by the English and Student Pilots when referring to an aircraft engine.

Nanosecond

The time delay between the low fuel light illuminating and the onset of carburetor icing. [Also see: carburetor icing]

Navigation

The art of flying from point 'A' to point 'B' while really trying to get to point 'C'.

Nose Wheel
   The wheel at the front of an airplane used by pilots unable and/or unwilling to fly airplanes with the third wheel at the tail of the airplane where it should be. [Also see: Training Wheel]

Nuremberg Defense
   The defense put forth by the Nazi henchmen during their post-WWII trials in Nuremberg, Germany: "I vas only following orders." (It won't work at your hearing or Review Board either – Ed.)

O-Club
   Officer's Club: The base watering hole where commissioned individuals may imbibe in FMB's and other assorted mind-altering beverages, tell lies, war stories and otherwise decompress from the stresses of the day.

Optimism
   A helicopter pilot who smokes thinking he's going to die from lung cancer.

Overhaul
   Cleaning the top spark plugs, adding a can of 'Upper Lube' and repainting the crankcase.

P-Factor
   What occurs when the IP shuts down one engine and the student feathers the prop on the other one. *What other definition came to your mind?*

Parker Pen
   The ONLY proper writing instrument for making 'important' entries in one's logbook.

Parking
Always try to keep the number of times you've parked an aircraft equal to the number of times you've gone flying.

Parasitic Drag
A pilot who bums a ride and complains about the service or doesn't offer to help with the fuel bill.

Pilot
A misguided individual who – if of the male persuasion – speaks of flying when with women and about women when flying.

Pilot in Command
The person who while seemingly protected by FAR 91.3 is actually the focus of attention when determining the extent of "Pilot error."

Pitch
The story a (male) pilot presents to the 'target for tonight'.

Plotter
Fixed Base Operator who connives to keep fuel prices above average.

Prang
1. (Verb) To damage an aircraft by contact with an immovable object (e.g. the ground).
2. A loud noise immediately preceding the termination of a flight, usually accompanied by a rapid descent.

Prop
What your buddies should do for you when leaving the club; like as not they need it themselves.

Propeller
The fan in front of an airplane that keeps the pilot cool...turn it off and watch him sweat.

Prop Wash
1. A cleaning agent the crew chief or plane captain sends 'Nuggets' in search of.
2. Refers to flying tales overheard in a 'Dive'.

Range
Usually about 30 miles beyond the point where all fuel tanks fill with air.

Rich Mixture
What you order at the other guy's promotion party.

Roger
Used when you're not sure what else to say.

Roll
1. The first design priority for a fully loaded KC-135A.
2. 'Ammo' at the end-of-deployment and/or squadron stand-down dinner (for Walt W. & the 69th SOG)
3. The money needed to take out that cute flight attendant

Rotorhead
A pilot who flies aircraft with the propeller on top of the aircraft rather than in front.

Runway
Cleared surface for departing from and alighting upon the face of the planet. Always too short and not wide enough for student pilots and those not adept at crosswind landings.

Safety Award
  The adult beverage consumed by pilots AFTER the planes have been de-armed and secured and the mission has been determined to be a 'success.'

Safety Belt
  Alcoholic drink for the instructor prior to dealing with a troublesome student.

Say Intentions
  Repost from that cute flight attendant after you ask her to dinner.

Scarf Up
  (Verb) To grab, rescue or capture (I was scarfed up by the Jolly Greens); unfortunately, can also mean "I was scarfed up by the V.C."

Sectional
  Any chart that terminates 25 miles short of your destination. [Also see: Chart]

Service Ceiling
  Altitude at which cabin crews can serve drinks.

Slow Flight
  That portion of the flight extending beyond bladder limits.

Spoilers
  [See acronym: FAA]

Squawk Ident
  Getting the wrong answer when asking if you're in the correct hotel room.

Stable Air
Atmosphere found over the stockyards of Chicago, IL; Omaha, NE; Fort Worth, TX; or Greeley, CO.

Stall
Technique used to explain to the bank why your car payment is late.

Stall Strip
Taking longer than normal to undress.

Steep Bank
Banks that charge pilots more than 10% interest.

Stick Actuator
Pilot

S-Turn
Course flown by a Student Pilot going from point 'A' to point 'B'.

Supercharger
Pilot with eight credit cards (all maxed out).

Sweat
What a pilot does when the 'fan' up front (or above, for you rotorheads) isn't rotating anymore and keeping him 'cool'.

Taildragger
1. An older pilot after a long flight.
2. A young pilot who over-rotates a tricycle-gear airplane during takeoff.

Tail Wind
Results from eating beans and/or cabbage, often causing oxygen depletion in the immediate vicinity.

Takeoff Distance
Length of the runway plus 150'.

Tango-Uniform
[See acronym: TU]

Test Pilot
Any unemployed aviator more than 50 nm from home.

Thermal
Atmospheric phenomenon blamed when a pilot cannot hold altitude.

Touch and Go
Your love life after age 60.

Touchdown
Achieved after passing Decision Height.

Trim Tab
A device student pilots use to control the airplane instead of using the flight controls.

Turn & Bank Indicator
An instrument largely ignored by pilots.

Useful Load
1. Volumetric capacity of the aircraft, disregarding weight
2. About four scotch whiskeys (doubles, natch!).

WAC Chart
Directions to the Army Post's female barracks. *You must be of a 'certain' age to appreciate this one.*

Walkaround
What to do when waiting for the weather to clear.

Wilco
Roger's brother, the nerd.

Wingman
#2 in the flight who protects the tail of flight lead. The member of the flight or crew who says "You have the steak, Skipper; I'll take the chicken" or "I'll take the fat one, boss."

Wing Span
Pilot with arms long enough to reach the charts on the floor behind the pilot's seat.

Wing Strut
Peculiar, ritualistic walk performed by Student Pilots after their first solo.

Yankee
Any pilot who asks Atlanta tower to "Say again."

Yaw
Answer given by a pilot (mouth full) during happy hour when asked if he's a pilot.

Zero
Style and artistry points earned for a gear-up landing.

Recommended Movies

In this list you will find what are, in my opinion, movies and films which present many features, events, and personages, of aviation history about which everyone who claims an interest in aviation should know. How can one claim a fascination with a subject and not be interested in the history of that endeavor, how it came to be, how it came forth out of the mists of the past to be what it is today? Does not an all-consuming interest and fascination in today's technology require of us a familiarity with the past, how we who now enjoy and employ this technology arrived at today?

I will admit to favoring the older examples, for in them actual airplanes are flown, and the roar of engines is the real thing, not computer-generated imaginings presented as reality.

In chronological order:

1903 *Kitty Hawk: Wright Brothers Journey of Invention*
A definitive documentary about the inspiration, hardships, perseverance, and true genius of Orville and Wilbur as they experimented with 'flying machines', both gliders initially and then powered with a home-made engine of their own design. Neil Armstrong [first man on the moon] and John Glenn [first American to orbit the planet] lend their voices as Orville and Wilbur.

1911 *Those Magnificent Men in Their Flying Machines*
The tongue-in-cheek recreation of the first London-to-Paris air race of 1911. The producers built actual flying replicas of these very early aeroplanes for the movie. Family fun.

1916 *Wings [silent film with musical accompaniment]*
Received the very first Oscar® for best picture in 1929. Director William Wellman was a pilot in the Lafayette Flying Corps during WWI, bringing a there-I-was sense of realism to the movie. Great flying scenes only slightly marred by a goofy love triangle sub-plot.

1917 *The Blue Max*
WWI story of a German soldier who looks up from the trenches and sees airplanes; desiring to get out of the mud and blood of the battlefields, he becomes a pilot in the German Air Force. But there's a hitch - he's a 'commoner' and his squadron mates are from the aristocracy. Great flying here starring George Peppard; lame love interest secondary plot, but Ursula Andress is a hottie [1917 style].

1918 *Hell's Angels*
Howard Hughes, multi-millionaire and pilot, bought up all the flying WWI original airplanes in Europe for this 'blockbuster' epic made in the late 1920's. Just to see and hear original WWI planes fly is worth the price of admission.

1927 *Spirit of Saint Louis*
Retelling of Charles Lindbergh's preparations, challenges, and ultimate success in being the first pilot to fly solo across the Atlantic Ocean. Considering the 100th anniversary of that event is not far away, it's a great depiction of how far aviation has come. His flight set off an 'aviation craze' in the US. Stars Jimmy Stewart. Might be boring for younger children.

1931 *The Great Waldo Pepper*
"What are you going to do, Newt? Build highways in the sky?" "Yes, Waldo, we are." One of my favorite films depicting the days, and ultimate demise, of the 'Barnstormer Period' in American aviation history - the wild and wooly 1920's, when WWI veteran pilots,

looking for flying jobs, scoured the country hopping rides, performed dare-devil stunts, and began the early 'air meets'. Stars Robert Redford with Susan Sarrandon in her next role after 'Rocky Horror Picture Show.' Family fun.

1937 *Amelia*
Biopic of Amelia Earhart, who is still missing from an around-the-world flight attempt in 1937. Explains her determination and persistence to show the world what a female pilot can do. Family film, especially for young girls interested in aviation.

1940 *Battle of Britain*
Actual German bombers and fighters from the Spanish Air Force compliment the in-flight action depicting Britain's 'Finest Hour' where 'Never was so much owed by so many to so few." - Winston Churchill speaking of the RAF pilots who fought the German Luftwaffe to a standstill in the summer of 1940. Cast of many famous actors of the day [1968], consultants to the film's accuracy were several pilot veterans from both sides of the battle.

1941 *Tora, Tora, Tora*
Vintage airplanes filmed in Pearl Harbor depict the 'Day of Infamy' - December 7th, 1941 - when the Japanese committed an attack on the US Pacific fleet without warning, pulling the US into WWII. The Japanese segments were filmed by Japanese cinematographers and the film is an even-handed, no vitriol or nation-bashing retelling of that fateful day. Many great actors of the day [1970] have cameo roles.

1942 *Thirty Seconds Over Tokyo*
Excellent film depicting the 'Doolittle Raid', the first bombing of Japan after the disaster of Pearl Harbor. Colonel James P. Doolittle [played by Spencer Tracy] is charged with the task of retaliating for

the 'Day of Infamy' during the dark days after December 7th, 1941 when Imperial Japan was running wild across the Pacific. The answer was Army B-25s taking off from a US Navy aircraft carrier; the result was a huge morale boost to the country. A classic film of a true event.

1943 *The Dam Busters*
Recreating the training and execution of a British raid to destroy German dams throughout the industrial Ruhr of Germany. Excellent retelling of the commitment and sacrifice of the crews. Guy Gibson, the unit commander, was awarded the Victoria Cross, Britain's highest military award, for leading the raid. Not for younger ones.

1944 *12-O'Clock High*
8th Air Force Bombers under a tough commanding officer fly dangerous missions over Germany in WWII. Accurately depicts the flying hazards the young pilots and crew went through. Look for the great Paul Mantz [legendary stunt pilot] crash a B-17 for real. Stars Gregory Peck. Not for younger viewers.

1960 *The Right Stuff*
Depicts the journey into space during the late 1950's through early 1960's based on Thomas Wolfe's great book [highly recommended!]. There was so much we didn't know and had to find out, the people depicted herein led America's way into space. Look for Chuck Yeager - who was first to 'break' the sound barrier - portraying an old ranch hand in the bar scenes at Pancho Barnes' Happy Bottom Riding Club.

1980 *Airplane!*
A great parody of the many aviation disaster films popular in the late 1970's - early 1980's which use, reuse, and use again every

airline cliché known to man. "Surely, you can't be serious." "Yes, I am ... and don't call me Shirley." Leslie Nielson stars.

1996 *Fly Away Home*
Enchanting family film follows a young girl traumatized by her mother's death caring for a flock of orphaned goslings [baby Canada geese]. She uses an ultralight aircraft to teach the birds their traditional migratory routes so they can return to the wild. Great aircraft/ geese-in-formation flying scenes. Family fare at its finest.

2000 *Hot Shots*
Spoof of 'Top Gun' starring a still sober Charlie Sheen where most every military aviation cliché was used to great comedic effect. For those who have 'been there, done that', it's a great send-up of the life. Younger ones may not get the jokes and puns, but you can explain it to them ... once you quit laughing.

2005 *One-Six Right*
A stupendous presentation of the glories of flight by detailing the myriad number of pilots and unique airplanes at Van Nuys Airport [KVNY] in Los Angeles' San Fernando Valley. One of the best films about aviation ever made. [I attended high school with Howard Keck, jr. who is interviewed therein, RIP]

2009 *Sully*
Recreating the "Miracle on the Hudson" where a commercial jet piloted by Chesley 'Sully' Sullenberger [portrayed by Tom Hanks] had to ditch 'dead-stick' in New York's Hudson River after taking off and flying into a flock of geese, flaming out both engines. The 'miracle' part was there were no casualties. Good family fare.

2010 *Les Chevaliers du Ciel [Knights of the Sky]*
French version of 'Top Gun' with incredible aerial scenery using modern French Air Force airplanes. "Mon Dieu, le avions du France ... c'est magnifique!"

The following is an editorial opinion expressed solely for the nefarious purposes of the author. Questions and comments might be responded to; criticism you keep to yourself.

Now, conspicuous by its absence from this list, let's address the movie of which many sing praises but I, for one, will not include on any 'top ten' list of great aviation films. That movie is *gasp* "Top Gun". While the flight sequences are thrilling and all, a fellow pilot with whom I was familiar - Art Scholl - lost his life filming a scene for the film. That automatically puts a damper on enthusiasm for the film for me. I realize I am treading on dangerous ground here but as an avowed iconoclast [look it up], and with so many icons to clast, I'm going to stick to my [top] guns for the following reasons:

1. I cannot for the life of me see anyone performing the anti-authoritarian antics of Maverick remaining in the service one minute later from the time of touch-down. What he does is so out-of-limits that he would be in front of a Board of Inquiry in a nano-second and, if not cashiered out of the service immediately, would in all reality find himself the PLO [Permanent Latrine Orderly] in some shit-hole deployment for the rest of his life. I find no glory or bemused tolerance for his deeds which endanger other airplanes and their crews. Hot Shots, part Deux has more realism than this. Call me a curmudgeon, but that's how I feel about it.

2. Has ANY fighter jock had an air warfare instructor the likes of Kelly McGillis in their entire career? Never in my lifetime! It was pure Hollywood to have her there - and we all recognize how

correct Hollywood gets aviation matters in film, don't we? Like - not at all. Again, realizing some kind of 'love interest' fills in the time when the hero isn't flying but really, now, is any fighter pilot worth his squadron patch going to give any credence whatsoever to someone who has only a theoretical knowledge of air combat? I think not. But in Hollywood, sex sells; the flying and/or a good plot is secondary to all that ... *sigh*.

Recommended Books

There are SO many good books about aviation, it would take another volume this size to mention them all. For that, then, you're on your own. Whether you like non-fiction, enjoy fiction, or read books just for the pictures, there's something out there for everyone.

Four books for which I will shout out are:

Kill Devil Hill - Harry Combs
The story, told in great detail, of the Wright Brothers journey of invention to create the first powered 'flying machine' and take it aloft.

Unlocking the Sky: Glenn Curtiss & the Race to Invent the Airplane - Seth Shulman
After the Wright Brothers proved powered manned flight was possible, they spent the next seven years in lawsuits attempting to 'keep it all to themselves'. Glenn Curtiss not only fought them but continued the development of the aeroplane right up to WWI. Frankly, he did more to advance the cause of flight post-1903 than the Wrights. An amazing saga of inventiveness, courage, and perseverance.

Fate is the Hunter - Ernest K. Gann
An absolute classic relating his first job with an airline just prior to WWII, the lessons taught to him and learned through trials and hardship, to ferrying airplanes during the war. Part history, part aviation philosophy, part inspirational musing. One of the best.

Stick and Rudder - Wolfgang Langewische
The penultimate instructional book about flying, what it is and how to accomplish it. A must-read for ANYONE who will be, is, or has acted as, Pilot-in-Command.

The Right Stuff - Thomas Wolfe
An outstanding overview of the early days of American space program, where oh-so-much was either unknown and/or had suppositions viewed as facts. Details the efforts from 'breaking' the sound barrier through the X-15 sub-space flights to the first seven Mercury astronauts riding a few hundred thousand pounds of propellant on a barely proven rocket into space. What could possibly go wrong?

Request for Assistance

If you have in your files, collections or ephemera other materials which you think could be added to another book like this, please feel free in sending them along to me. IF a sequel to this book is produced, IF your item is used, and IF you are the first one submitting it, I will include your name, city & state as contributor credit. Even better would be if you also include any relevant FAR or section from the AIM or any FAA publication so I may relate that which you send to a learning moment. You know – something which 'builds character'.

PLEASE be aware and VERY careful of submitting anything with an obvious copyright such as cartoons, pictures and/or illustrations as my begging for forgiveness in reproducing them can absolve me of just so much – then the copyright owners get pissy and nobody likes it when that happens. If you are sending along an original photo (Meaning: You are the photographer who took it), then I'd be pleased to include not only the picture but will also credit you for your photographic skills. If you photoshop something…ahhh… use your best judgment – and skills - if you submit it.

So, good and faithful reader, should you have something to contribute, please have some class and sense of appropriateness about it. After all, this book is being read by not only hard, cold, steely-eyed aviators who have been there and done that, but also by those innocents whose dreams we do not want dashed just yet. Let them figure it out on their own, okay?

Send what you have to: Drew@Coloradoskymaster.com

Thanks a lot…Stay cool…Right on…Roger-doger…Over & out.

ABOUT COLORADO SKYMASTERS

Colorado Skymasters is a loose – emphasis on 'loose' – confederation of pilots, mechanics, ATC personnel and yes, even retired FAA suits, who wish to remain active in aviation and give back to the community within which they have spent most of their lives.

The retired airline types have flown for airlines now long gone, absorbed by others or fallen by the wayside. The hottest aircraft our military types have flown are now either in museums, on a stick outside the entrance gate to the base or can be found in the 'Old Warbirds' section of fly-ins and airshows. The civil aviation sorts – who at times could hardly be called 'civil' – have logged time in airplanes only seen in the 'Classics' and 'Antiques' sections of Trade-a-Plane. In essence, we know how to start, keep running and maintain round and cantankerous engines in all their permutations.

We specialize in the esoteric and fringe areas of aviation, e.g. tailwheel training, aerobatics/upset-and-recovery, mountain flying in Colorado's Rocky Mountains (your airplane or ours), insurance-required instruction and experience-building for specialized and/or high-value airplanes, and most importantly the mentoring of youg aviators on their way up the aviation ladder. We also have a flight school on Denver's south side whereby those persons with time constraints or who are stalled in their efforts to gain a certificate and/or rating can come for a high-intensity training regime to quickly reach their goal(s) in aviation (Examiner on staff - natch!).

To view our programs or to contact us, please visit our website at:

www.Coloradoskymaster.com

ABOUT THE AUTHOR

In Memoriam – Peggy Ann Long
14 October 1946 – 15 April 2015

Andrew D. "Drew" Chitiea has been a pilot not only since well back in the last century but the last millennium as well. He has enjoyed, endured & experienced enough excitement, endeavors, assignments and so forth to righteously be entitled to say "Been there, done that" to much of aviation (He's got a number of corroborating T-shirts and has a supporting role in the video as further proof). Too modest for his own good, he will admit to nothing unless properly encouraged to spill his guts, usually by the profligate administration of some of Scotland's finest 'medicinal' beverage (Single Malt, Highland, minimum twelve-year old, vast quantities thereof) and or other ~~bribes~~ "creative inducements".

Adept at fooling all the people all the time, he has somehow managed to log PIC flight time in over 220 different makes and models of flying machines. After 12 consecutive designations as a "Master CFI" [24 years!], he was awarded the appellation of "Master Flight Instructor - Emeritus"; an honor currently held by very few. He sweet-talked the FAA into becoming a Designated Pilot Examiner (DPE), a position he held for 21 years (and over 5,000 flightchecks) until he retired from that duty. He conducts his activities from his secret ~~lair~~, ~~hideout~~, ~~man cave~~, Area of Operations in Colorado. He owns and operates his Cessna P-210 from his hangar at Colorado Air & Space Port [KCFO] just east of Denver, CO., aviating to the edges of the sky and the country with impunity and verve.

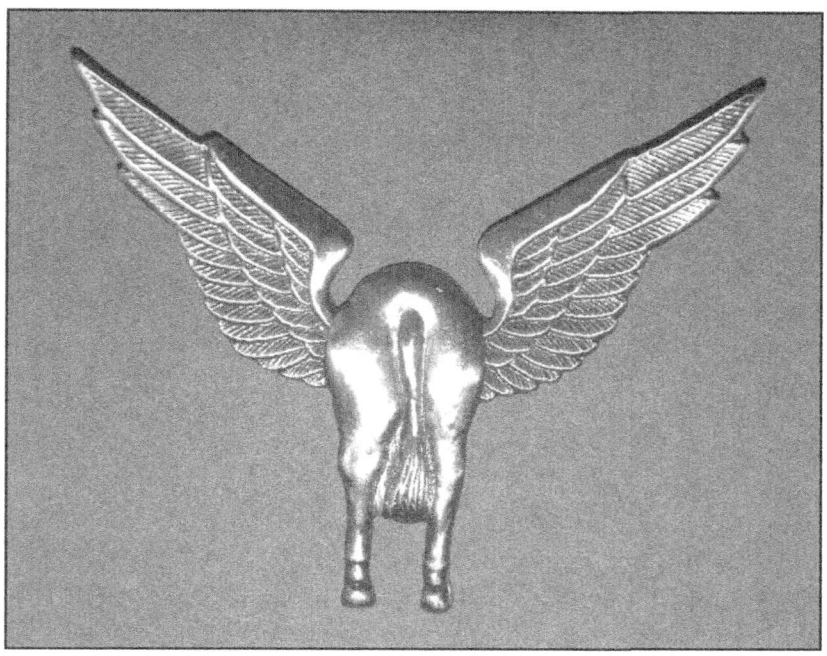

Retired Crusty Old Captain's Wings
Time Indeterminate
(Unauthorized)

HOW & WHERE TO ORDER MORE COPIES

www.Amazon.com

After entering this website, enter (Aviator's Bathroom Reader) or my last name (Chitiea) and you will be taken directly to the ordering page. Follow their prompts and in a few short days your own copy of this book will be delivered to the address stipulated in your order.

www.Coloradoskymaster.com

This is my company website; click on 'Products & Publications' along the left side, then scroll down until you see the Bathroom reader order page. You may then securely order this using Paypal AND you may ask for an inscription with signature from the author (surely in time to be a collectors' item!).

If you are an aviation bookstore, flight school or other retailer interested in volume discounts, please contact me at the address above or email:

Drew@Coloradoskymaster.com

Please use "ABR" in the message subject line.

PILOT'S TOASTS

Whenever good friends, colleagues, squadron mates, and others of that ilk meet up, a toast to old friendships and times gone by is often appropriate. Submitted here for your edification and enjoyment are two toasts recently heard at my hangar after a 'Burger Burn' followed by many 'Safety Awards'.

The clouds may float across the sky

The flower might kiss the butterfly

The sparkling wine may kiss the glass

And you, my friend ... Farewell.

Here's to the wine

Here's to the glass

And here's to the girl

With the pretty ... smile.

Printed in Great Britain
by Amazon